# PONYO

Original story and screenplay written and directed by
## HAYAO MIYAZAKI

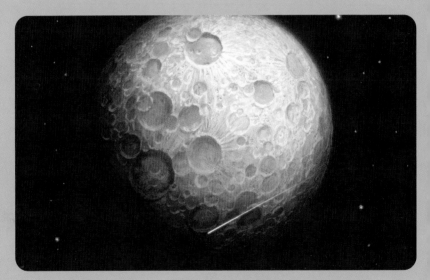

**3**

# MAIN CHARACTERS

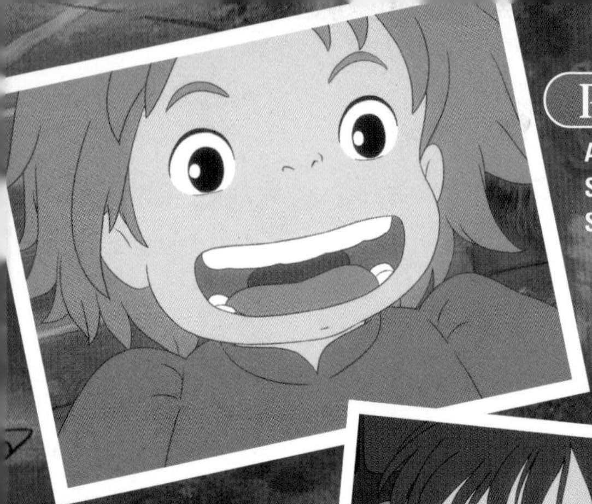

## PONYO

A young fish girl whom Sosuke named Ponyo. She loves ham.

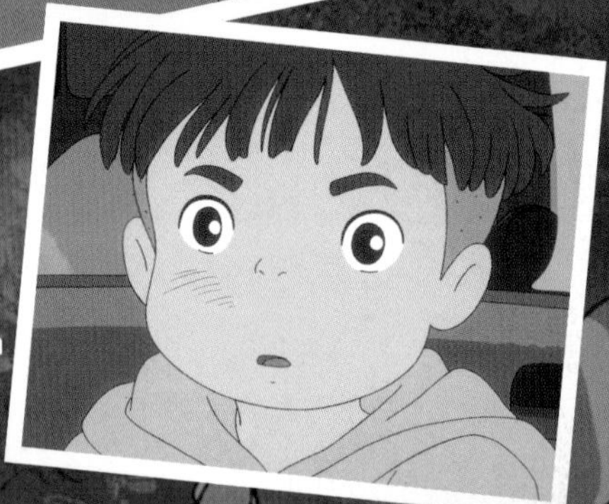

## SOSUKE

A kind and polite five-year-old boy. He is heartbroken when Ponyo's not around.

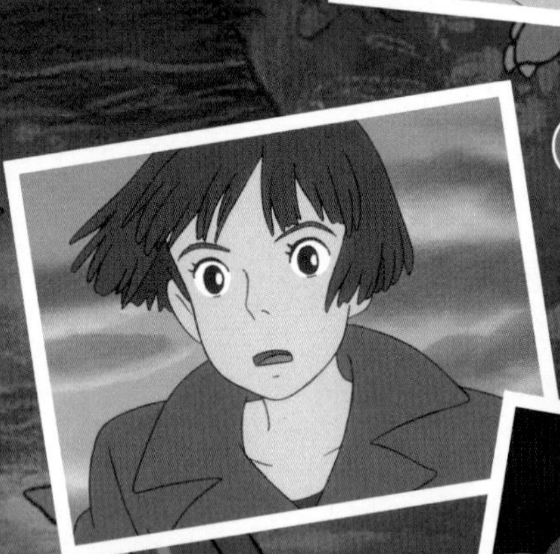

## LISA

Sosuke's mother. She's been looking after Sosuke and Ponyo.

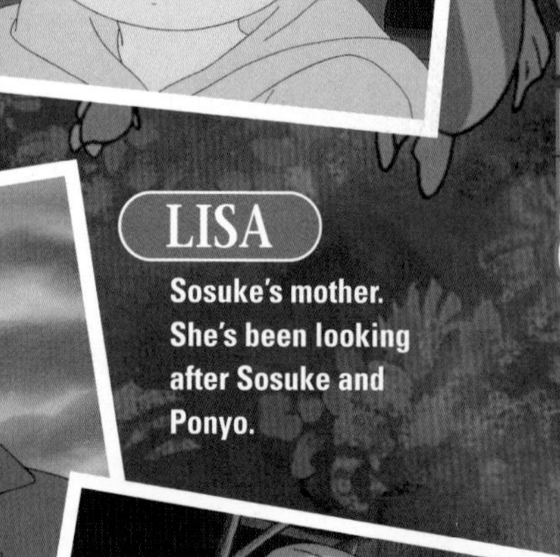

## KOICHI

Sosuke's father. He is the captain of the *Koganei Maru*.

## FUJIMOTO

Ponyo's father. He is studying how to reawaken the ancient seas.

## GRAN MAMARE

Ponyo's mother. She has magical powers.

## PONYO'S LITTLE SISTERS

There are a lot of them—and they are all cheering for their older sister, Ponyo.

## PREVIOUSLY...

The little fish that Sosuke found and named Ponyo was taken back to the ocean by her father, Fujimoto. Because Ponyo tasted Sosuke's blood, she is able to transform into a human and awaken the world above. However, Ponyo's actions have caused a huge storm...

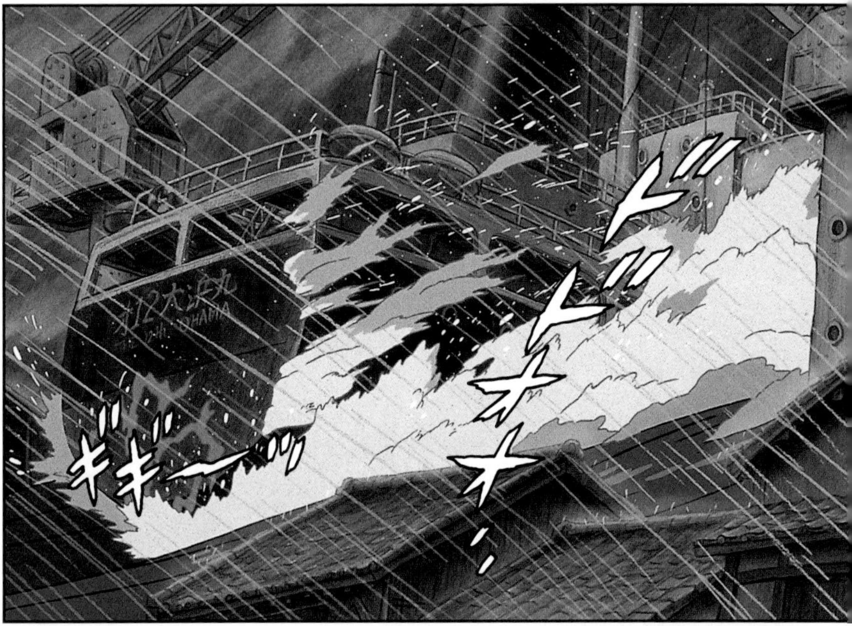
ドドオオー
ギギーッ
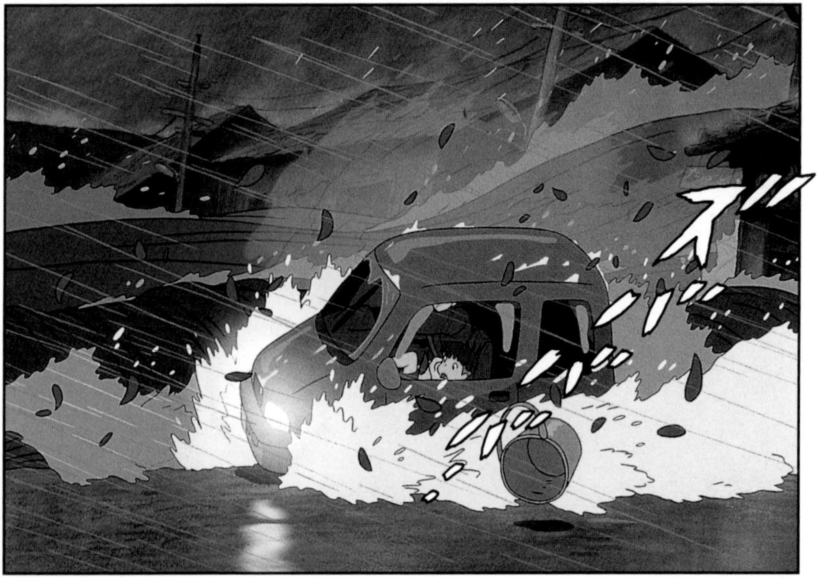
ズバババ

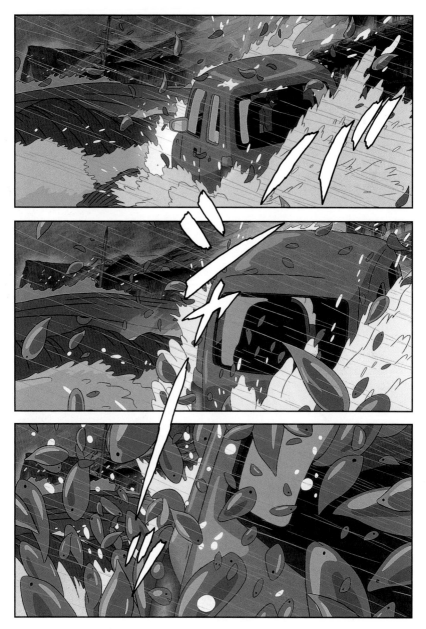

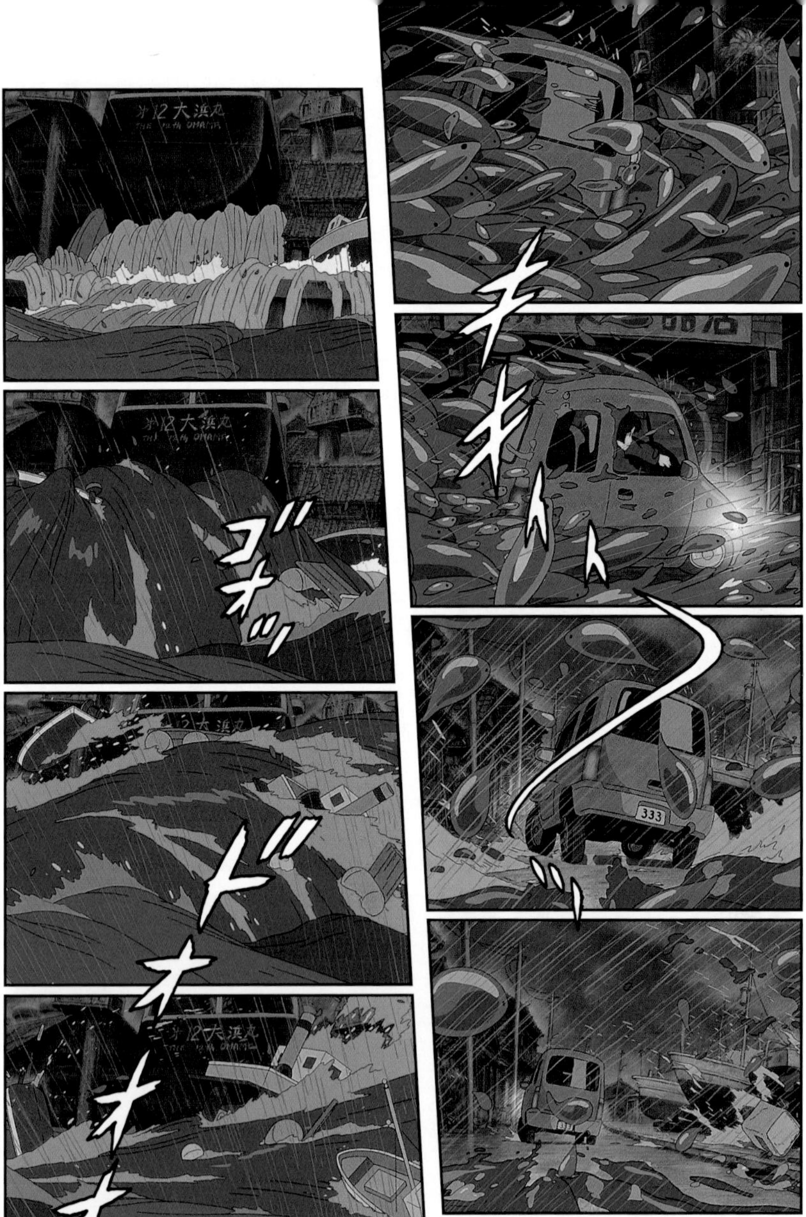
キキィィ
333
大浜丸
ゴボッ
ドドオオオオ

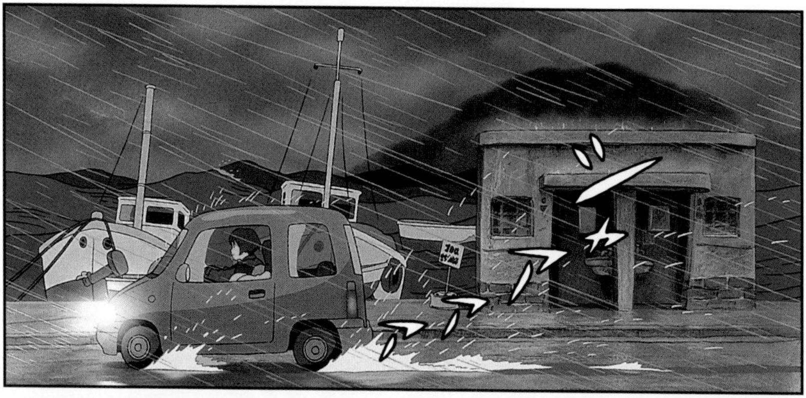

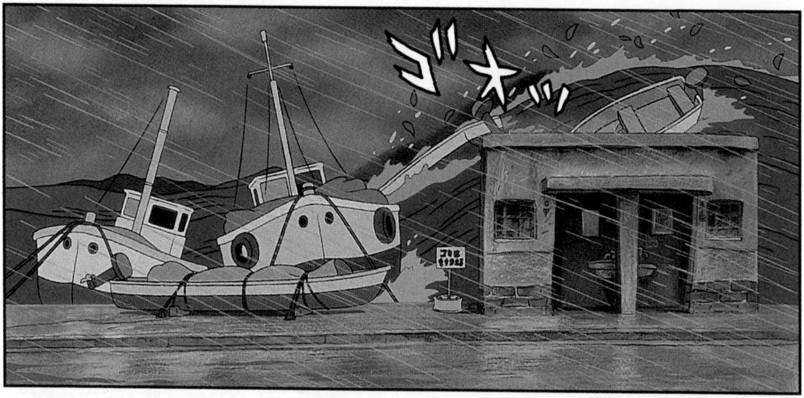
ゴオッ

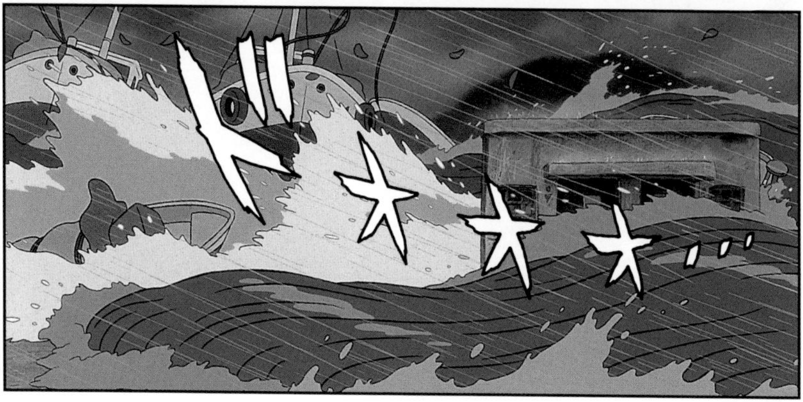
ドオオオ…

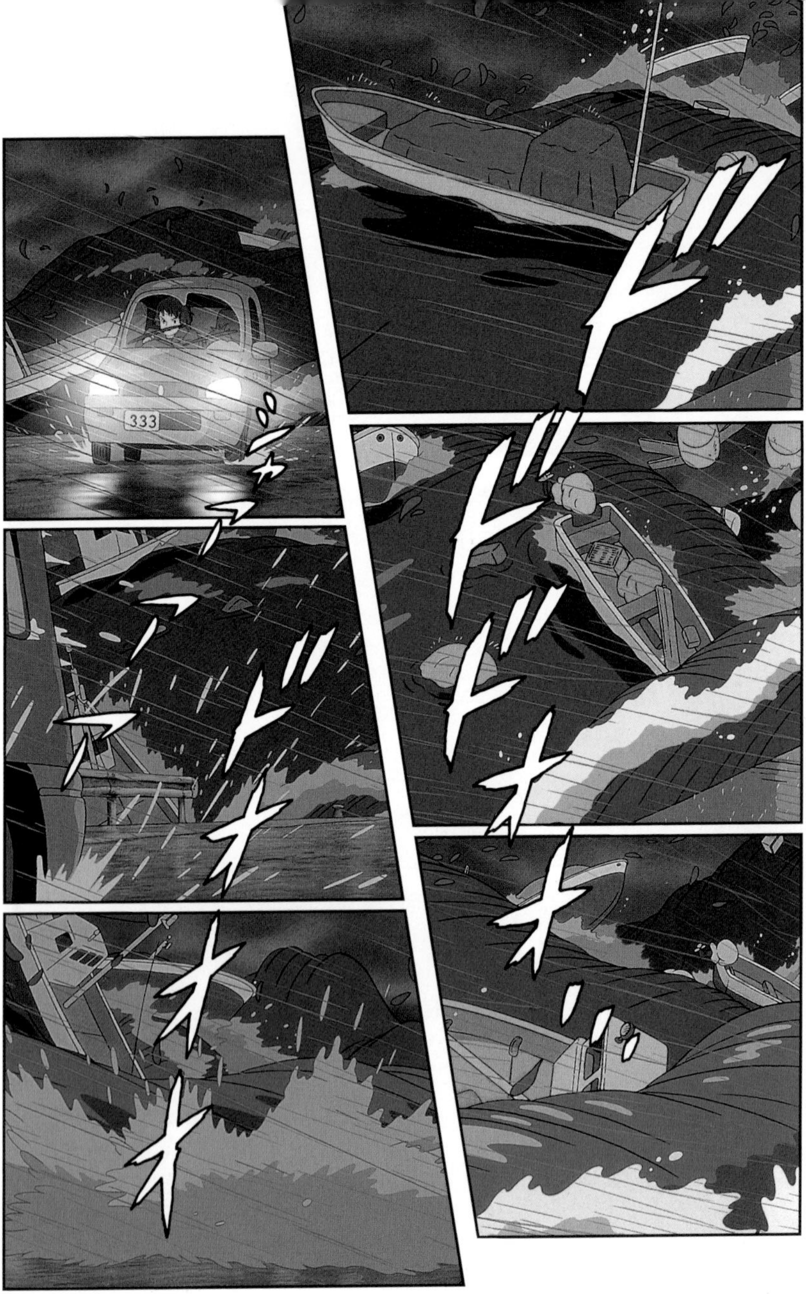
333
ドドドドオオオ…
ゴォアアア
ドオオオオ

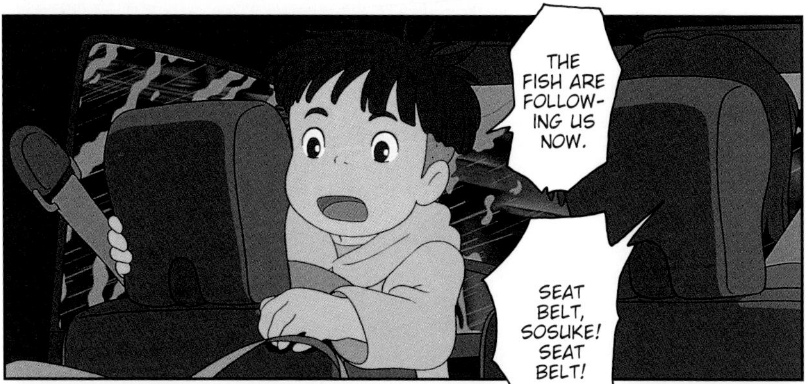
THE FISH ARE FOLLOW-ING US NOW.
SEAT BELT, SOSUKE! SEAT BELT!

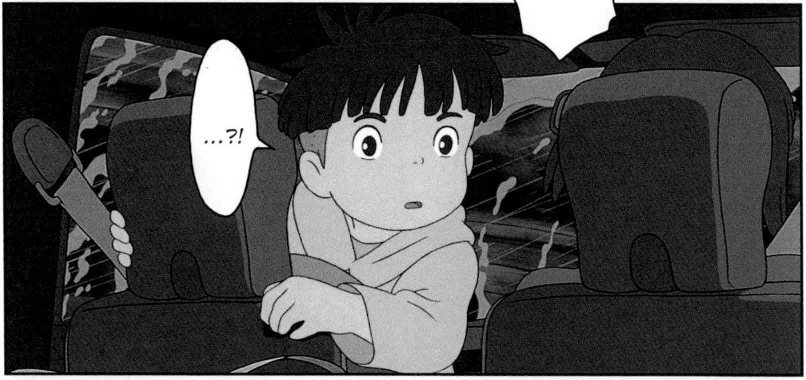
...?!

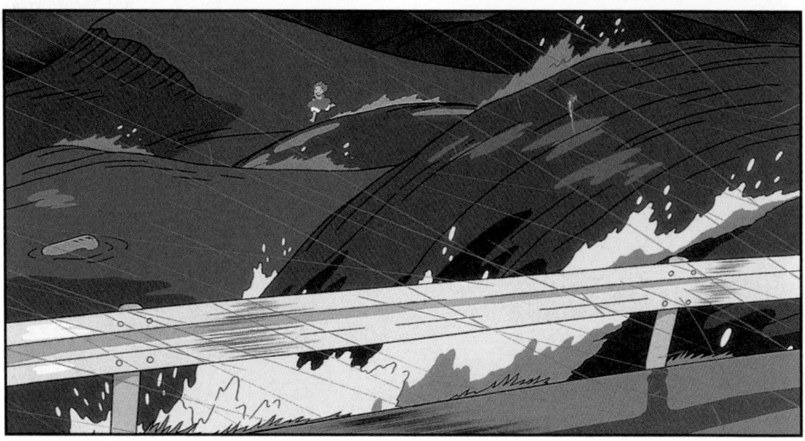

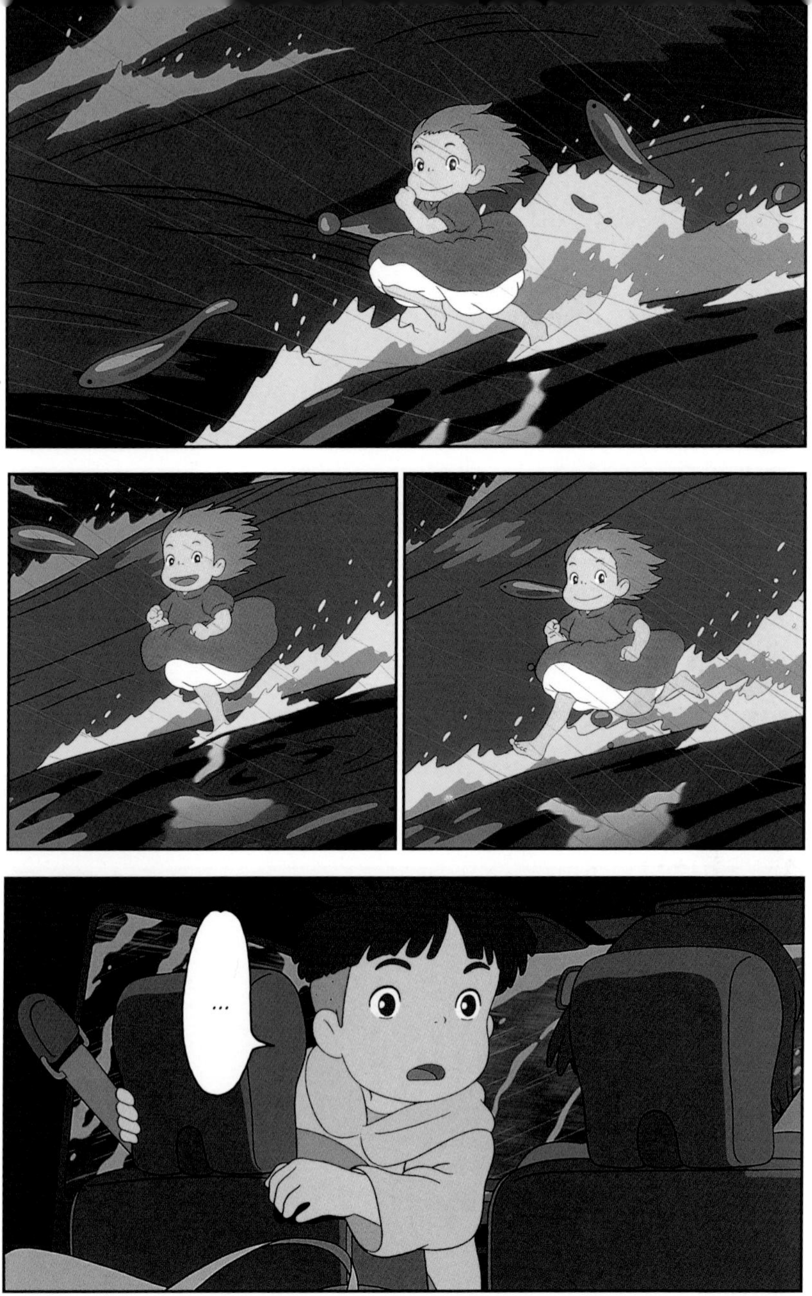
...

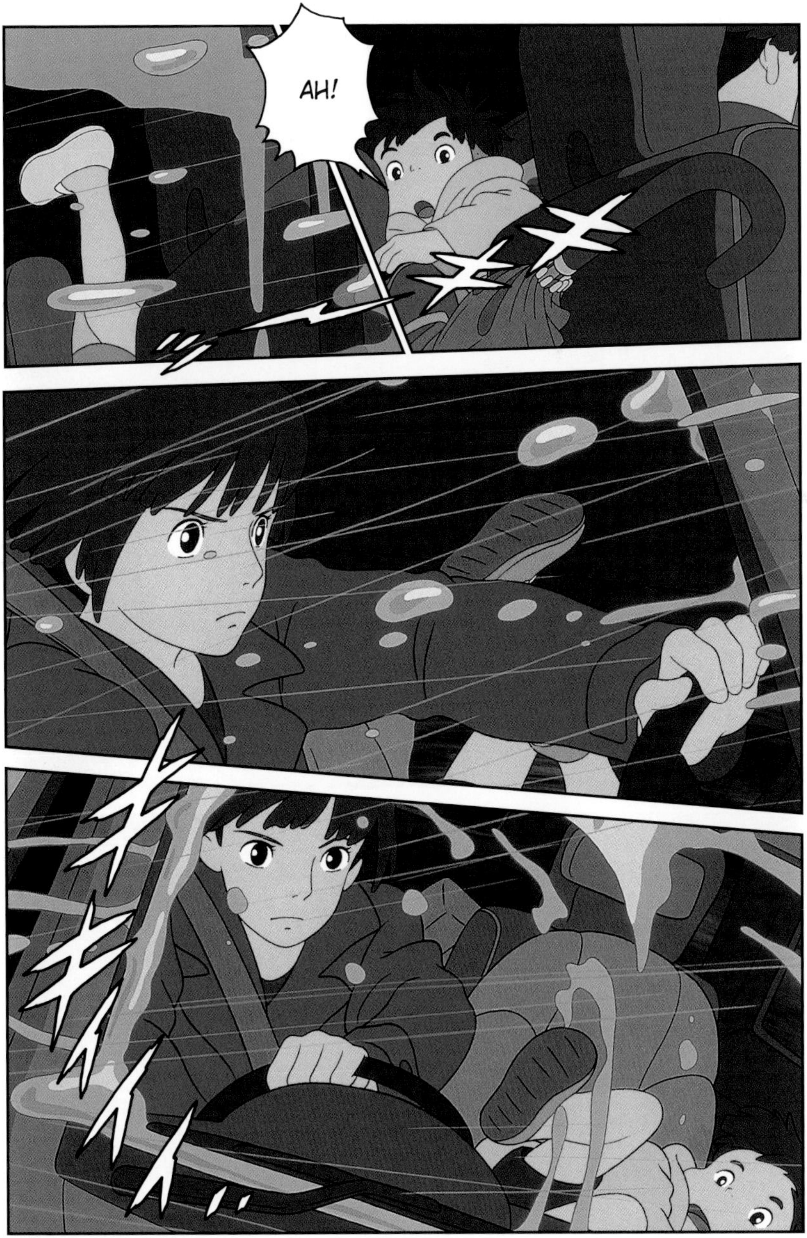
AH!

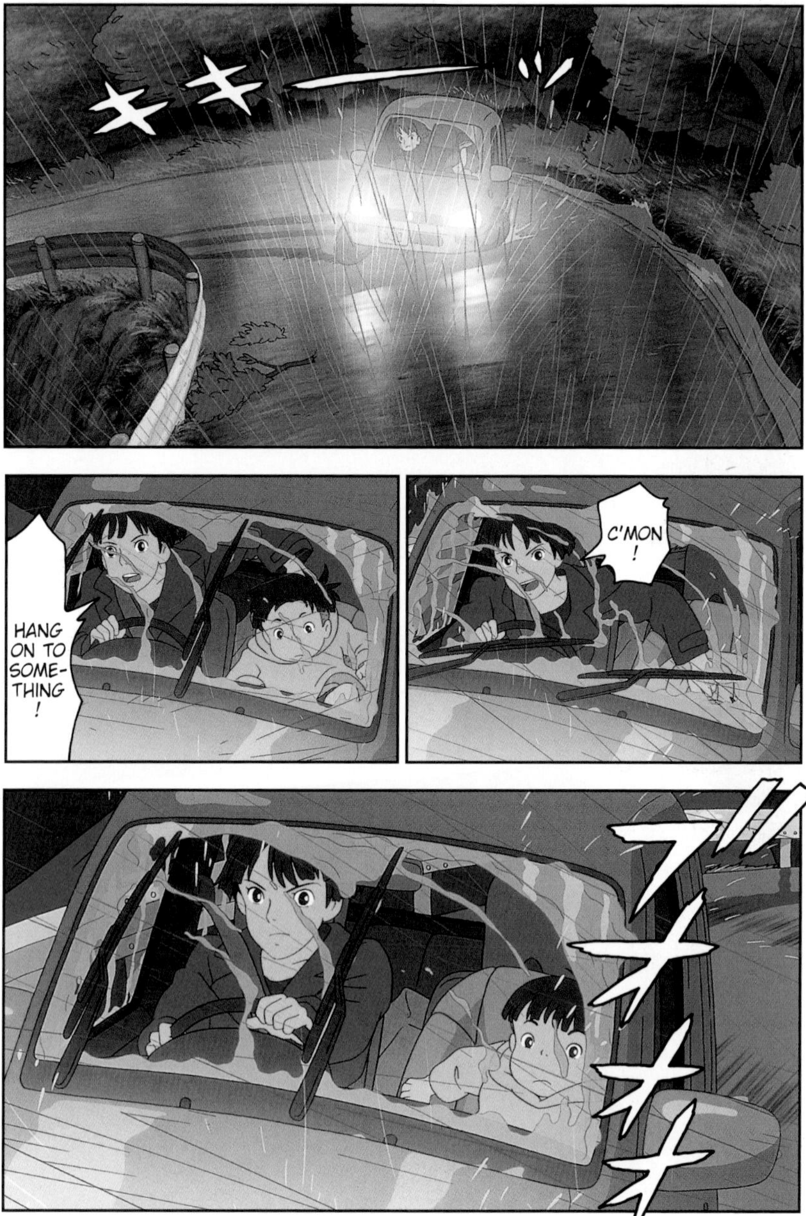
キキーッ
C'MON!
HANG ON TO SOME-THING!
ブオオオ

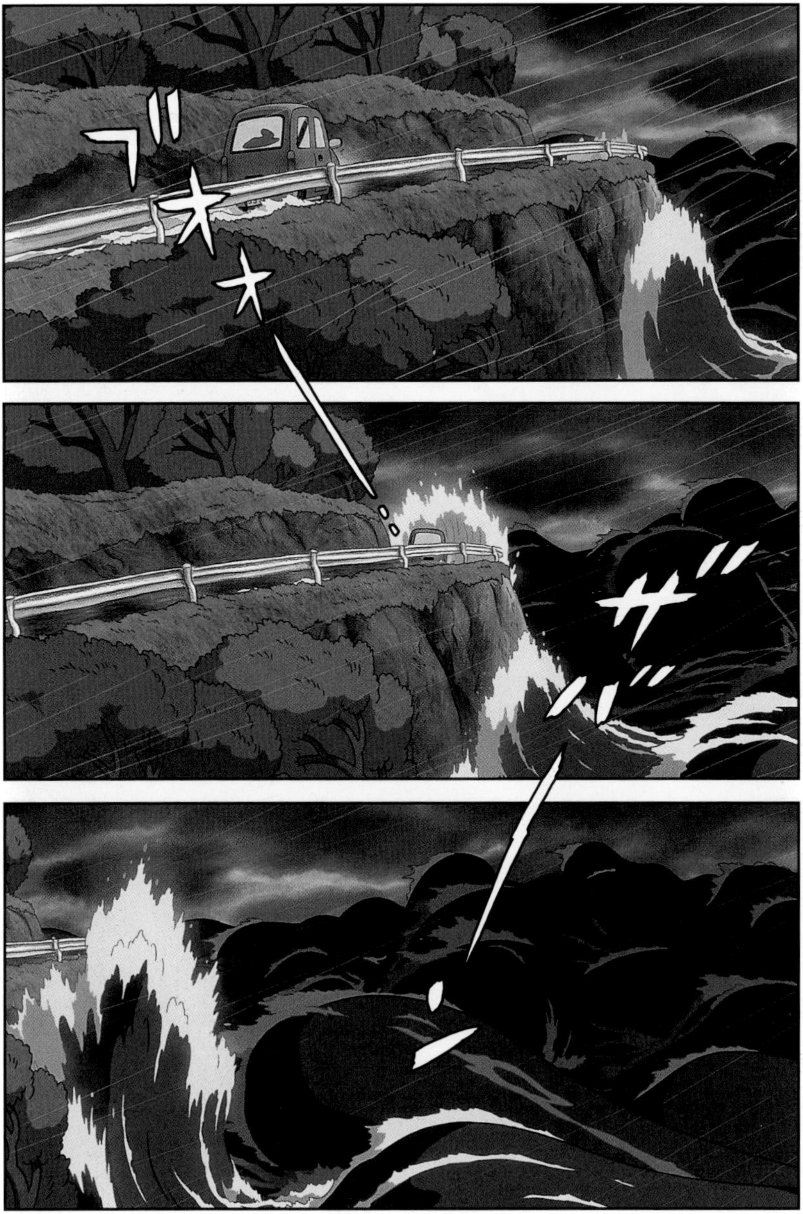
ブオオ
ザバーン

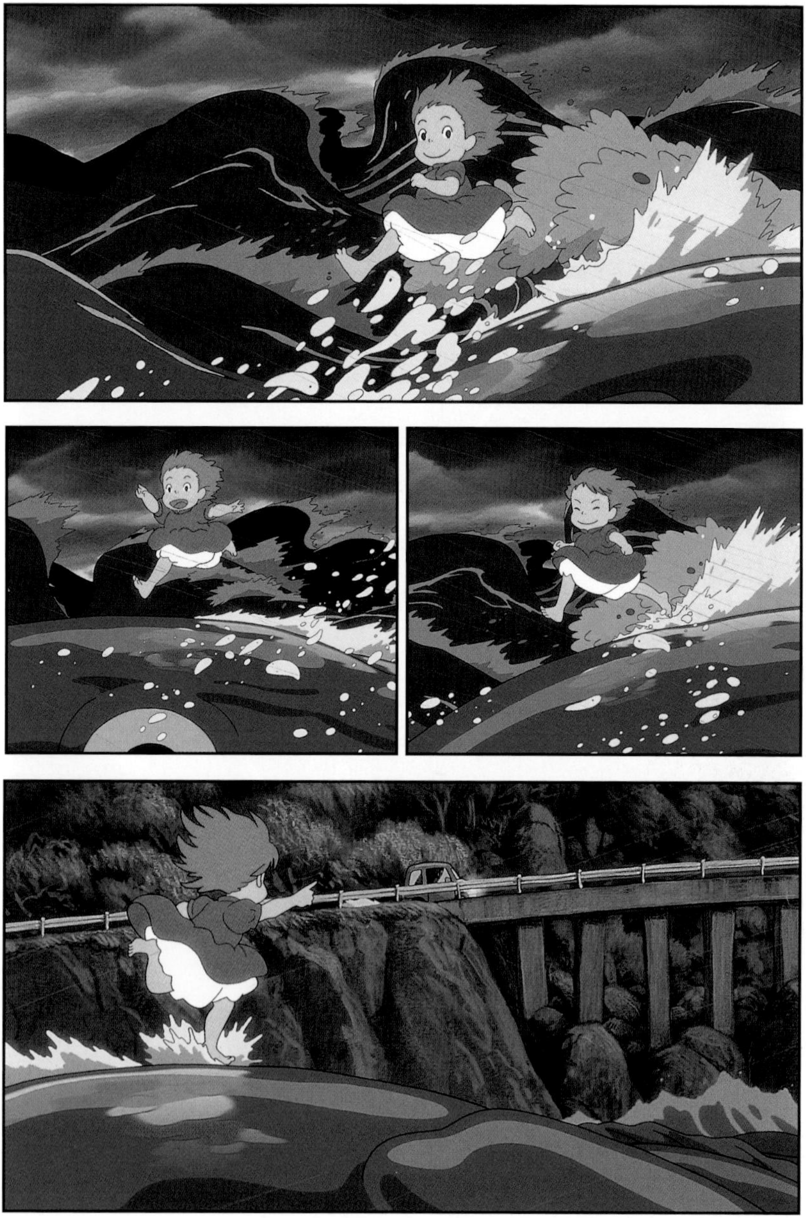

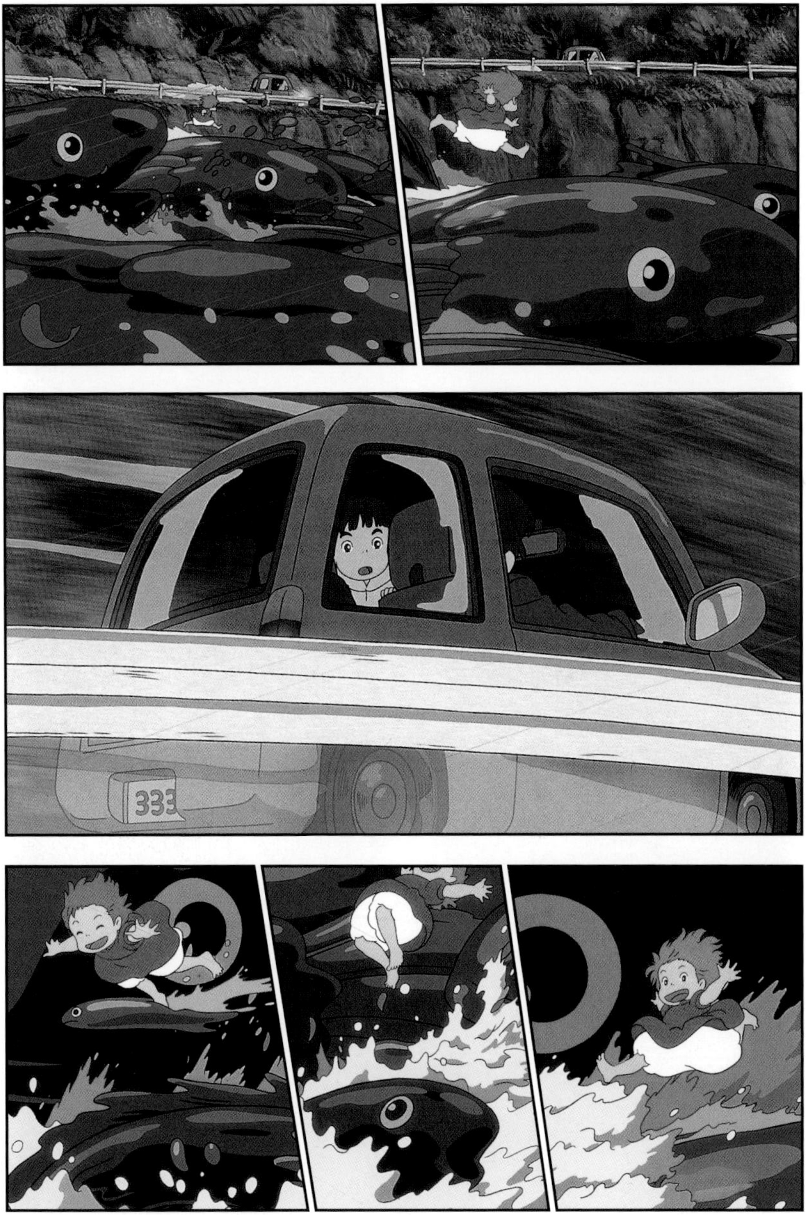
333

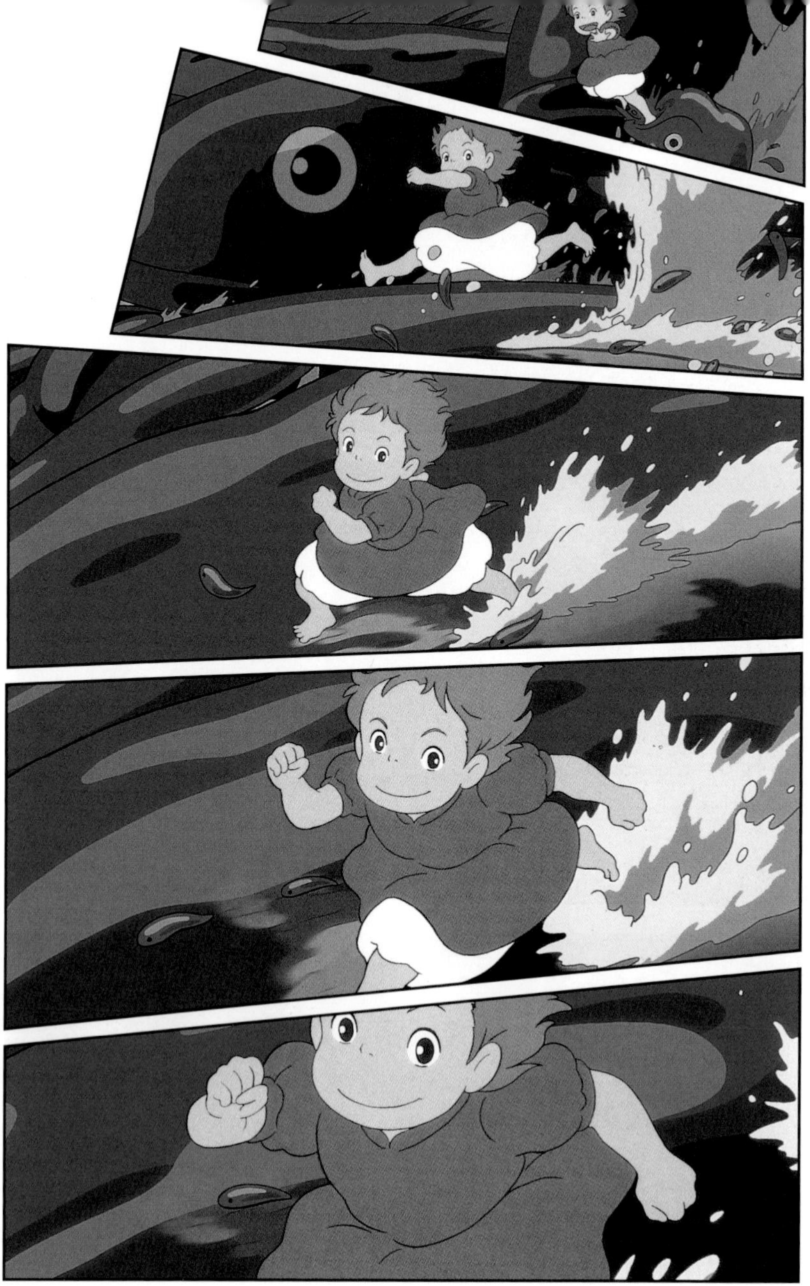

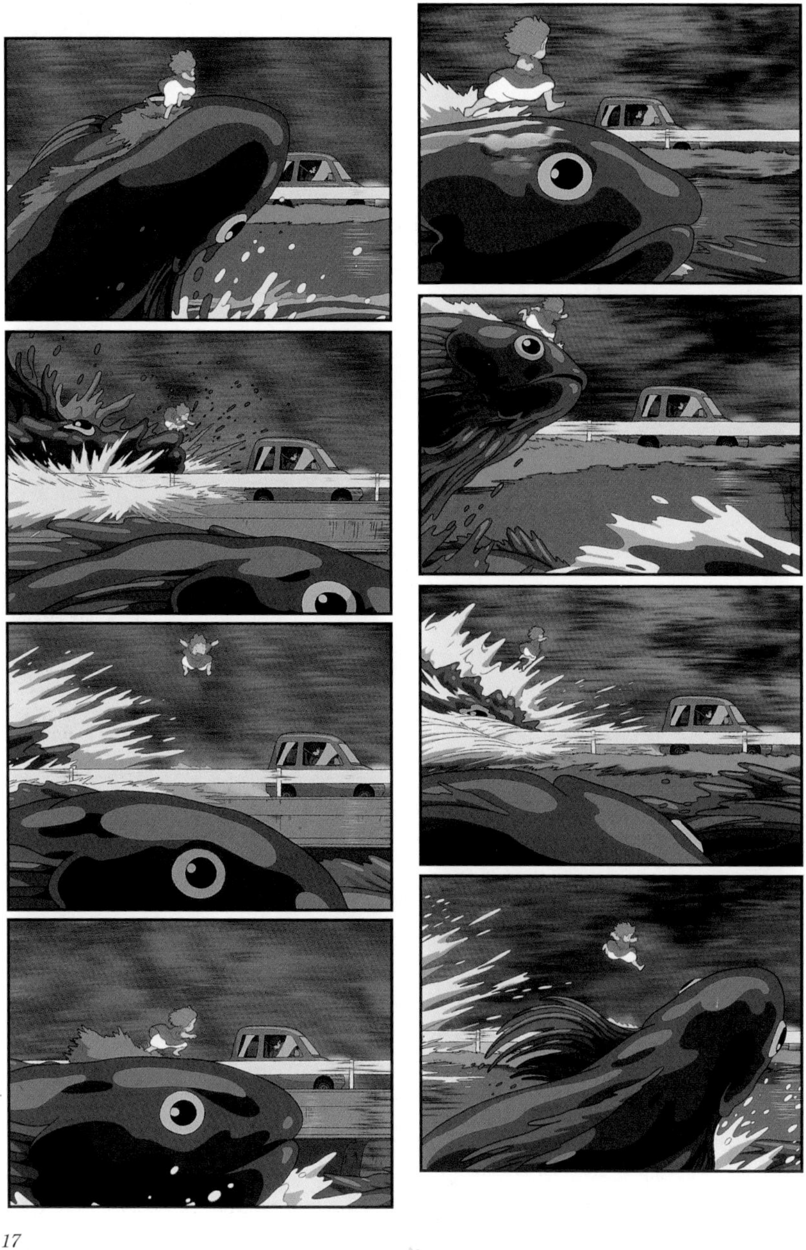

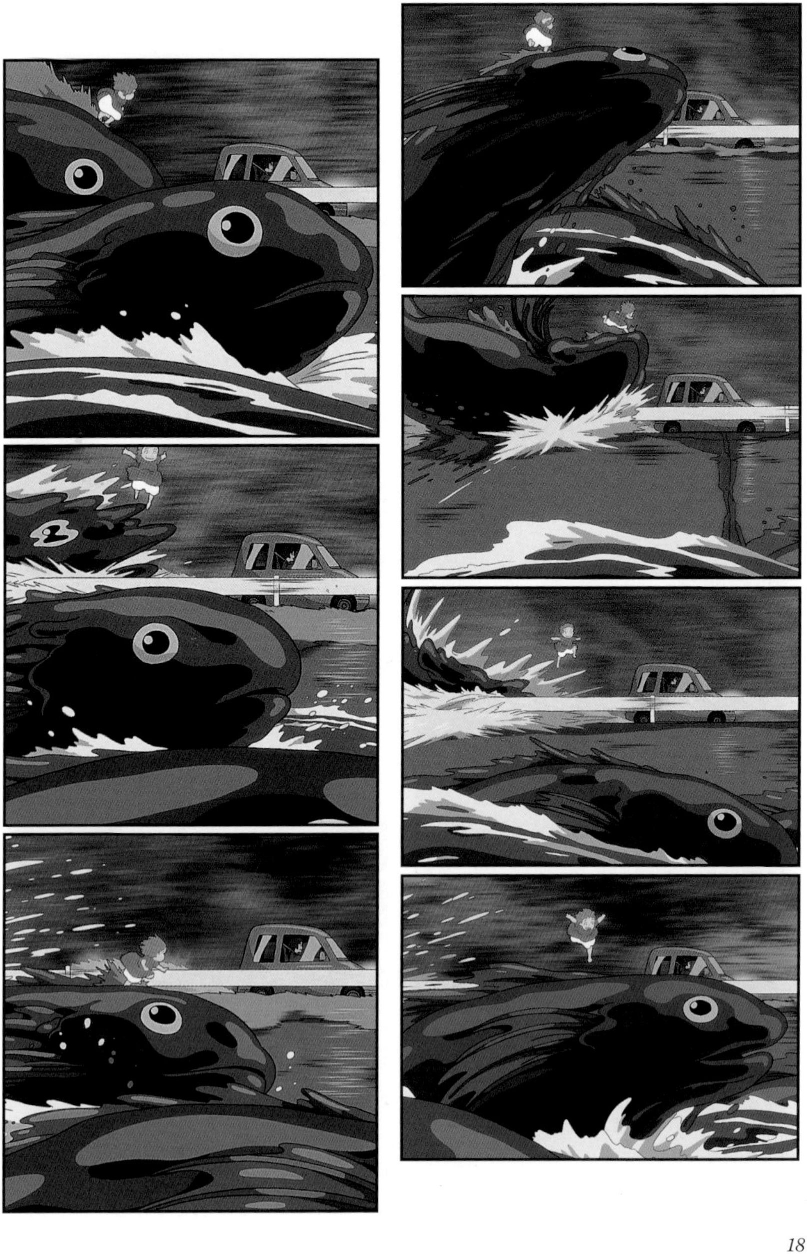

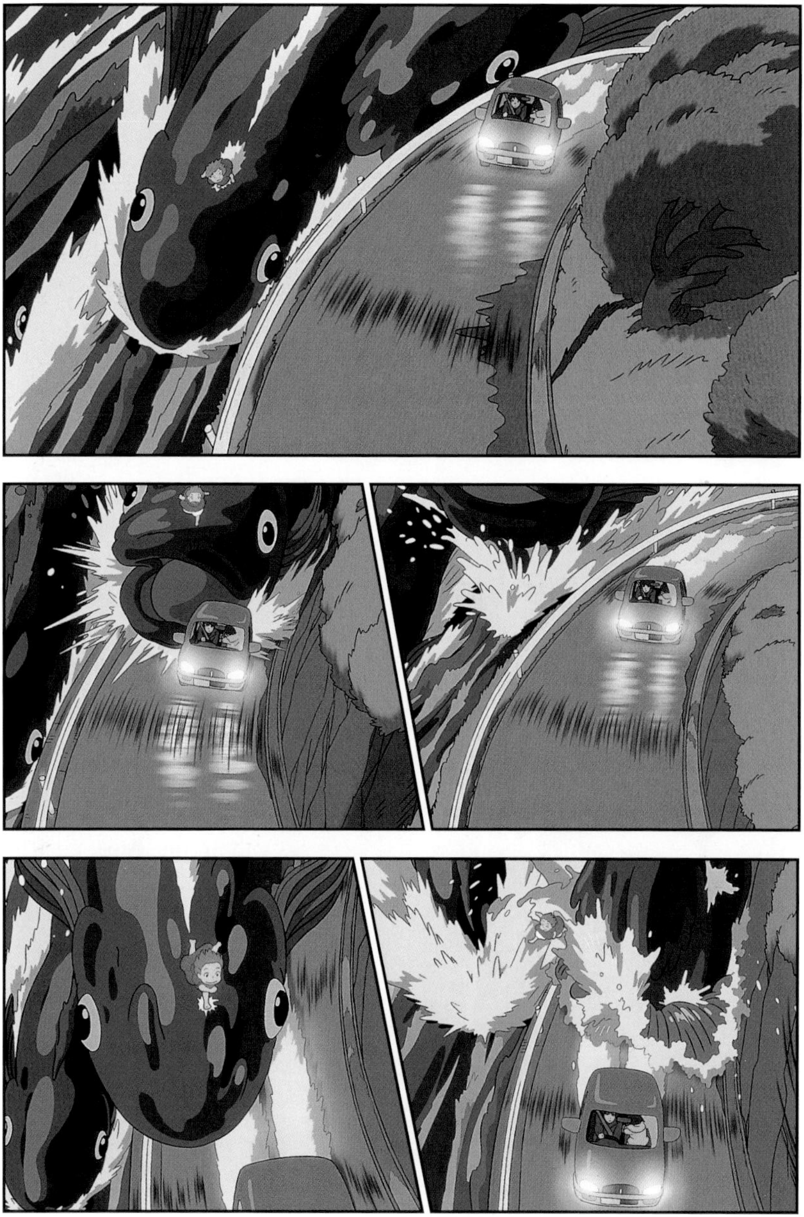

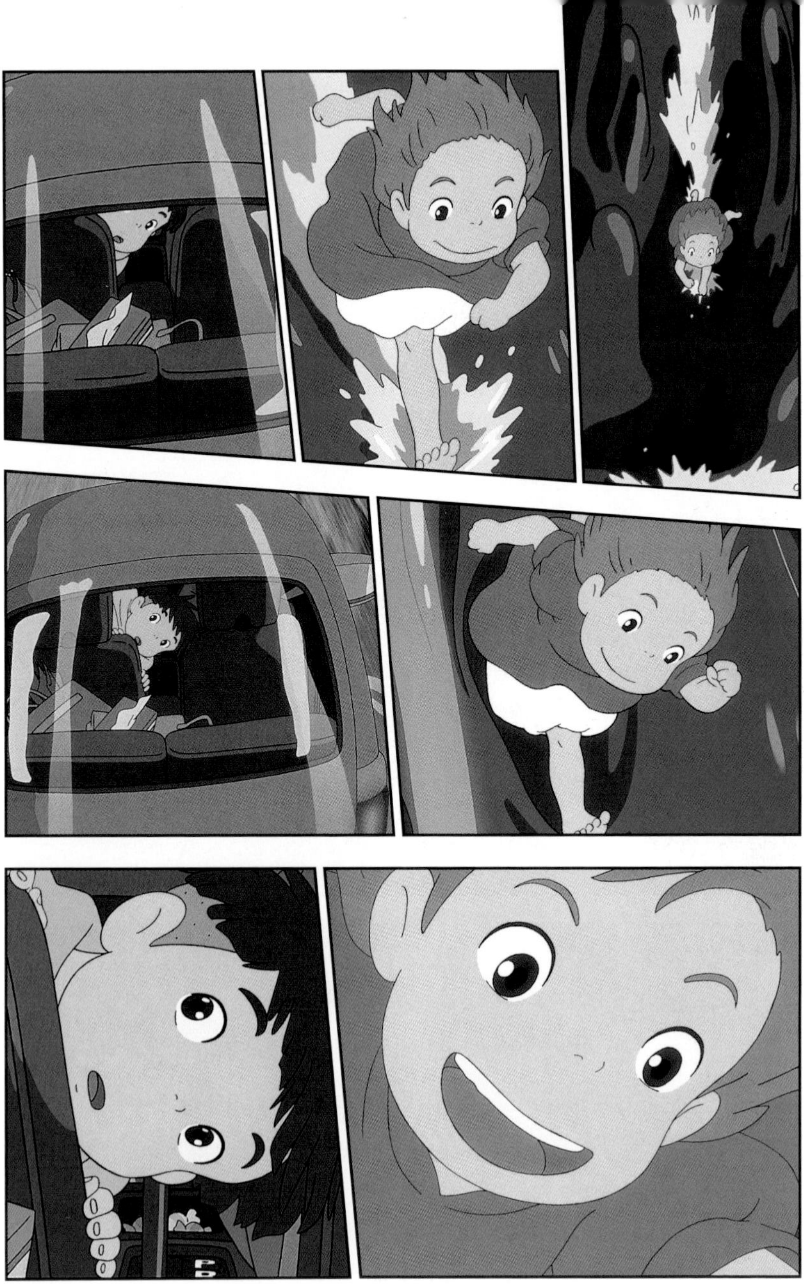

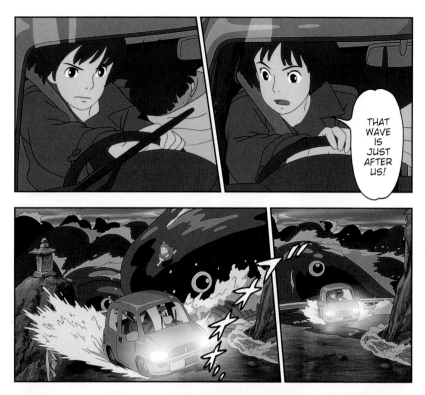

THAT
WAVE
IS
JUST
AFTER
US!

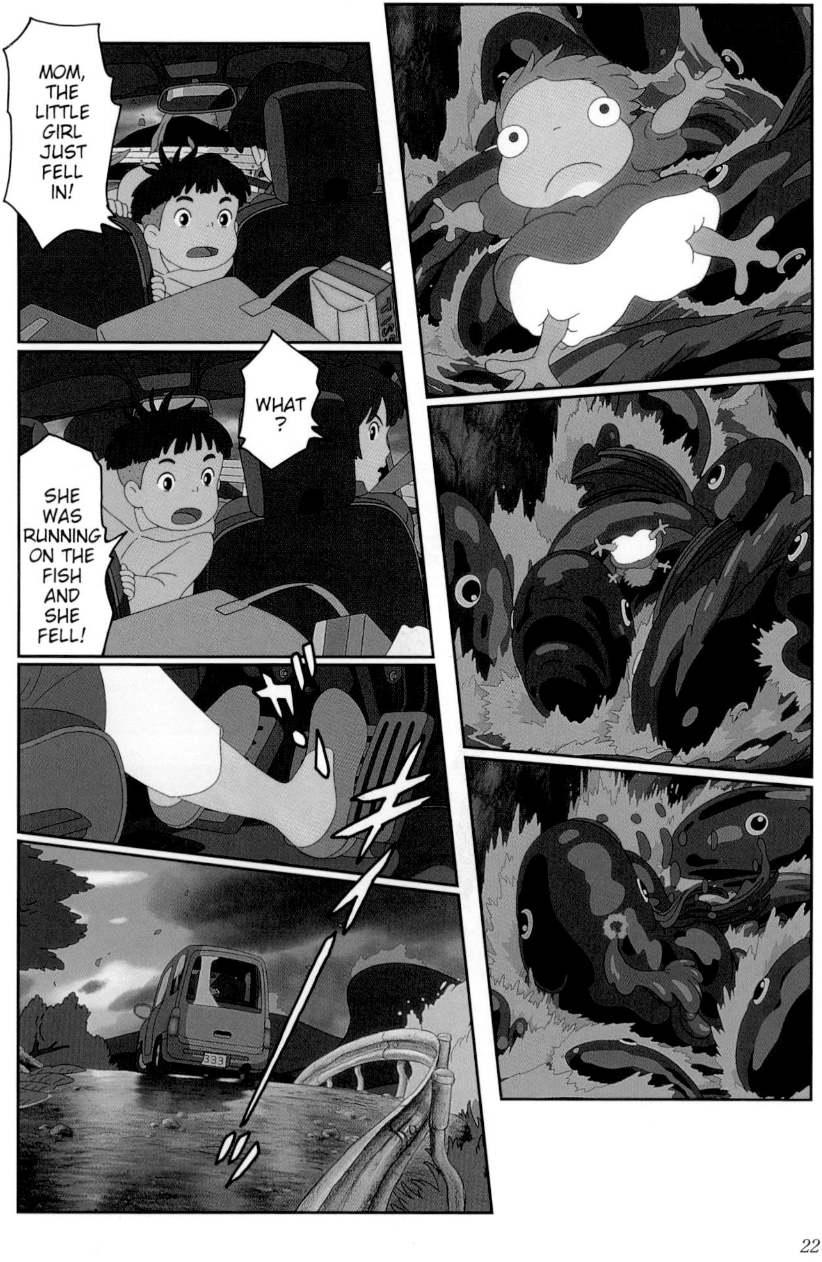
MOM, THE LITTLE GIRL JUST FELL IN!
WHAT?
SHE WAS RUNNING ON THE FISH AND SHE FELL!

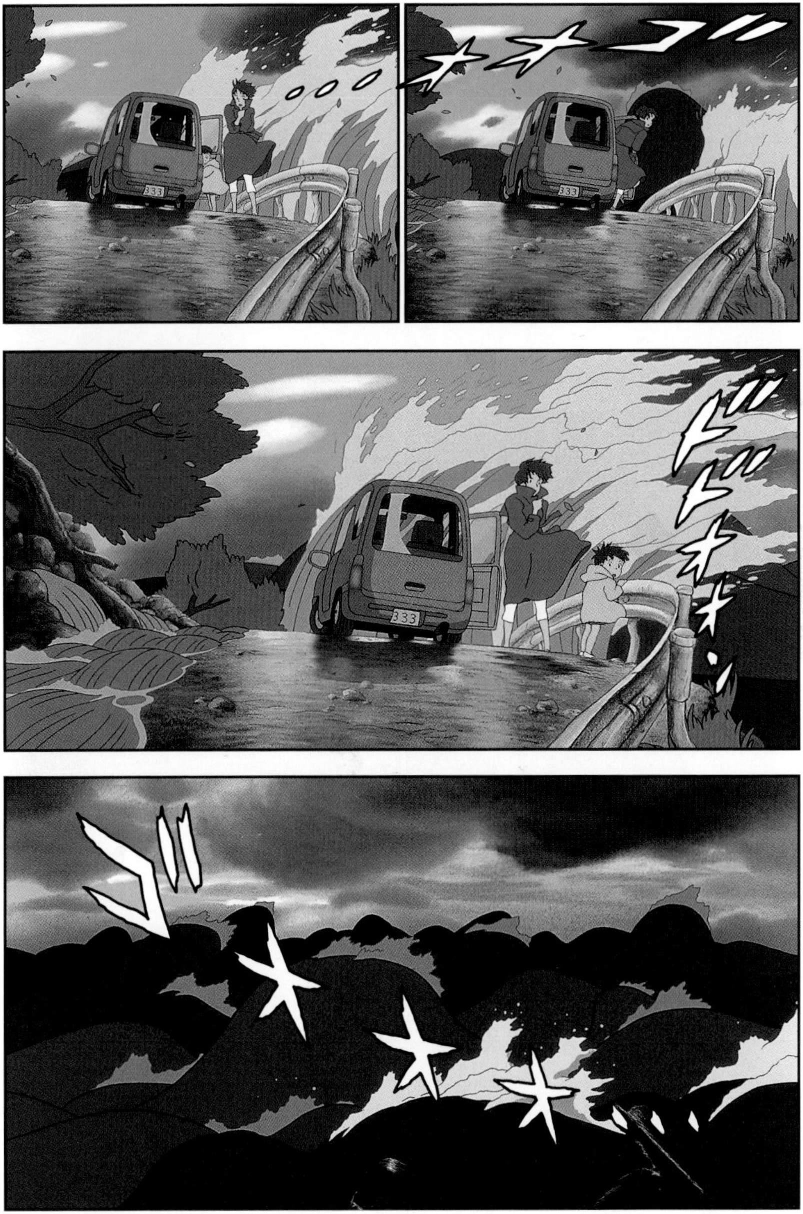
ゴーオオ…
ドドオオ…
ゴオオオ…

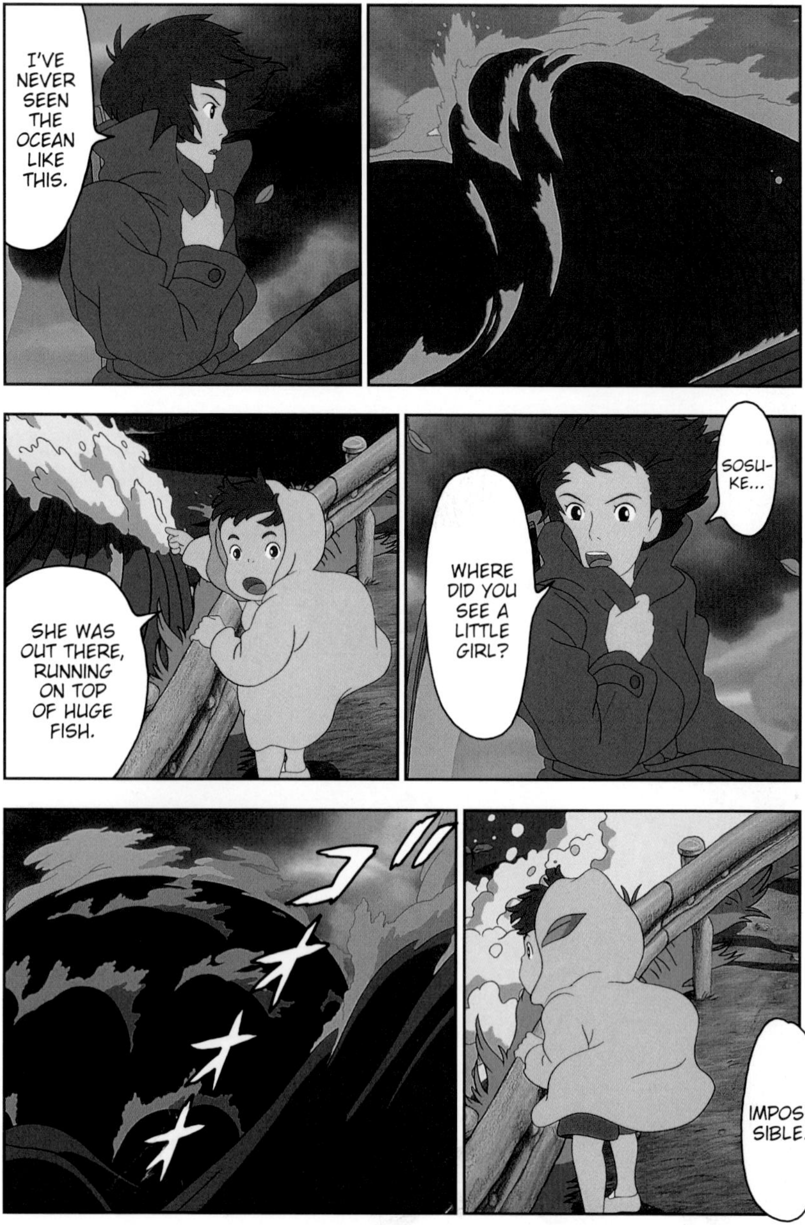
I'VE NEVER SEEN THE OCEAN LIKE THIS.
SOSU-KE...
WHERE DID YOU SEE A LITTLE GIRL?
SHE WAS OUT THERE, RUNNING ON TOP OF HUGE FISH.
IMPOS-SIBLE.

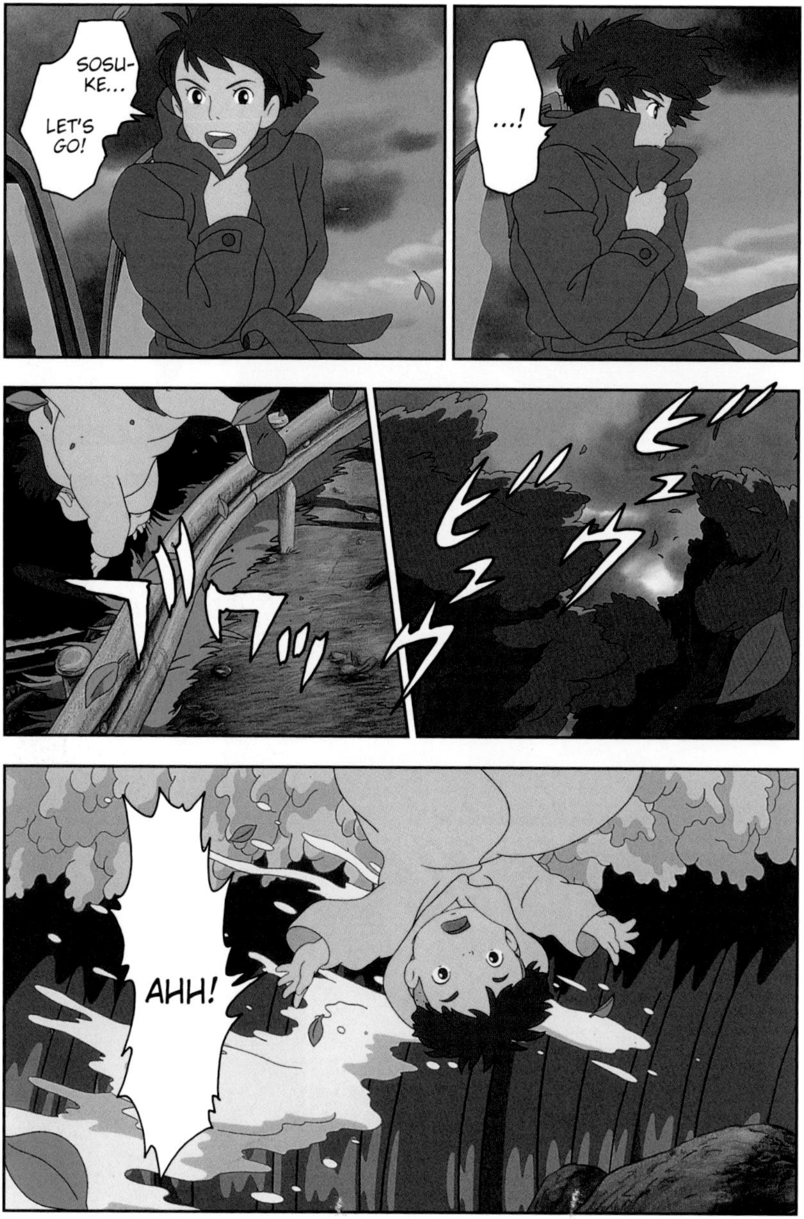
SOSUKE...
LET'S GO!
...!
ブワッ
ビュウ
ビュウ
AHH!

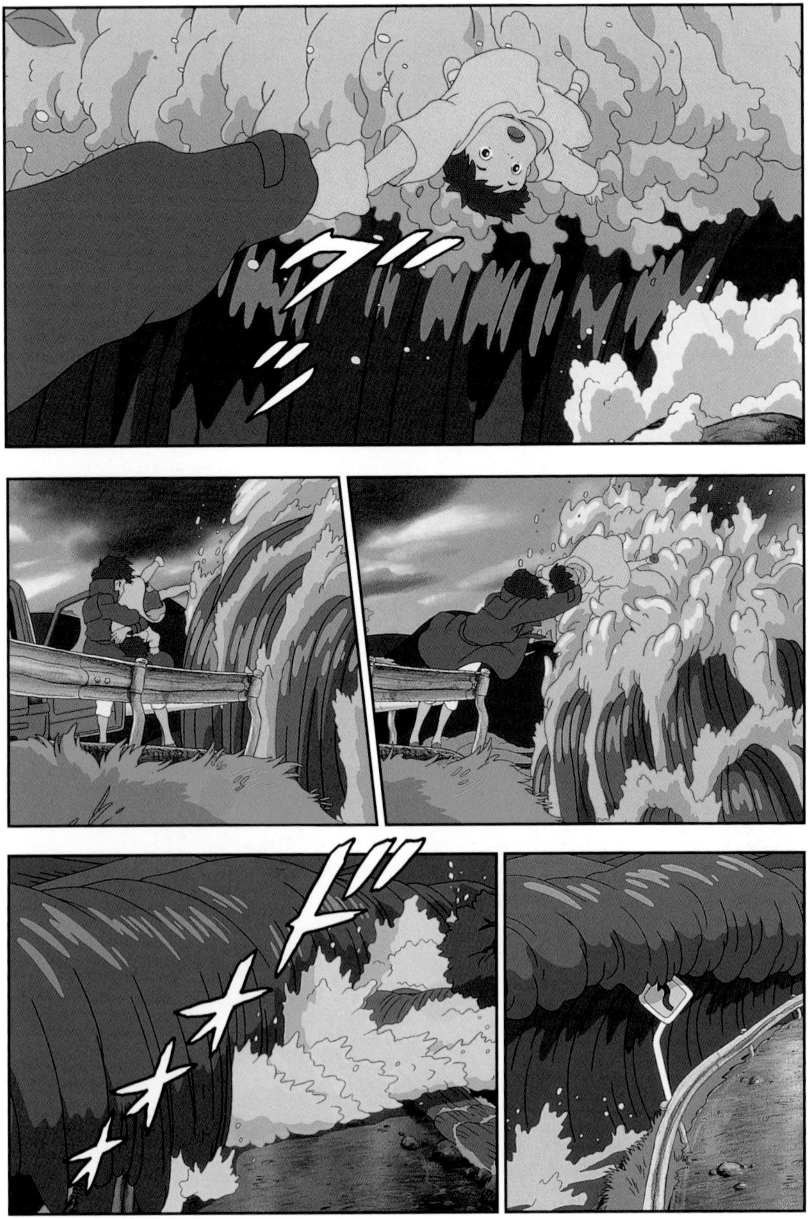

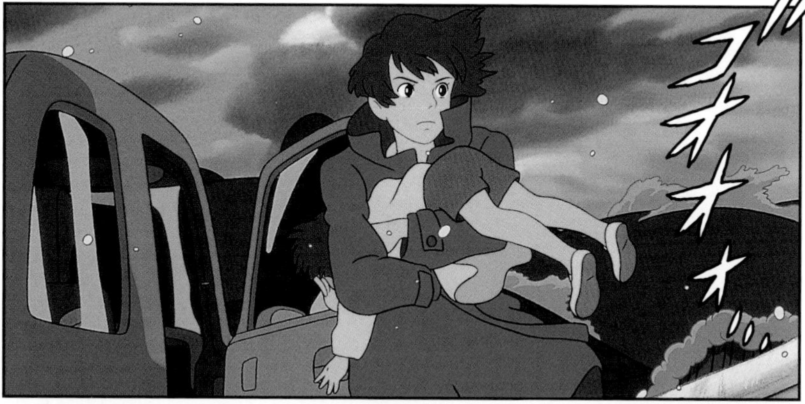
ゴオオオオ…
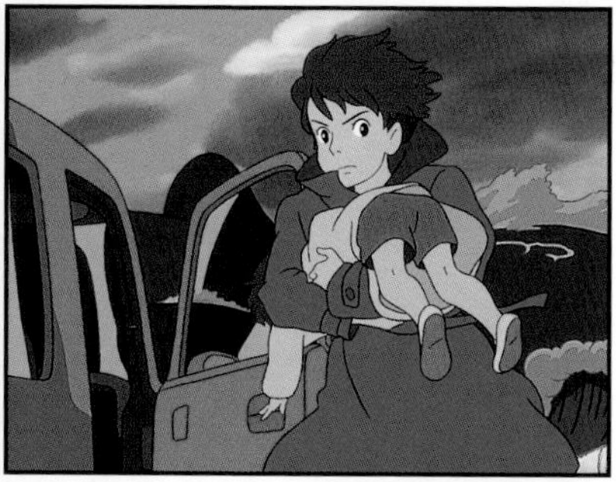
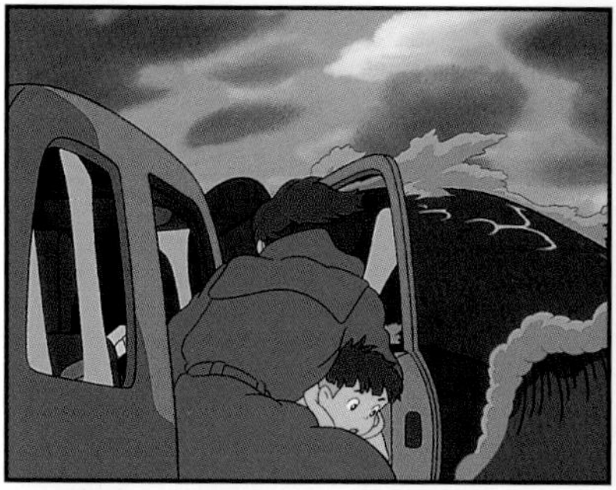
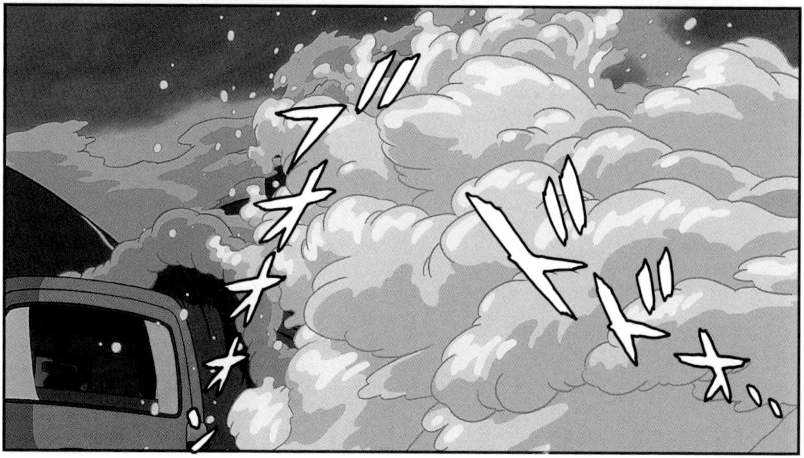
ブオオオオ…
ドドォ…

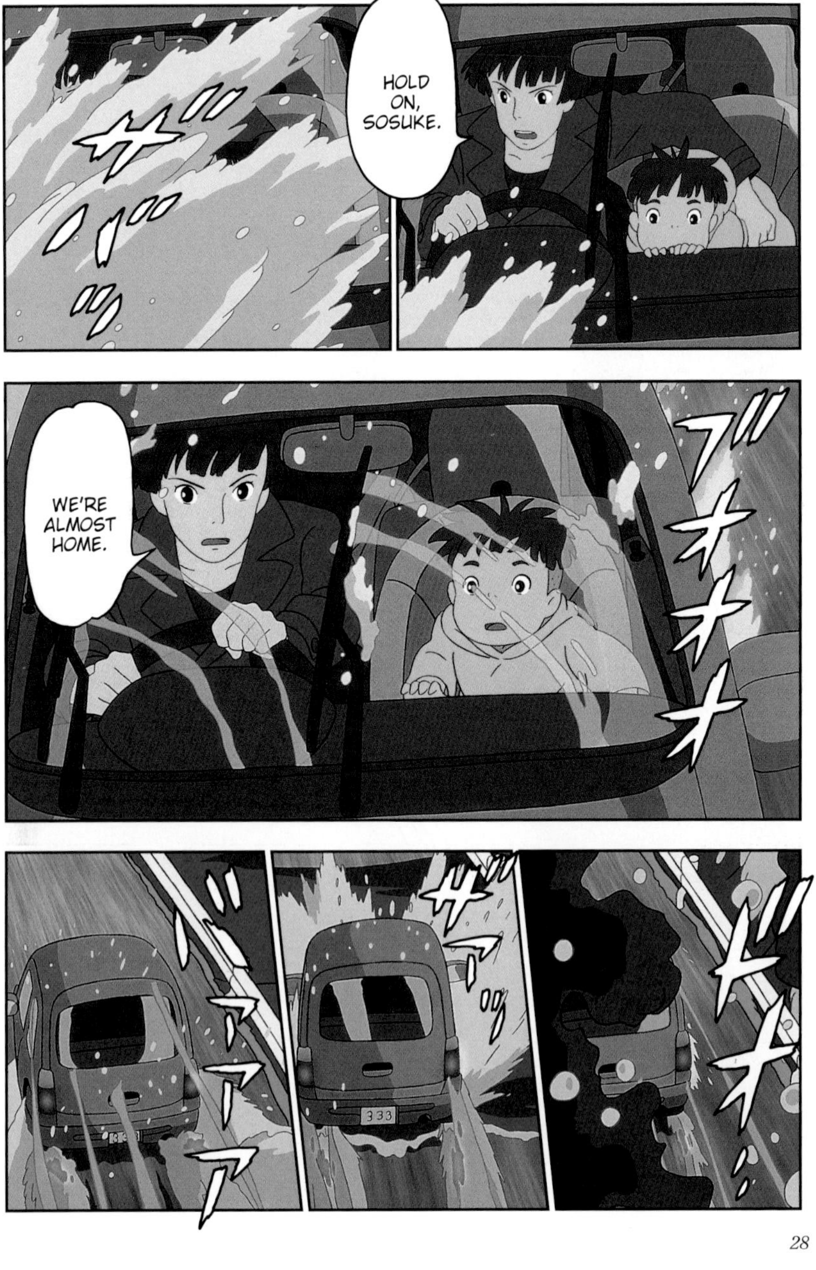
HOLD ON, SOSUKE.
WE'RE ALMOST HOME.

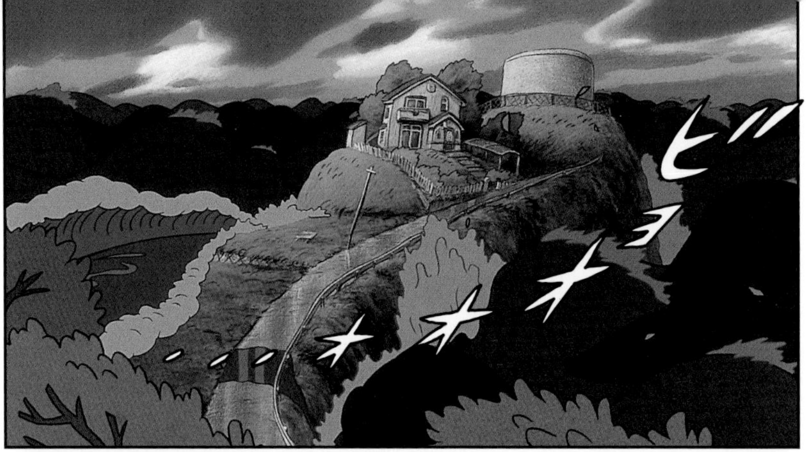
ビョオオオ…
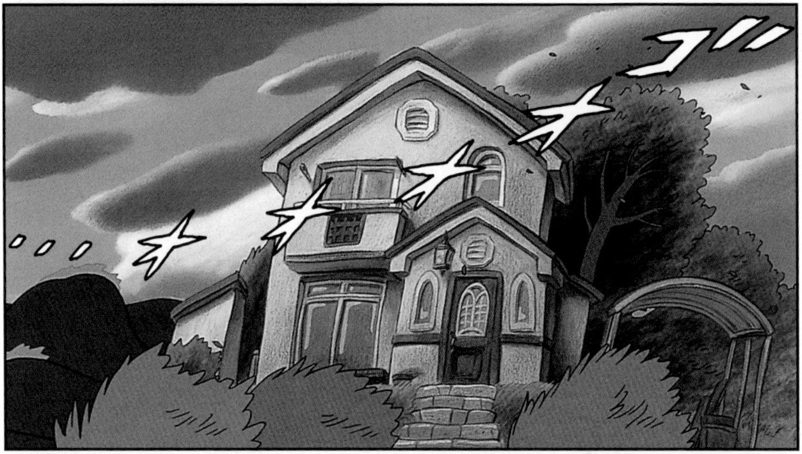
ゴオオオオ…
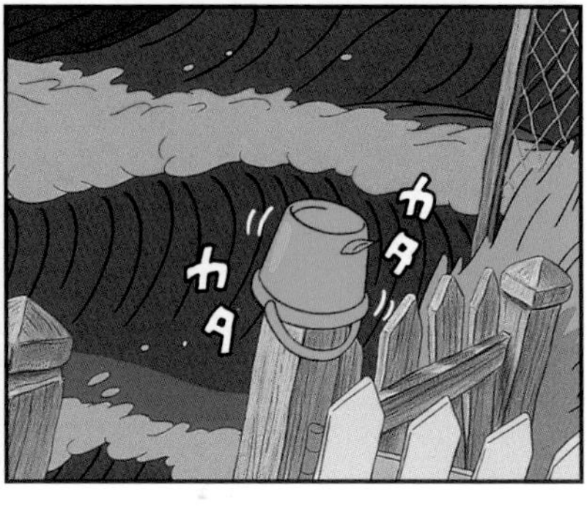
カタ
カタ
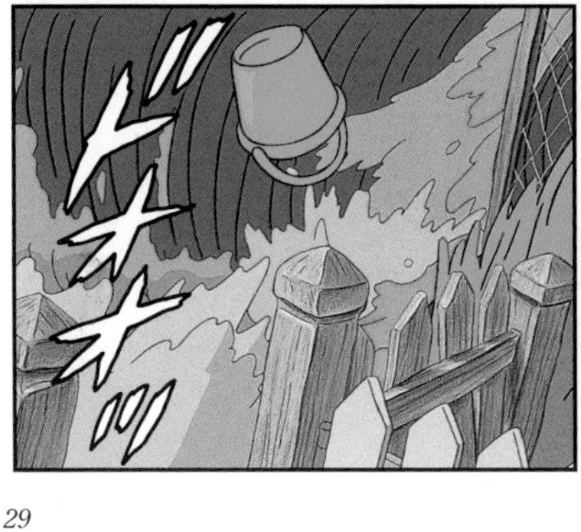
ドオオッ

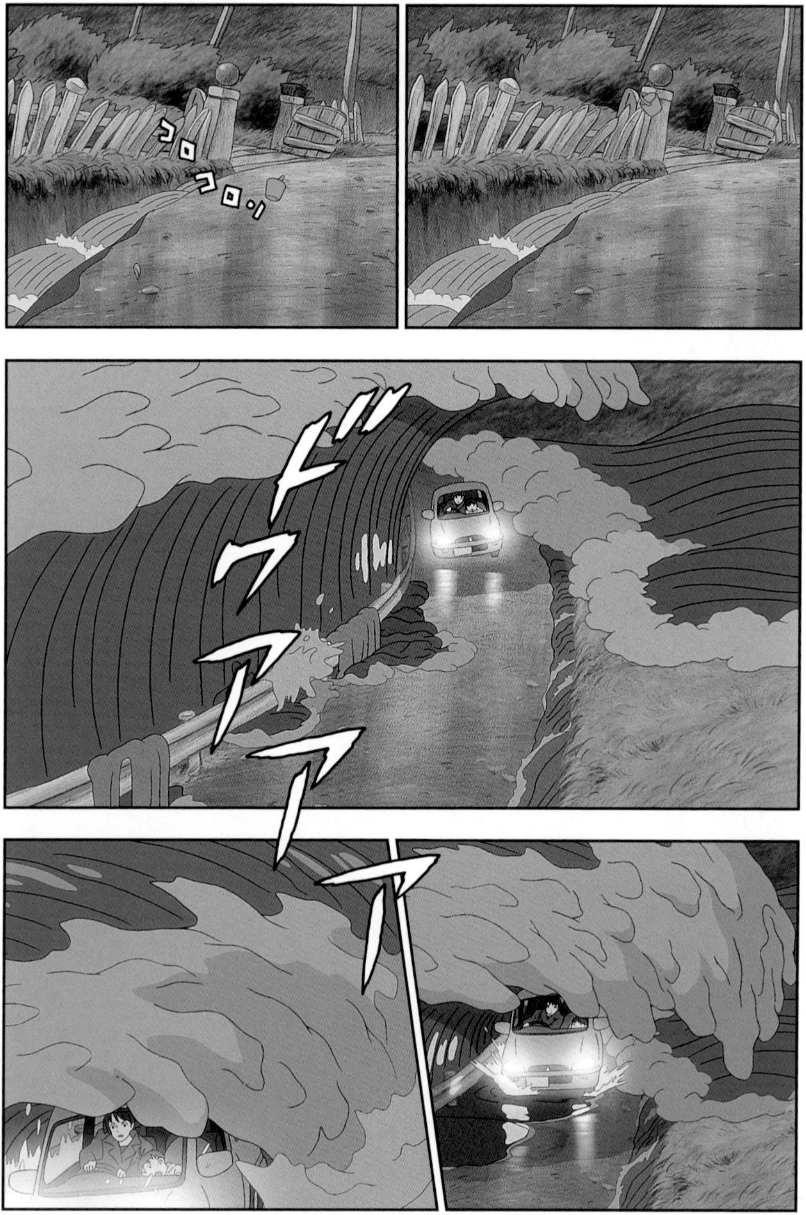
コロコロッ
ドワアアア

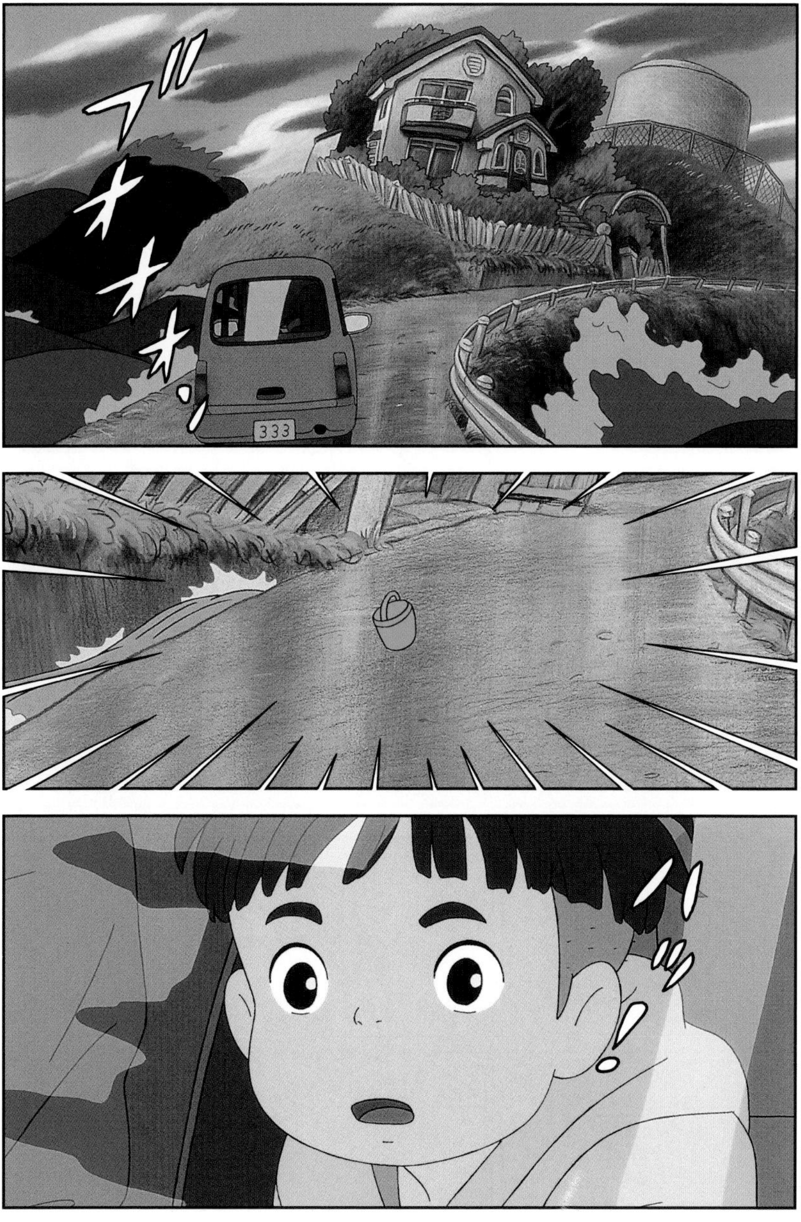
ブオォォ!
333

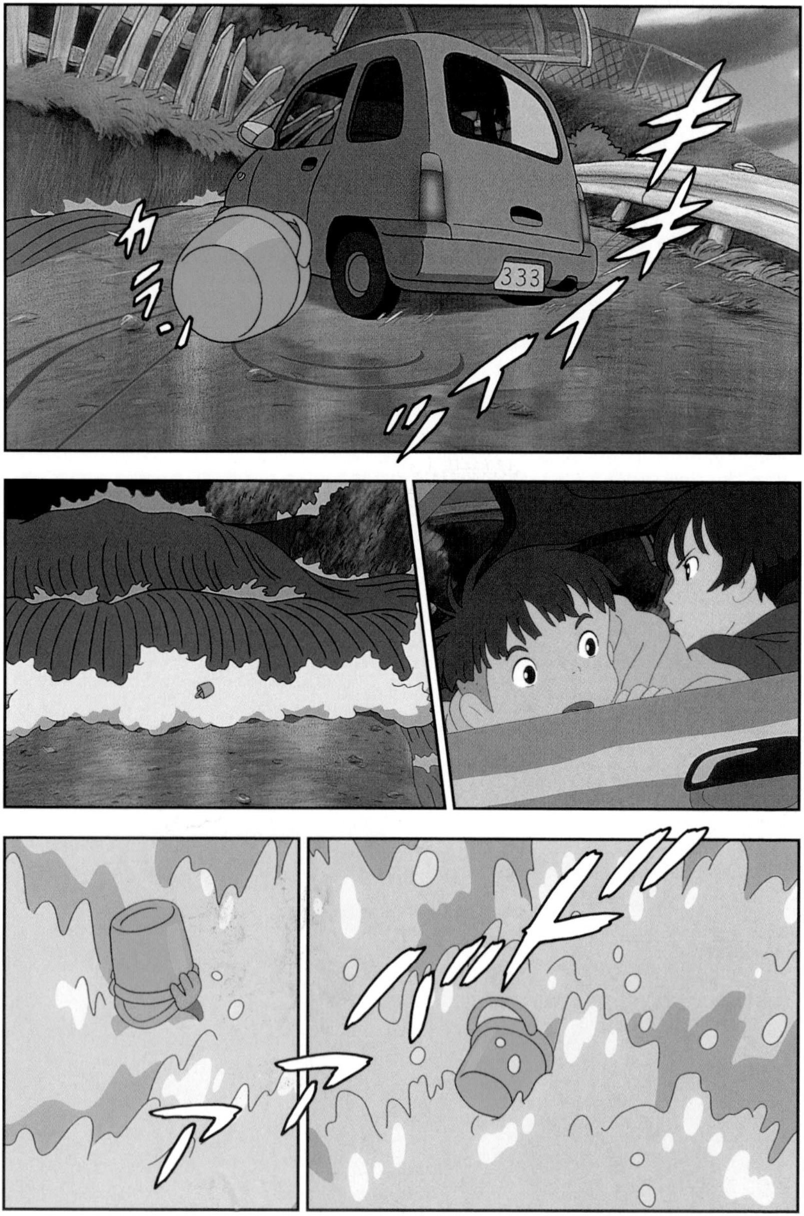
キキイイッ
カラン
ドバアア

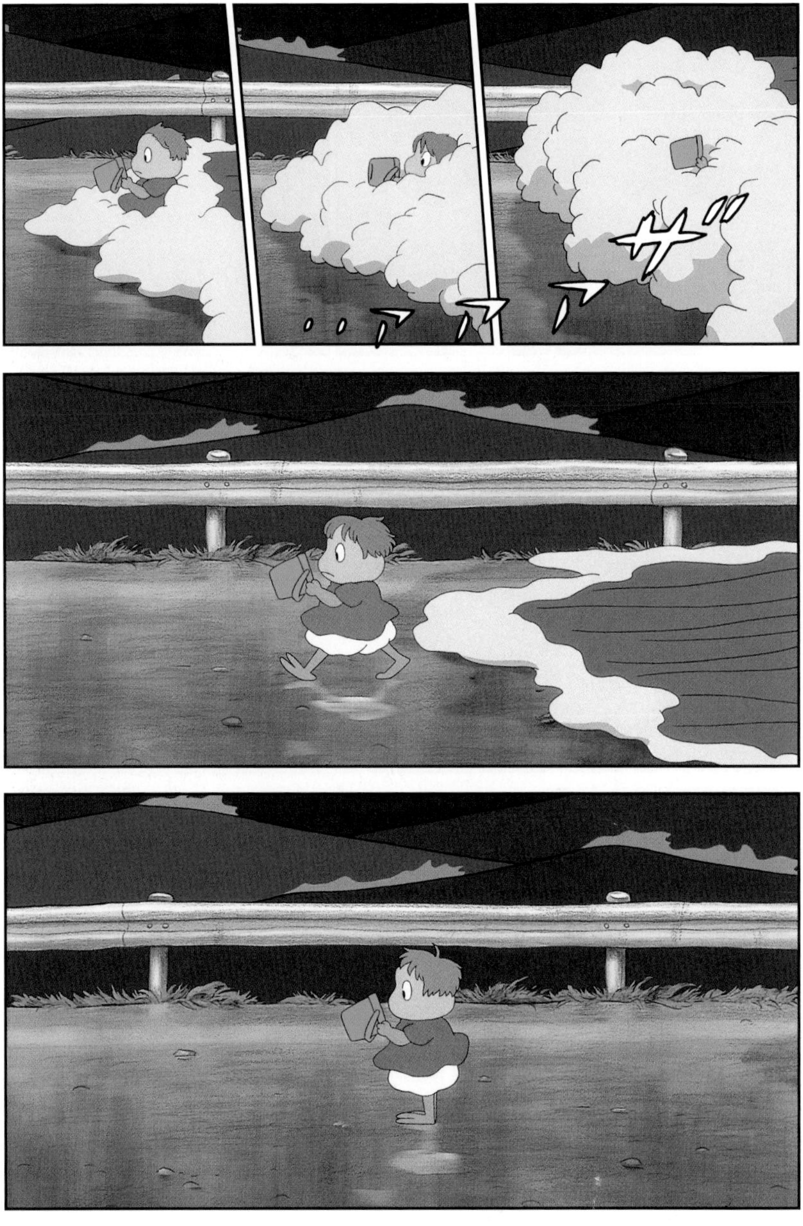
ザァァァ

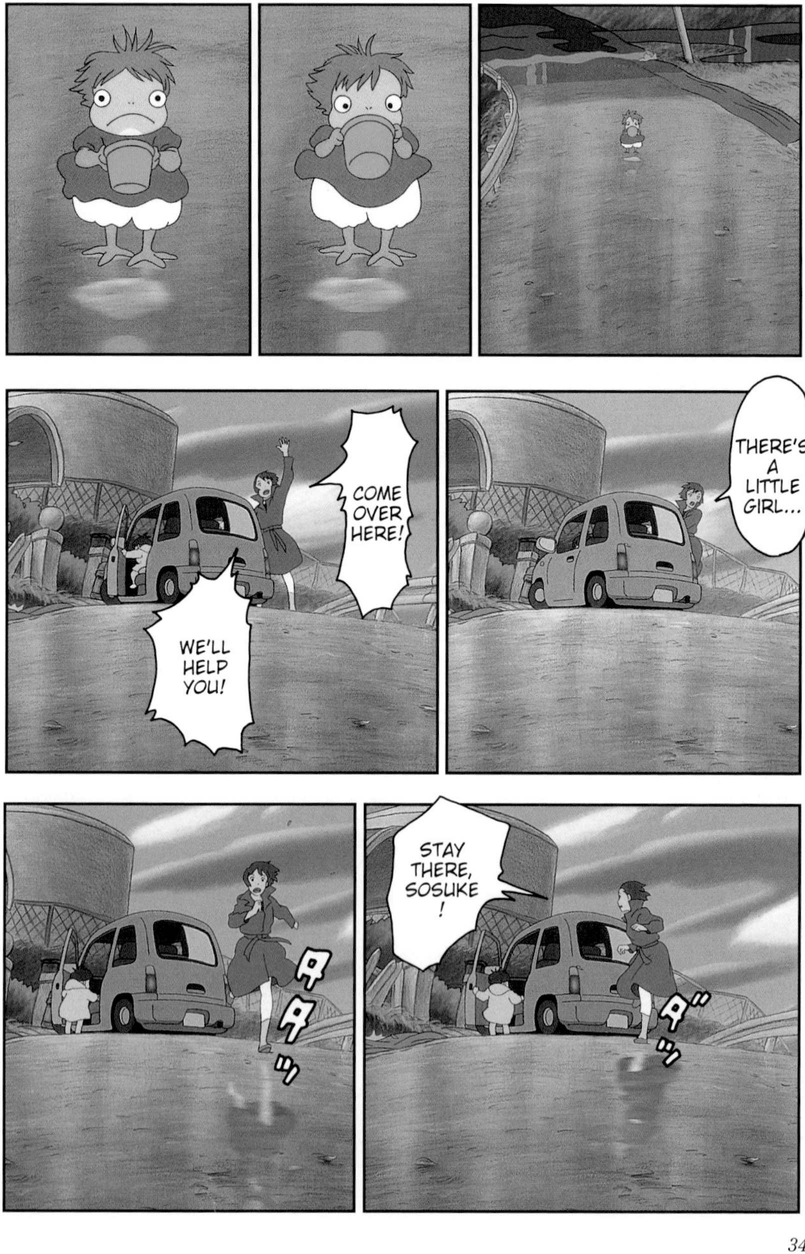
THERE'S A LITTLE GIRL...
COME OVER HERE!
WE'LL HELP YOU!
STAY THERE, SOSUKE!
ダッ
タタッ

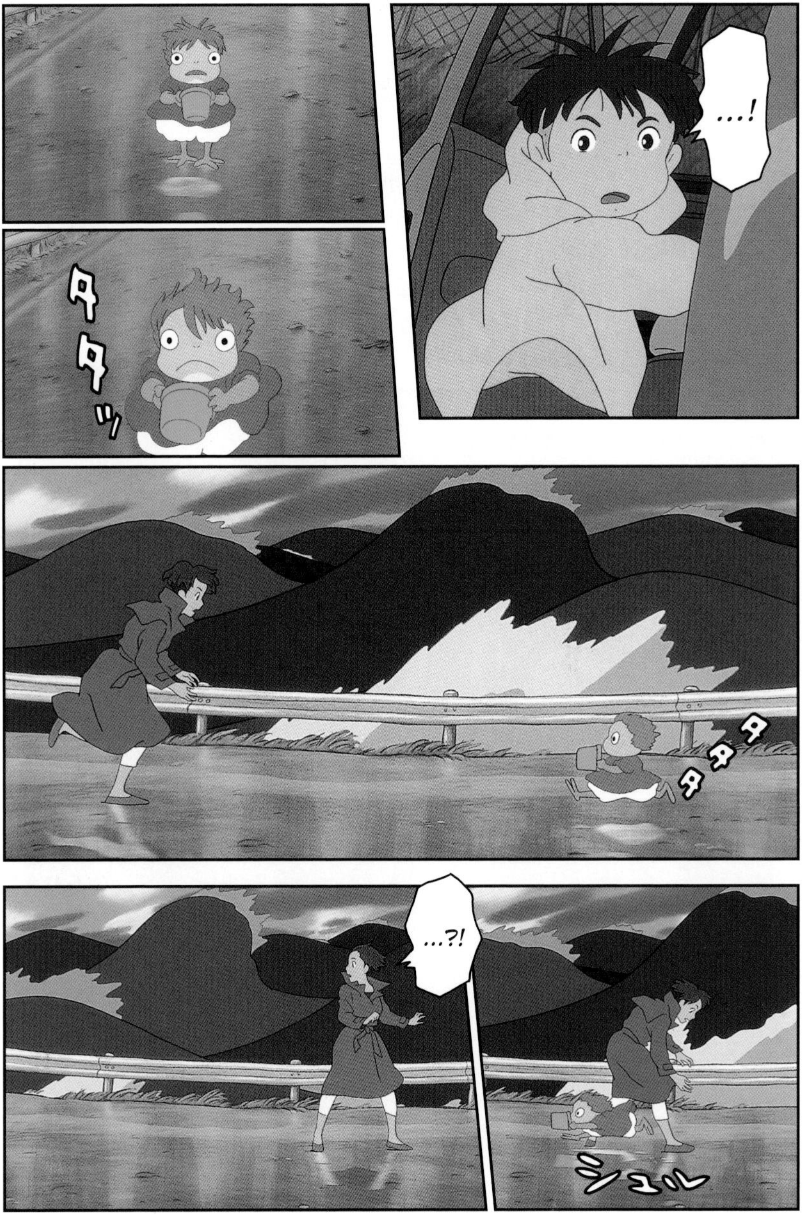
...!
タタッ
タタタ
シュル
...?!

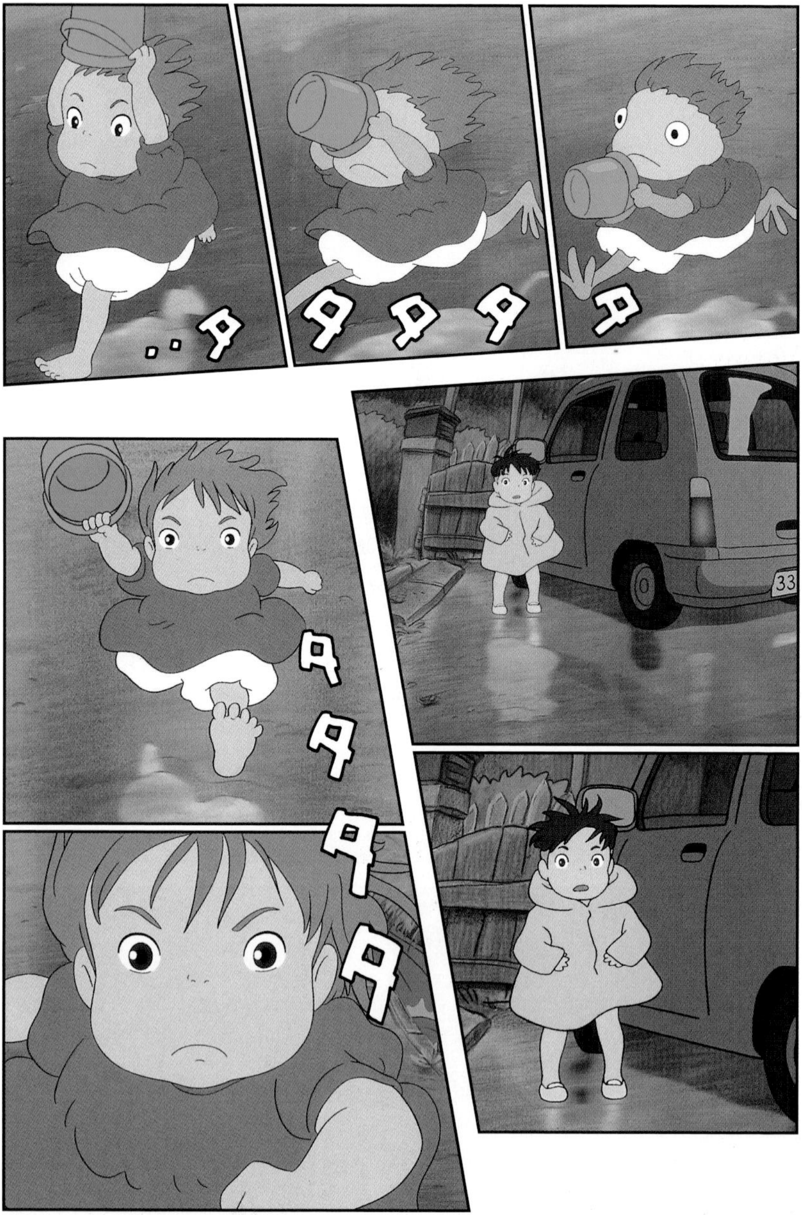
タ
タ タ タ
・・タ
タ
タ
タ
タ

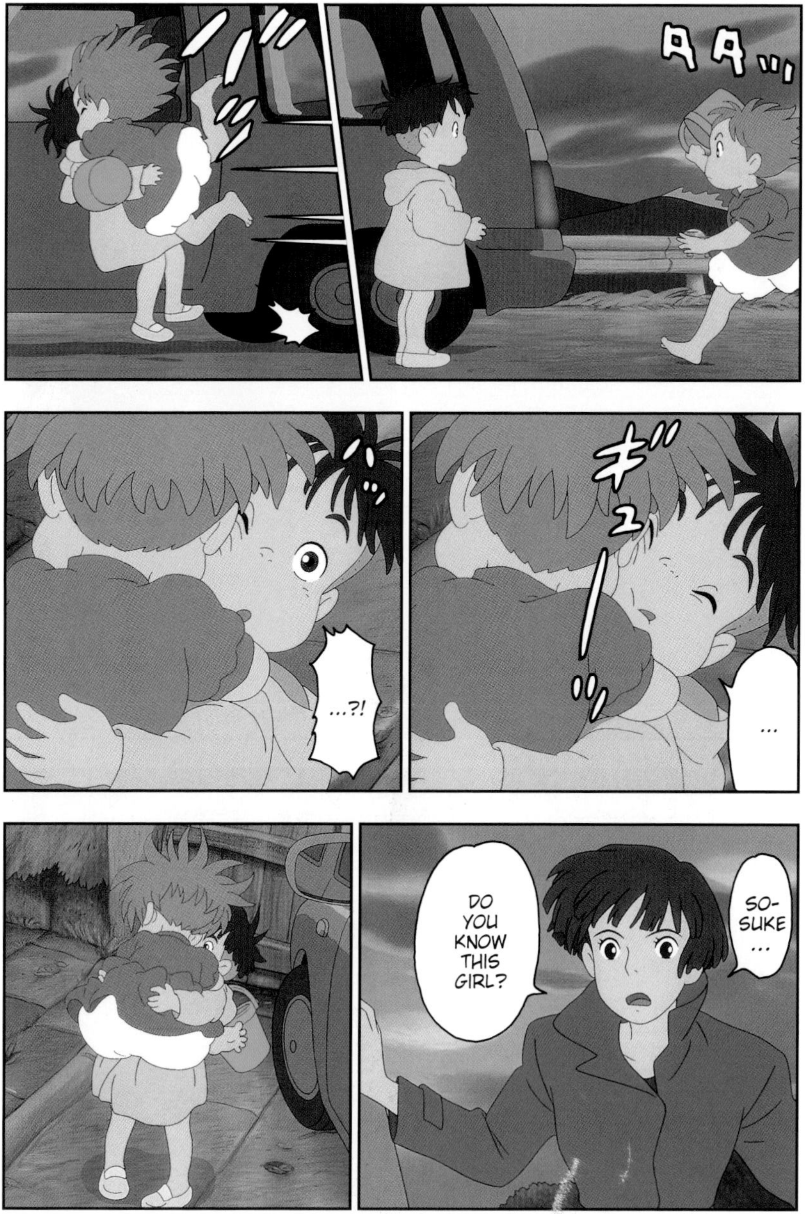
タタッ
ギュー
...
...?!
SO-SUKE ...
DO YOU KNOW THIS GIRL?

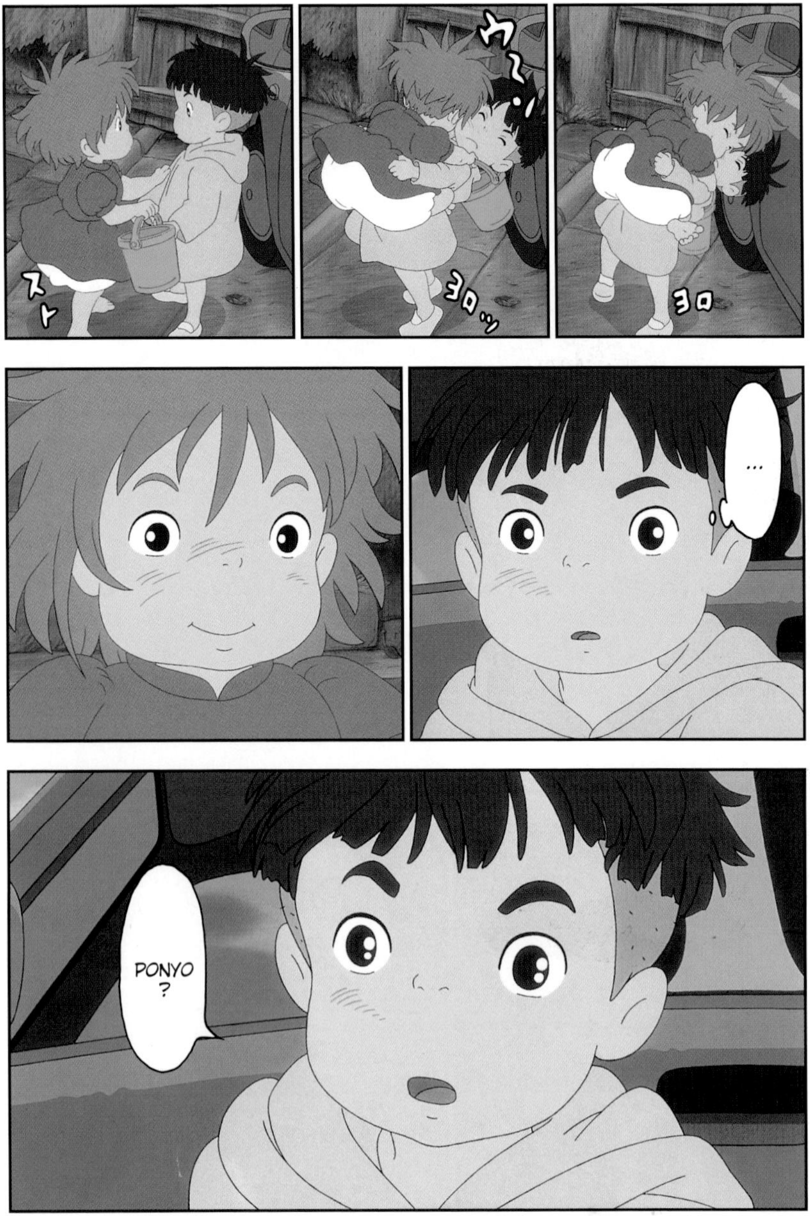
スト
わ〜!
ヨロッ
ヨロ
...
PONYO
?

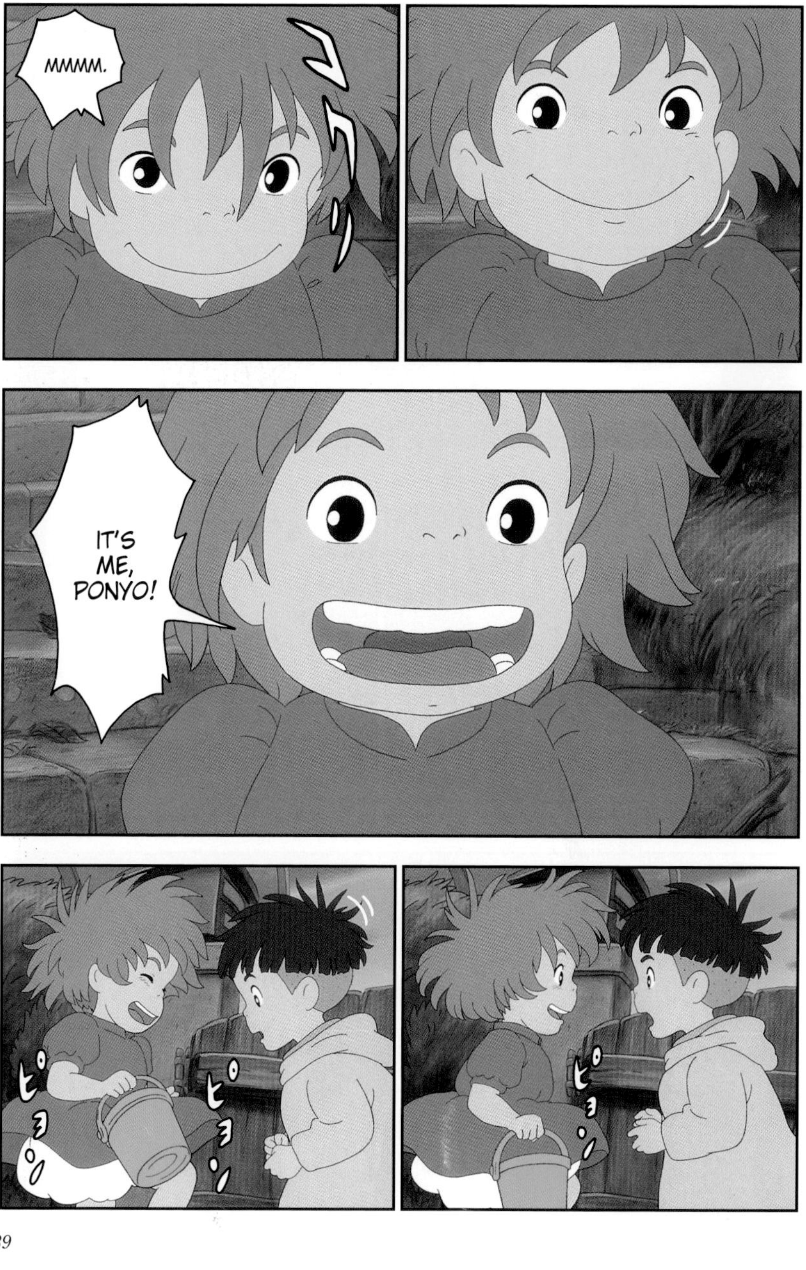
MMMM.
IT'S ME, PONYO!

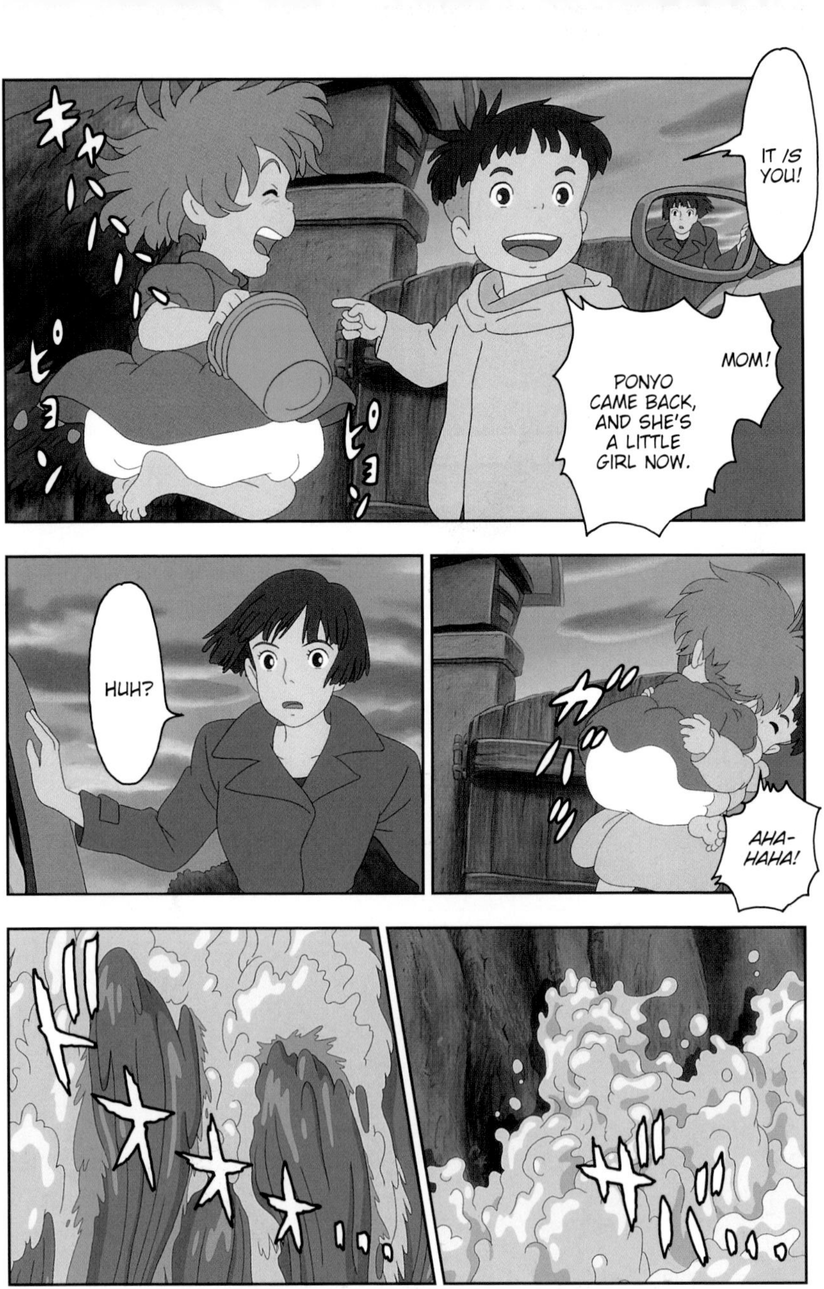
IT IS YOU!
MOM!
PONYO CAME BACK, AND SHE'S A LITTLE GIRL NOW.
AHA-HAHA!
HUH?

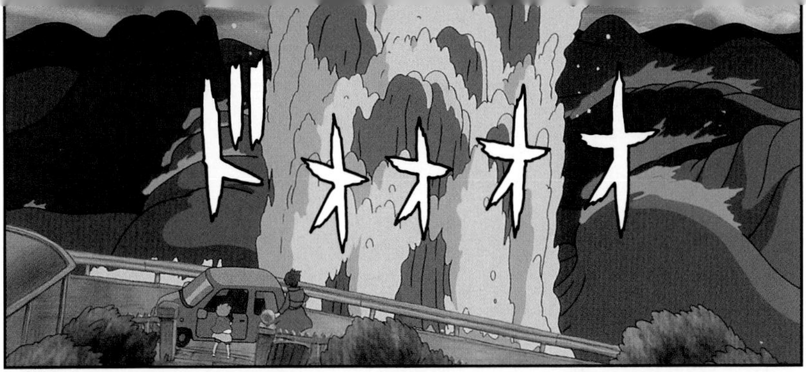
ドオオオオ

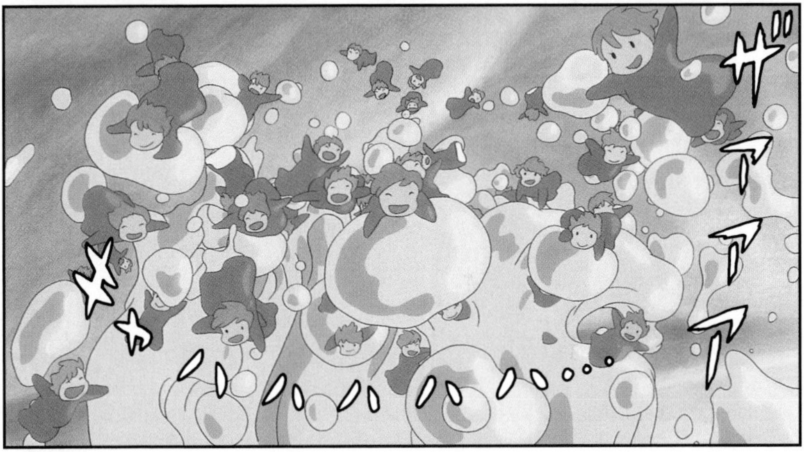
ザアアアア
キャ
ハハハハハ…

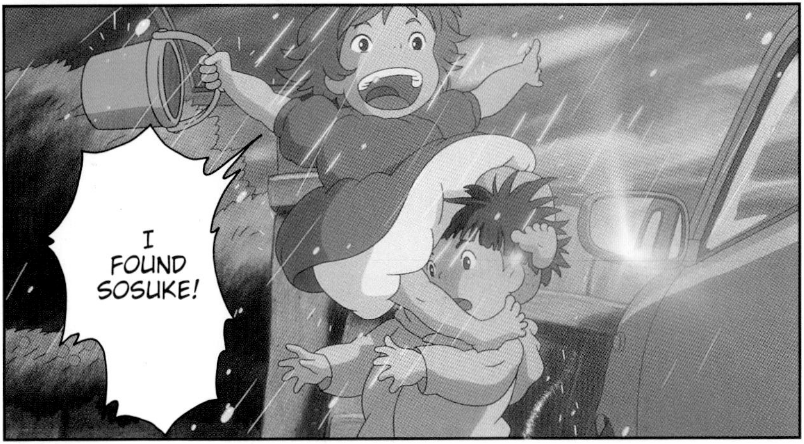
I FOUND SOSUKE!

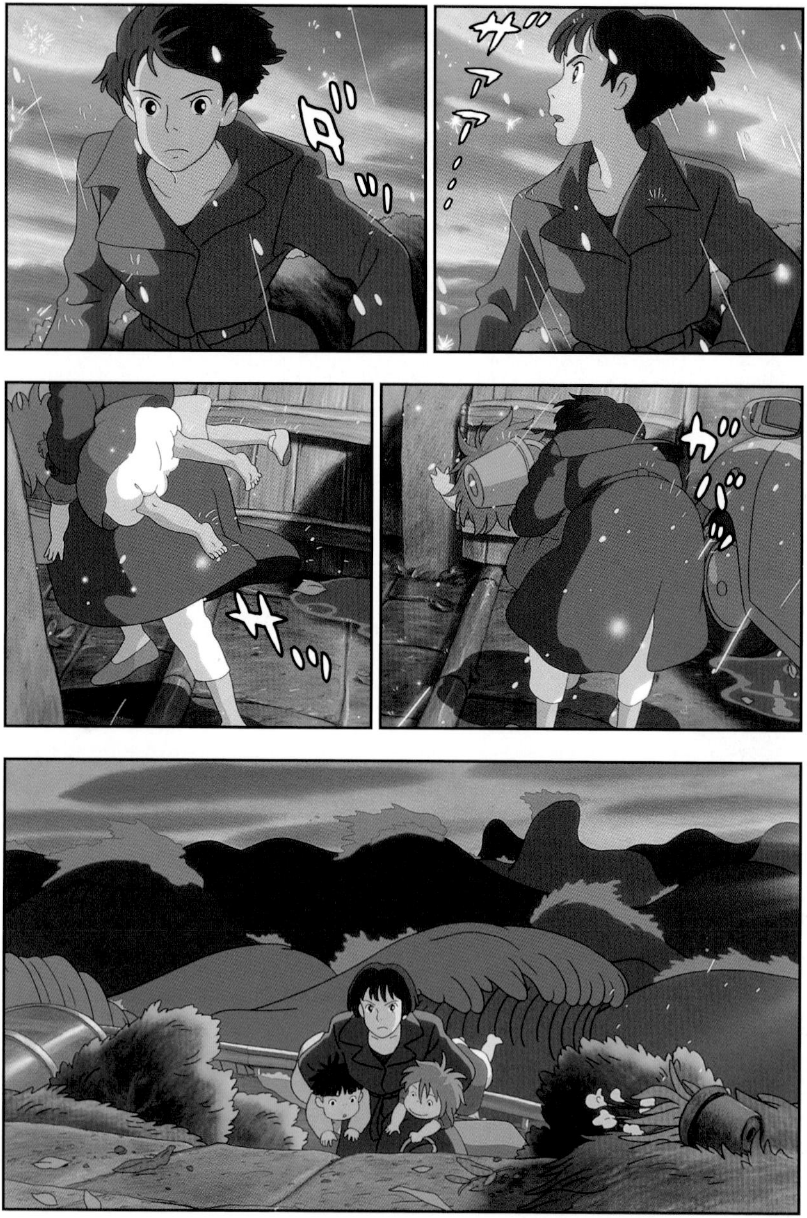
ザァァ…
ダッ
ガバッ
サッ

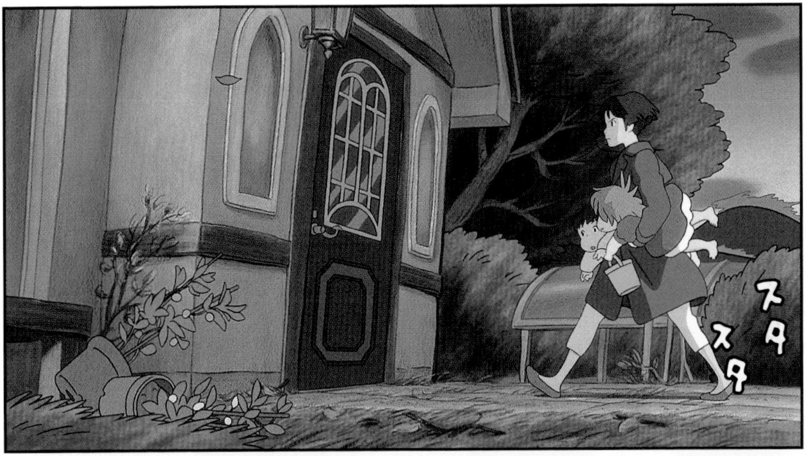
スタ
スタ
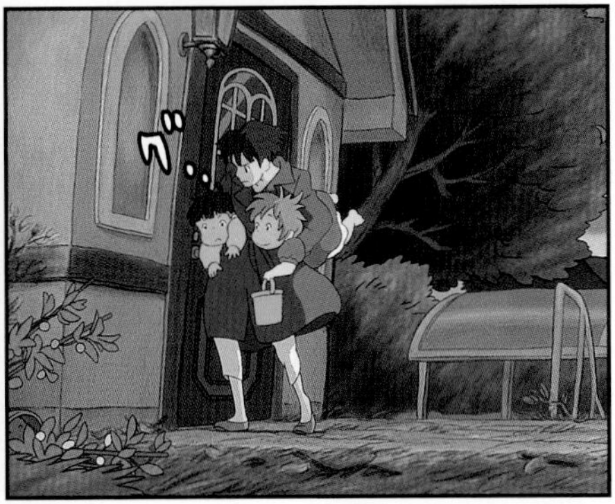
グ…
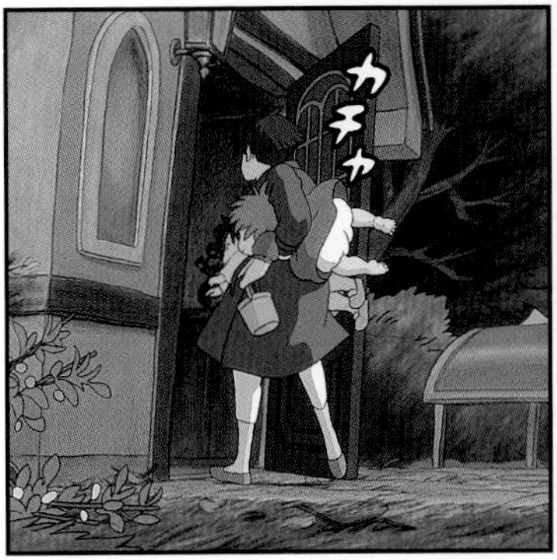
カチャ
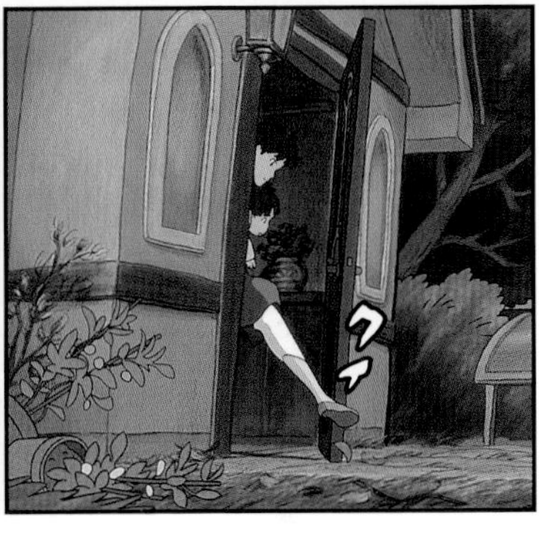
クイ
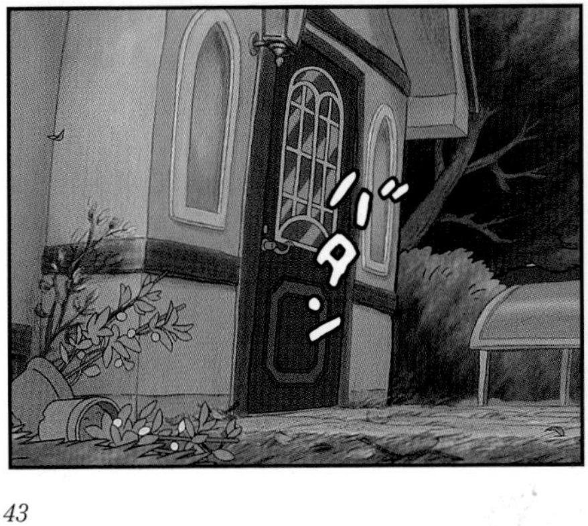
バタン

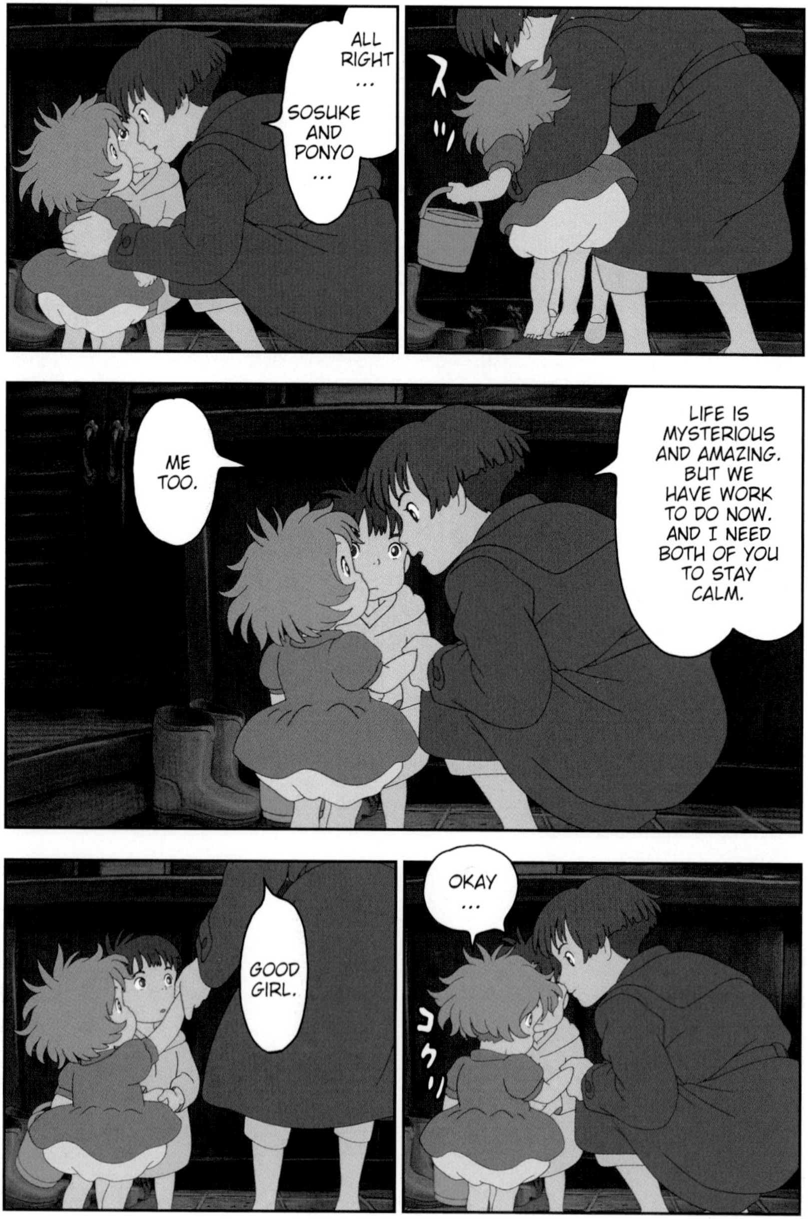
スッ
ALL RIGHT ... SOSUKE AND PONYO ...
LIFE IS MYSTERIOUS AND AMAZING. BUT WE HAVE WORK TO DO NOW. AND I NEED BOTH OF YOU TO STAY CALM.
ME TOO.
OKAY ...
コクリ
GOOD GIRL.

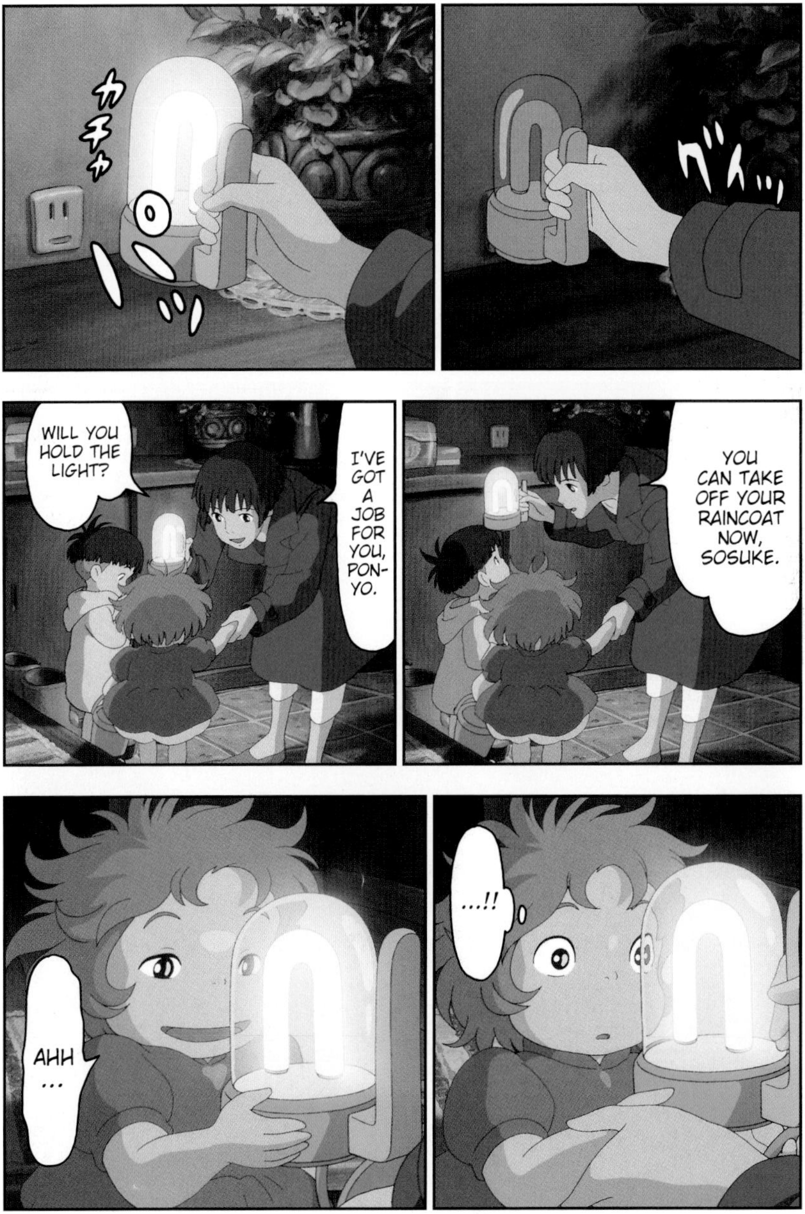
グイッ
カチャ
YOU CAN TAKE OFF YOUR RAINCOAT NOW, SOSUKE.
I'VE GOT A JOB FOR YOU, PON-YO.
WILL YOU HOLD THE LIGHT?
...!!
AHH ...

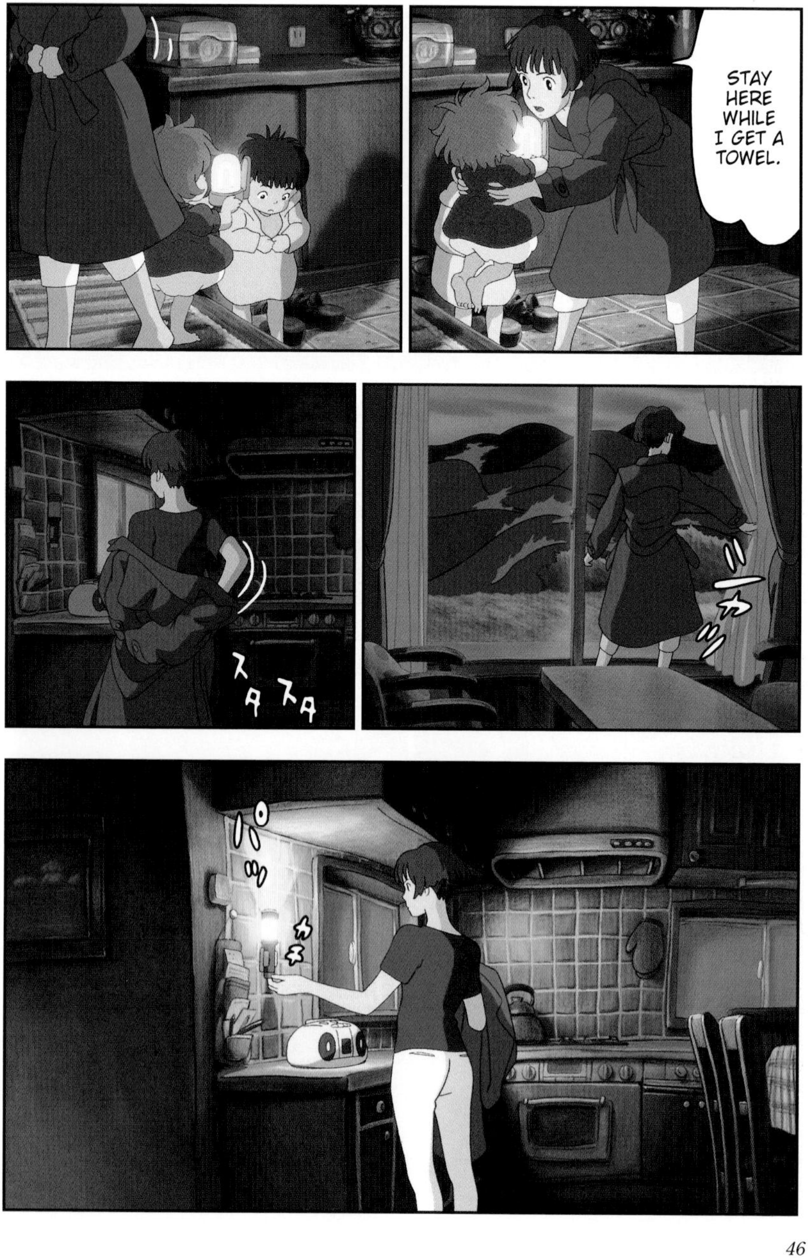
STAY HERE WHILE I GET A TOWEL.
スタ スタ
パッ
カチ

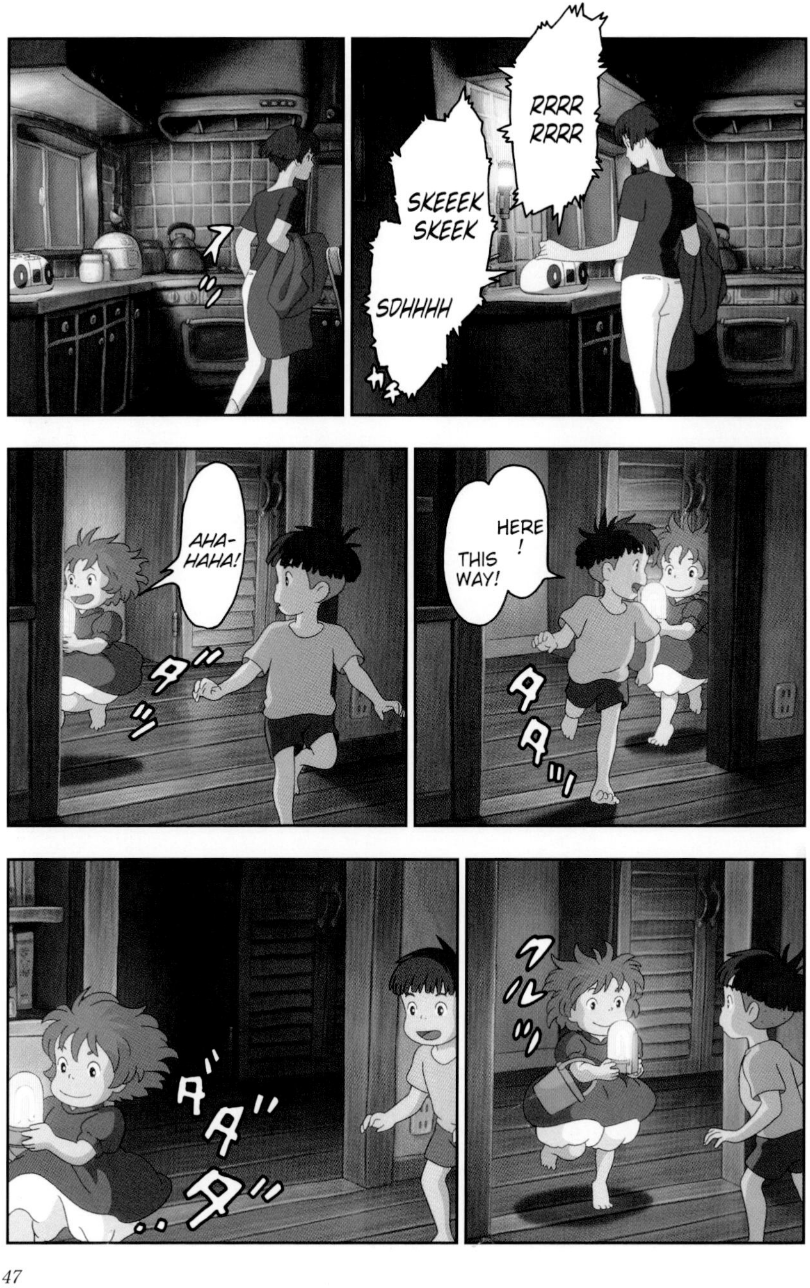

RRRR RRRR
SKEEEK SKEEK
SDHHHH
HERE! THIS WAY!
AHA-HAHA!

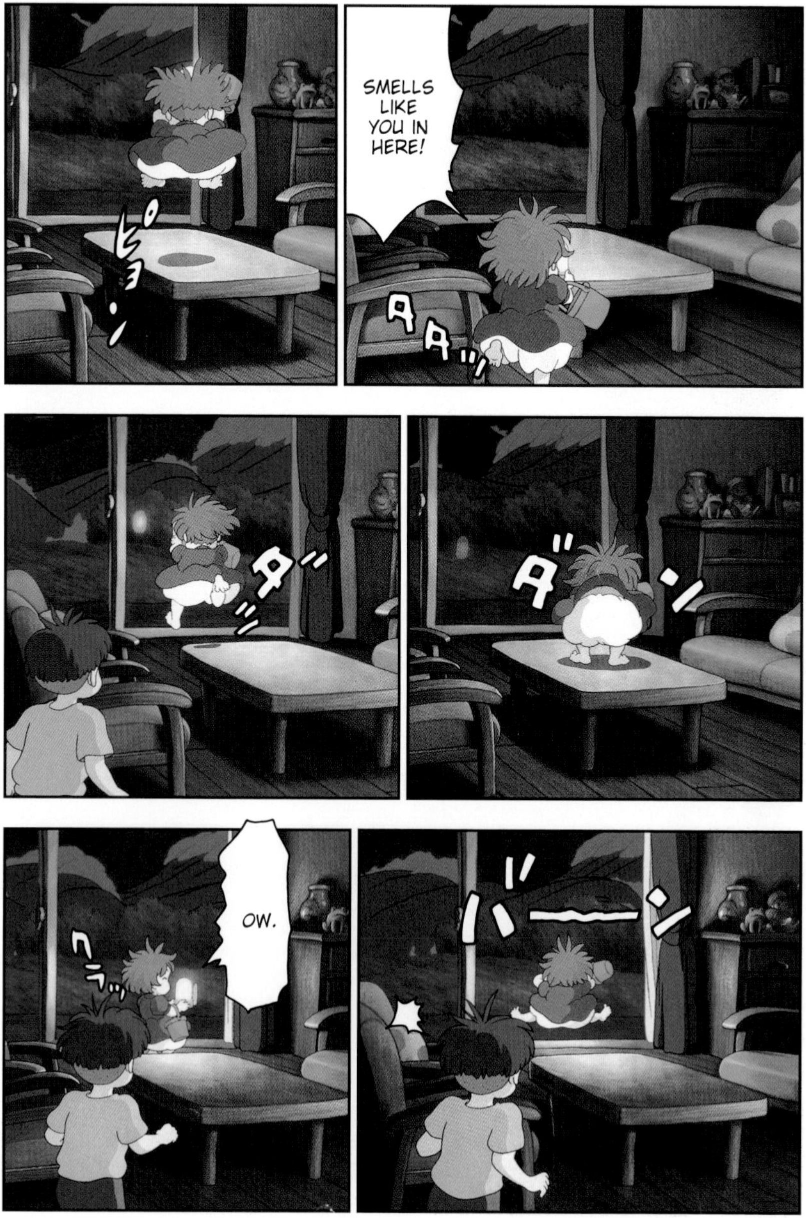
SMELLS LIKE YOU IN HERE!
タタッ
ピョン
ダン
ダッ
バーン
OW.

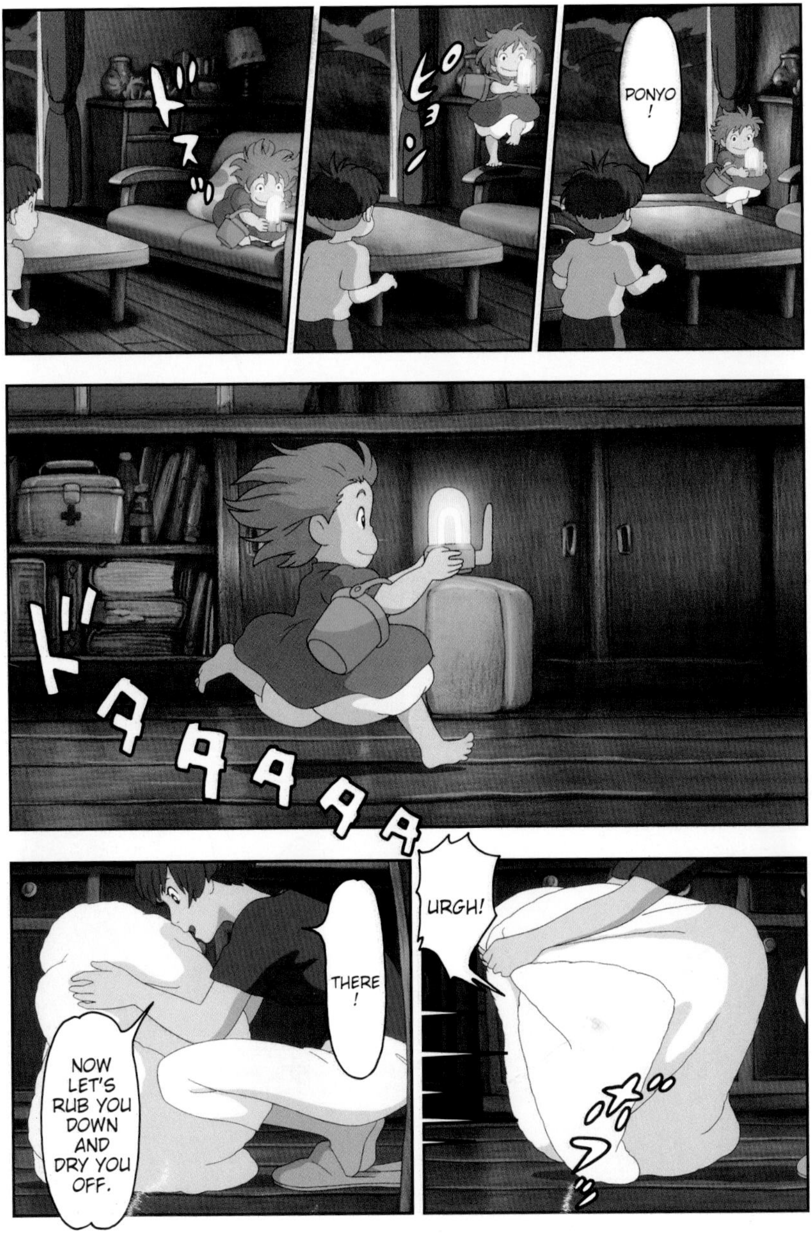
PONYO!
URGH!
THERE!
NOW LET'S RUB YOU DOWN AND DRY YOU OFF.

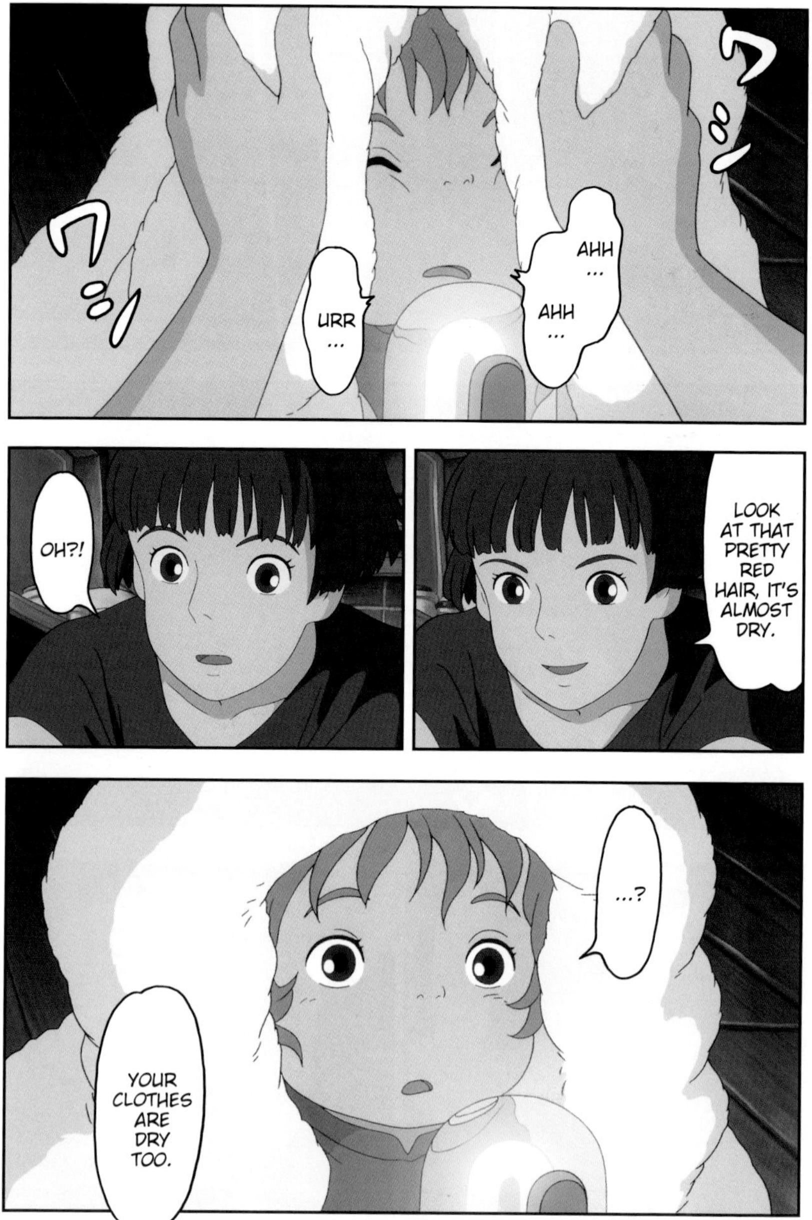
AHH ...
AHH ...
URR ...
LOOK AT THAT PRETTY RED HAIR, IT'S ALMOST DRY.
OH?!
...?
YOUR CLOTHES ARE DRY TOO.

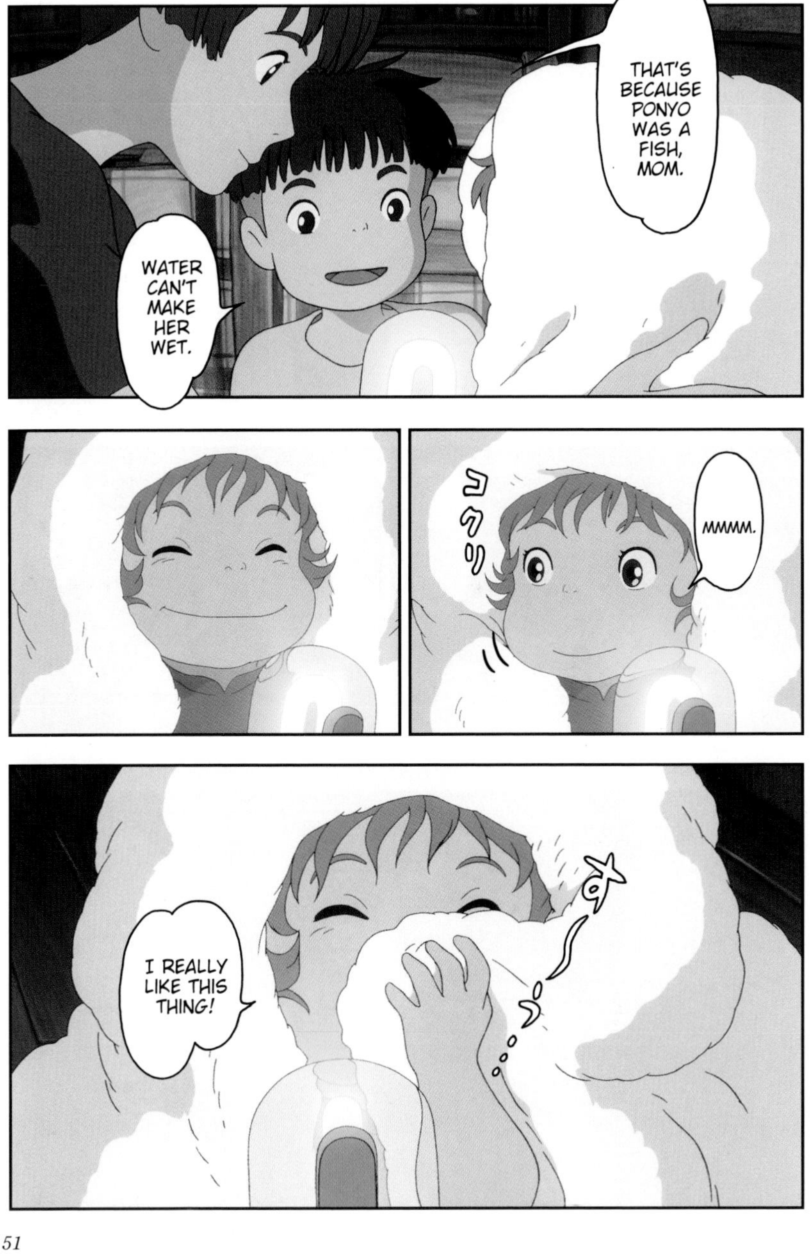
WATER CAN'T MAKE HER WET.
THAT'S BECAUSE PONYO WAS A FISH, MOM.
コクリ
MMMM.
I REALLY LIKE THIS THING!
すーっ

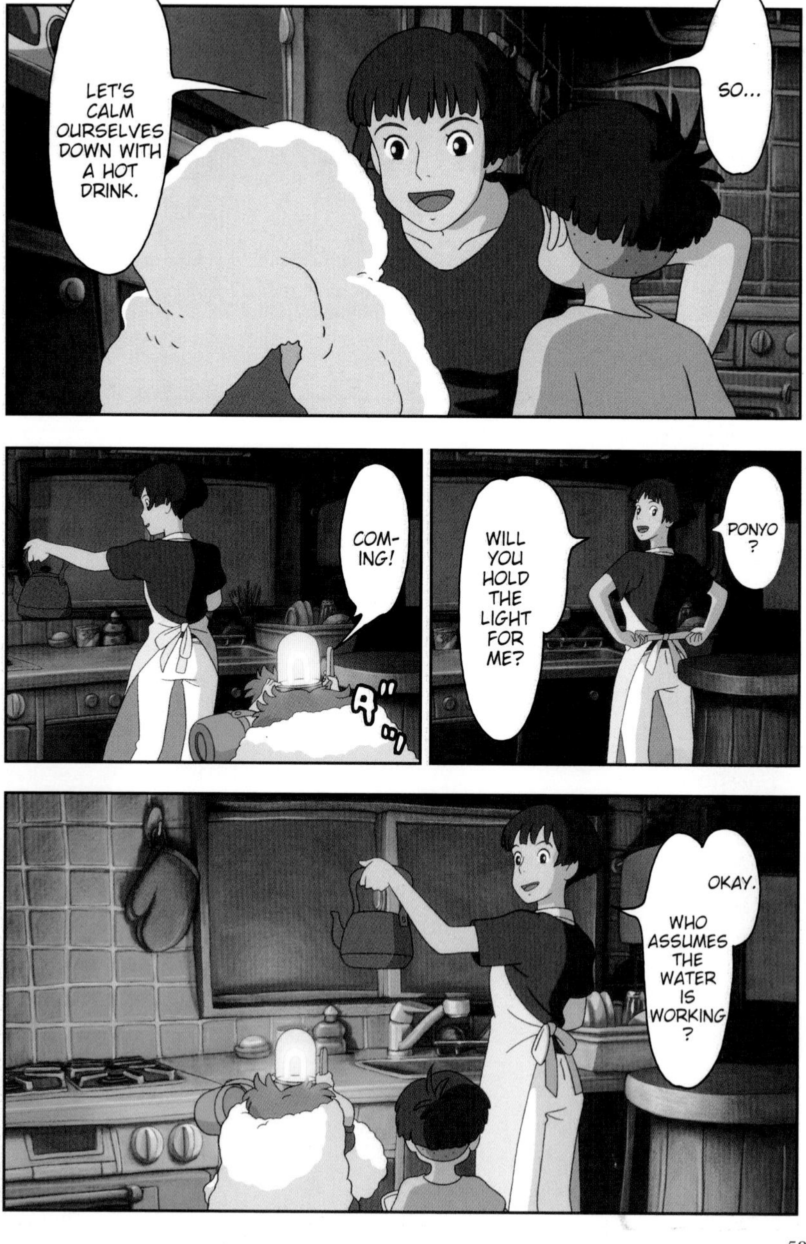
SO...
LET'S CALM OURSELVES DOWN WITH A HOT DRINK.
PONYO?
WILL YOU HOLD THE LIGHT FOR ME?
COM-ING!
OKAY.
WHO ASSUMES THE WATER IS WORKING?

I DO!

I DO!

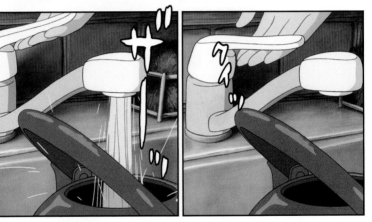

WE HAVE OUR OWN WATER TANK OUTSIDE IN THE YARD.

WATER!

WATER!

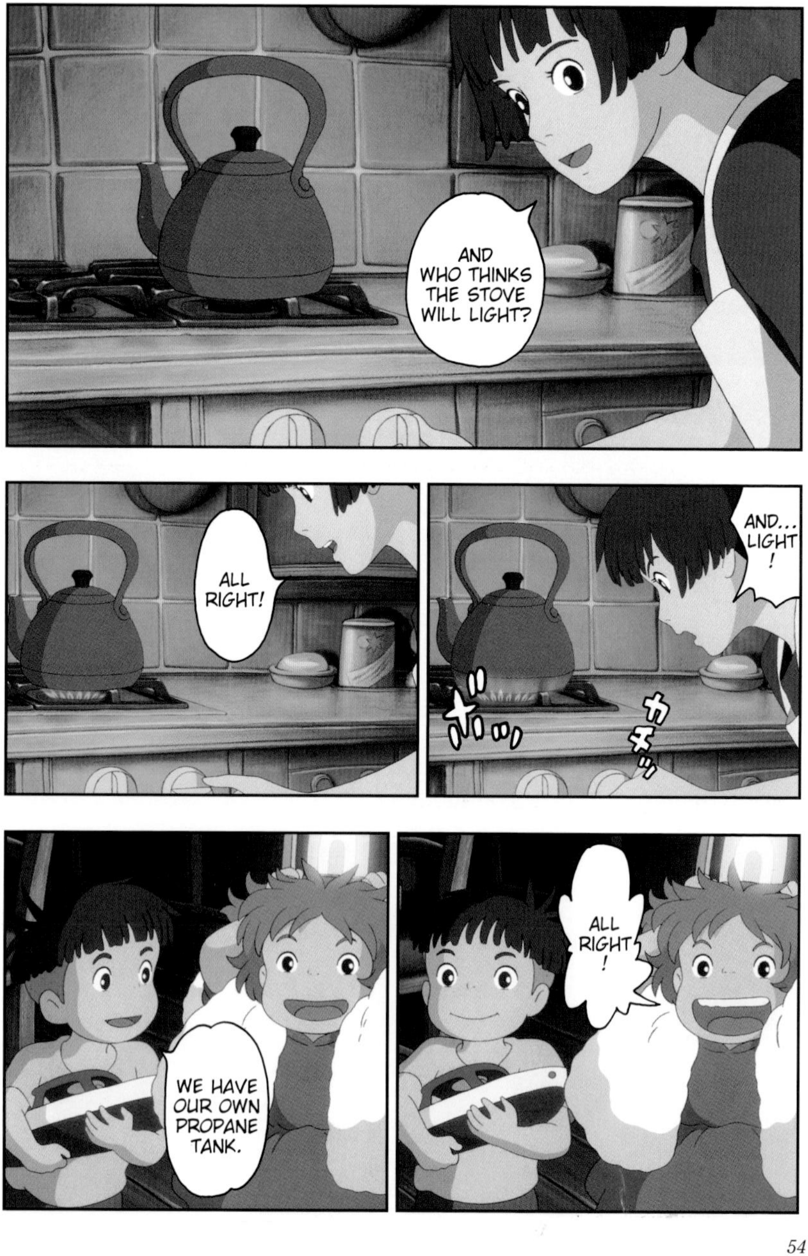
AND WHO THINKS THE STOVE WILL LIGHT?
ALL RIGHT!
AND... LIGHT!
ボッ
カチッ
WE HAVE OUR OWN PROPANE TANK.
ALL RIGHT!

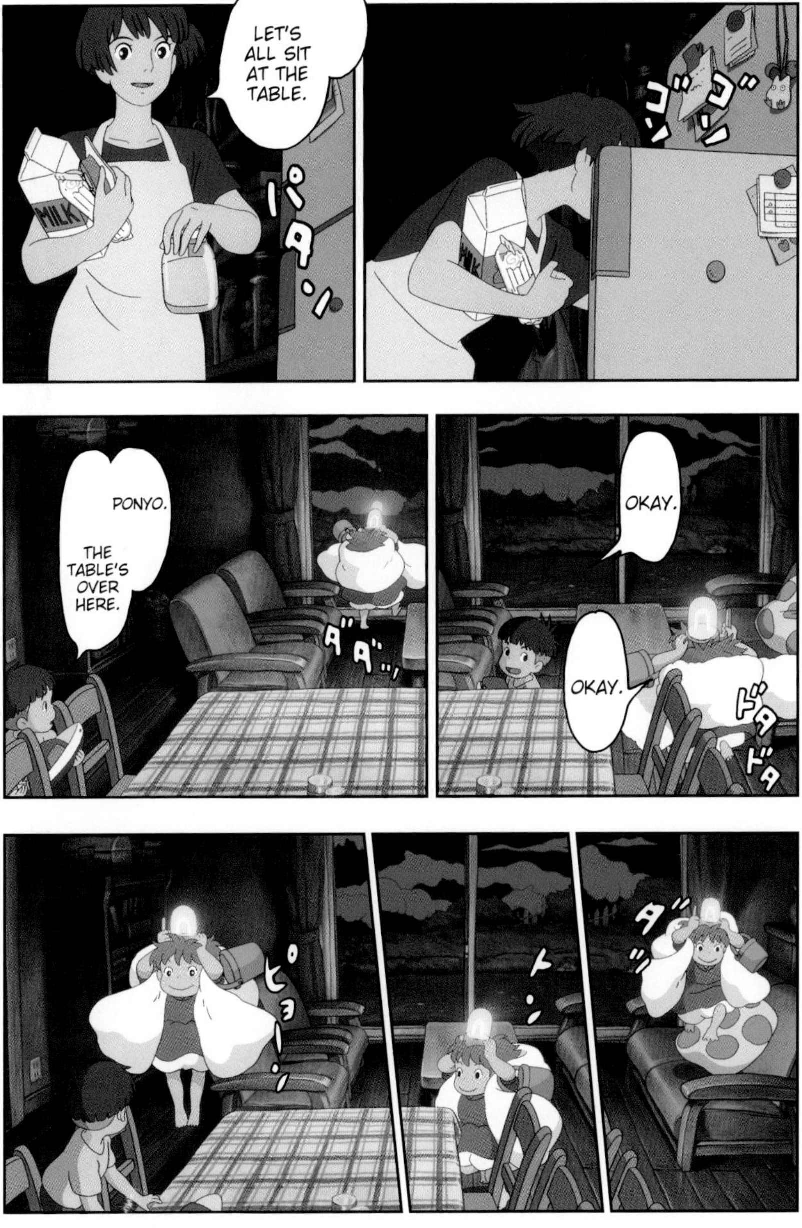
LET'S ALL SIT AT THE TABLE.
パタン
ゴン
ゴン
PONYO.
THE TABLE'S OVER HERE.
ダダッ
OKAY.
OKAY.
ドタドタ
ピョーン
ト
ダッ

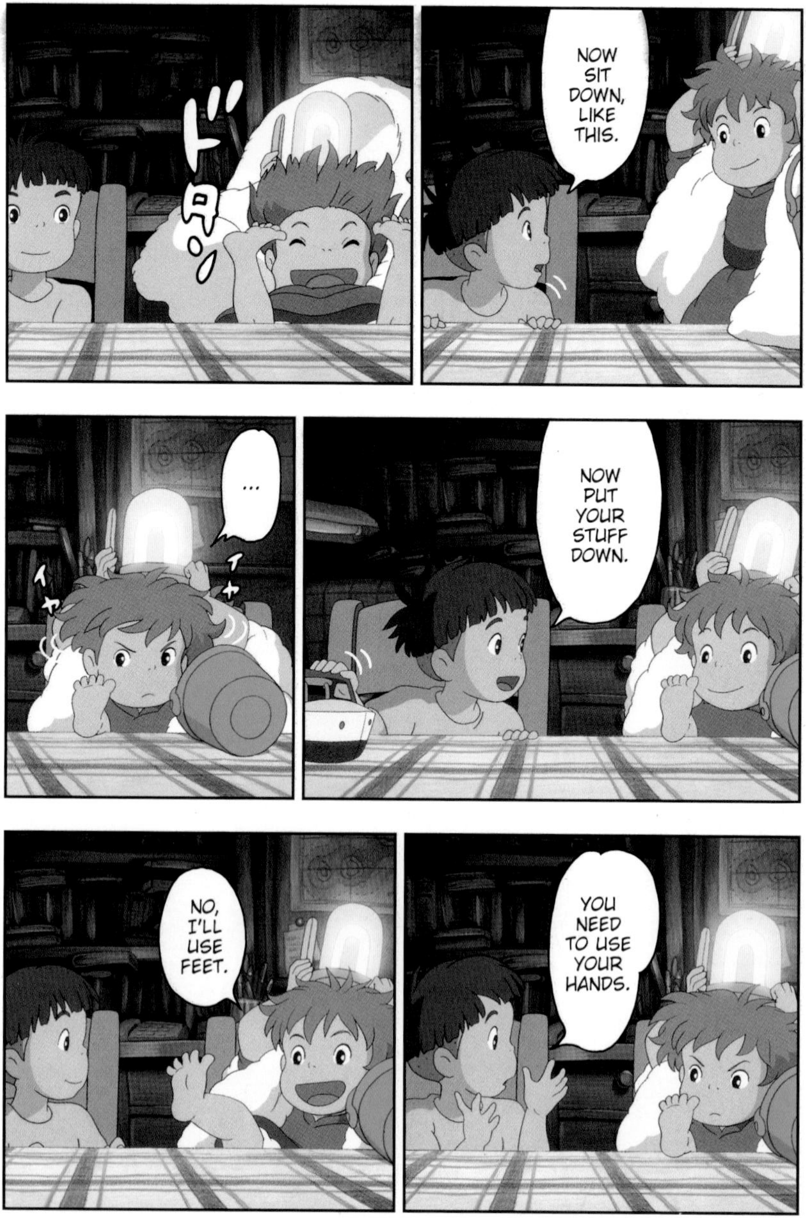
NOW SIT DOWN, LIKE THIS.
NOW PUT YOUR STUFF DOWN.
...
イヤ
イヤ
YOU NEED TO USE YOUR HANDS.
NO, I'LL USE FEET.

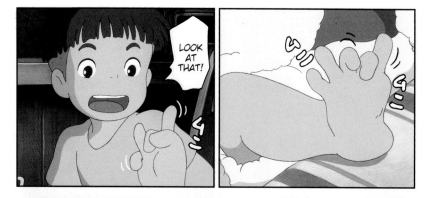

LOOK AT THAT!

MMMM.

WHAT ARE YOU DOING?

...?!

LOOK AT HER FEET! THEY'RE JUST LIKE HANDS.

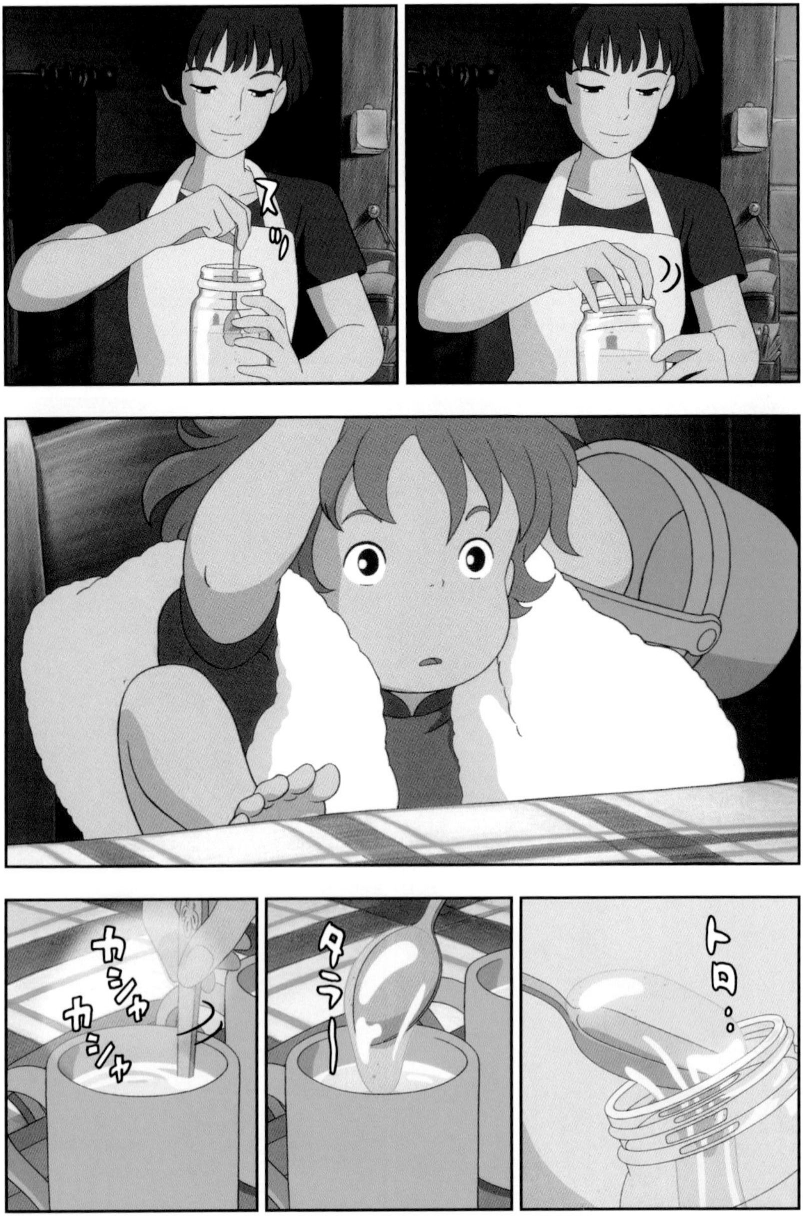
スッ
トロ・・
タラー
カシャ
カシャ

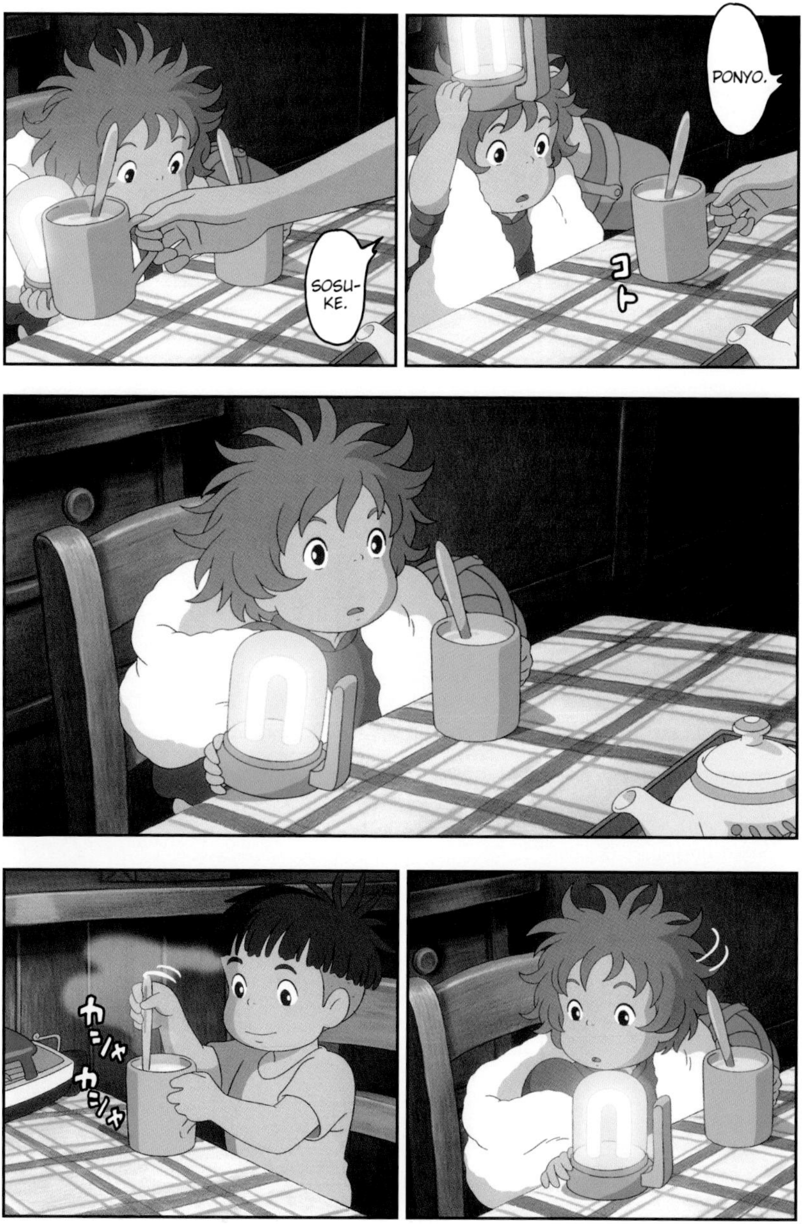
PONYO.
コト
SOSU-KE.
カシャ
カシャ

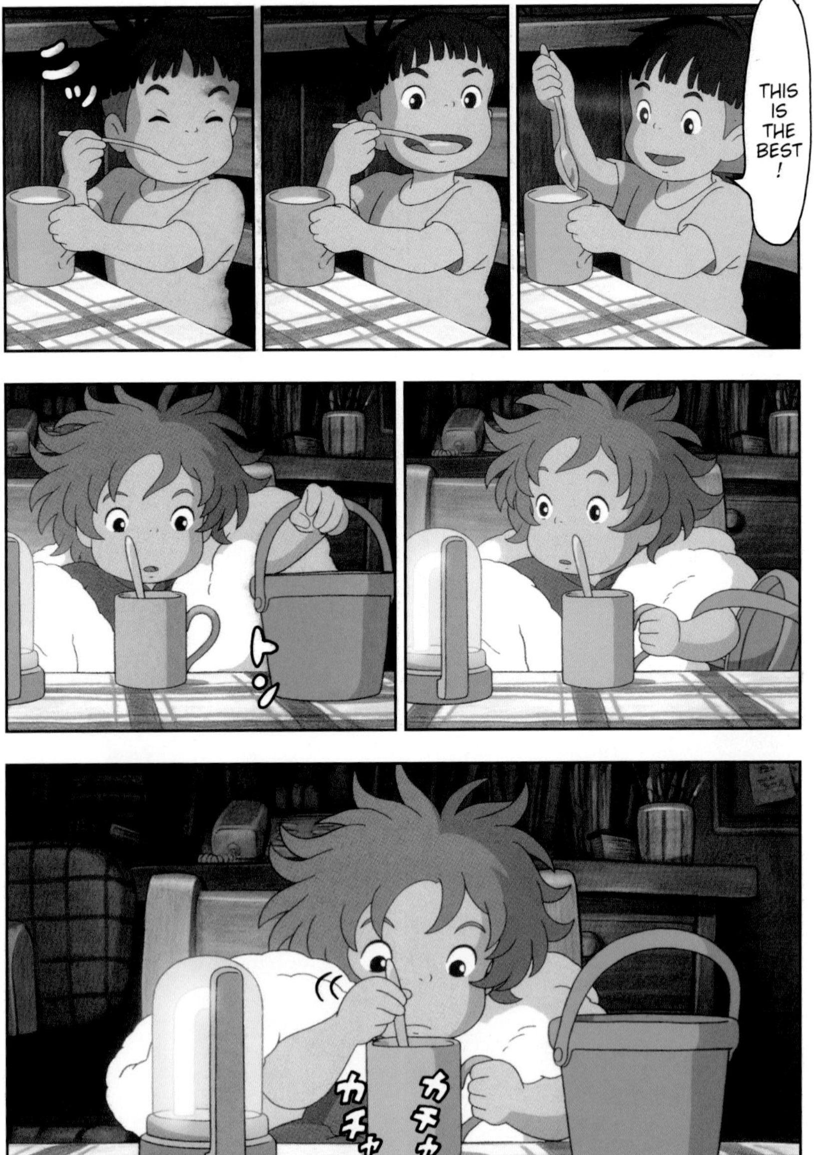
THIS IS THE BEST!
ニッ
トン
カチャカチャ
カチャ

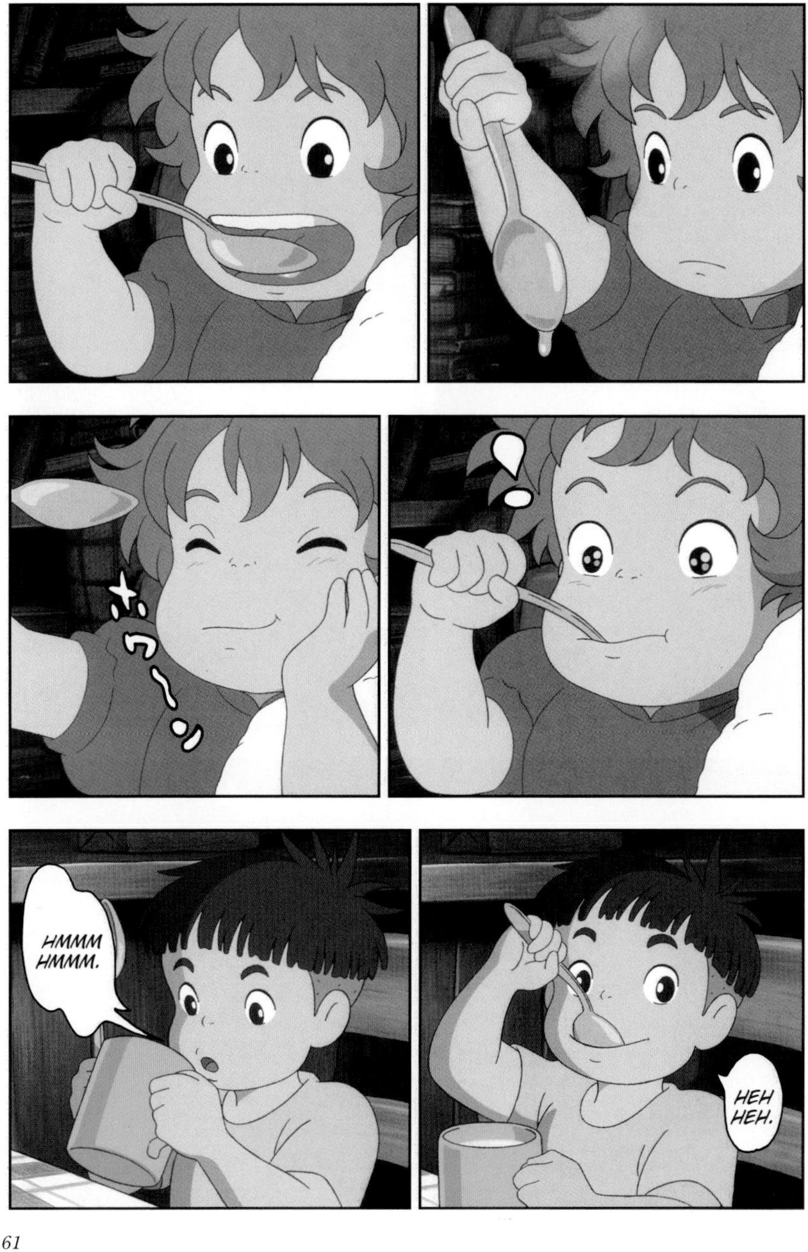
ボワ〜ッ
HEH HEH.
HMMM HMMM.

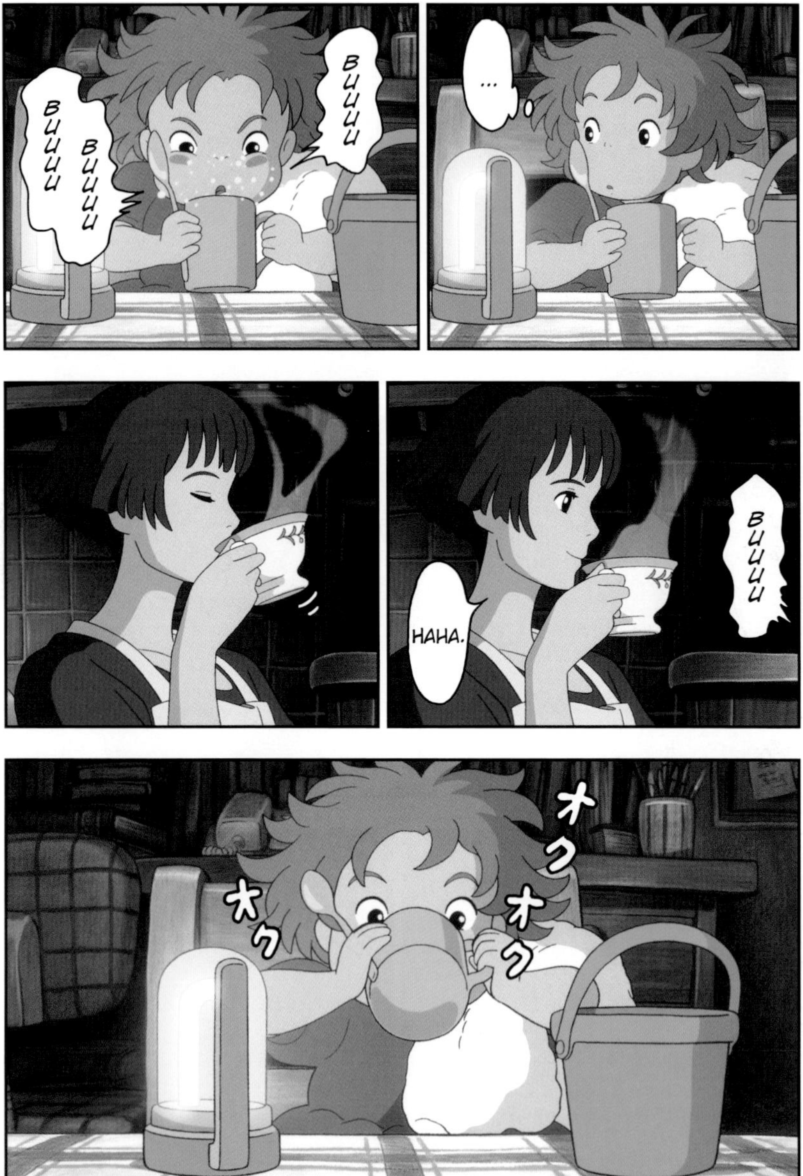
...
BUUUU
BUUUU BUUUU
BUUUU
HAHA.
オク
オク
オク

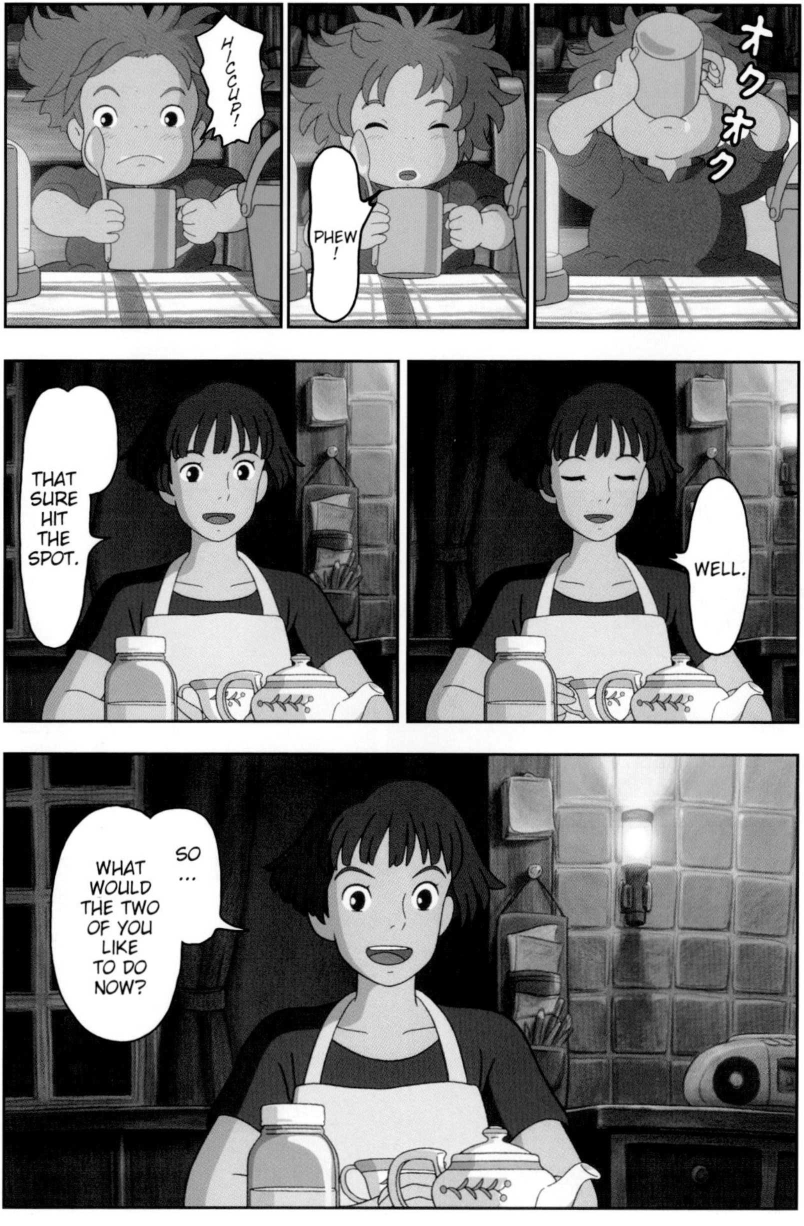

HICCUP!
PHEW!
オクオク
THAT SURE HIT THE SPOT.
WELL.
SO...
WHAT WOULD THE TWO OF YOU LIKE TO DO NOW?

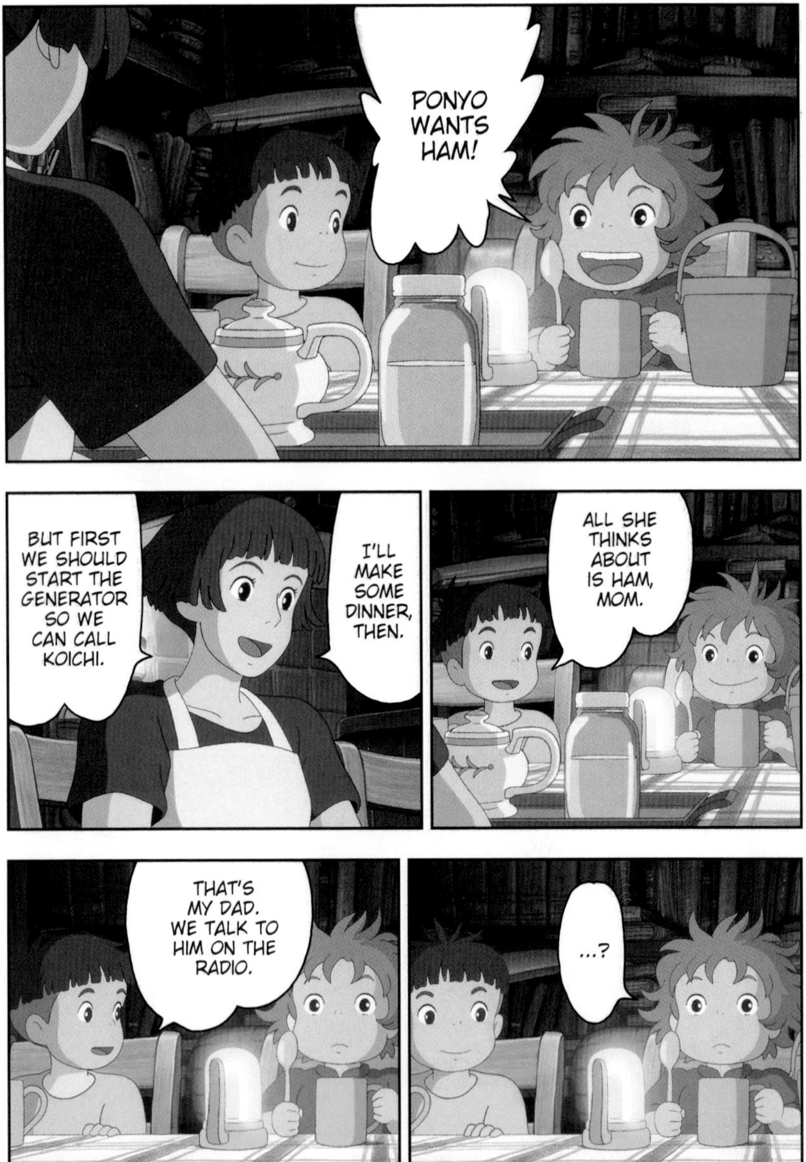
PONYO WANTS HAM!
ALL SHE THINKS ABOUT IS HAM, MOM.
I'LL MAKE SOME DINNER, THEN.
BUT FIRST WE SHOULD START THE GENERATOR SO WE CAN CALL KOICHI.
...?
THAT'S MY DAD. WE TALK TO HIM ON THE RADIO.

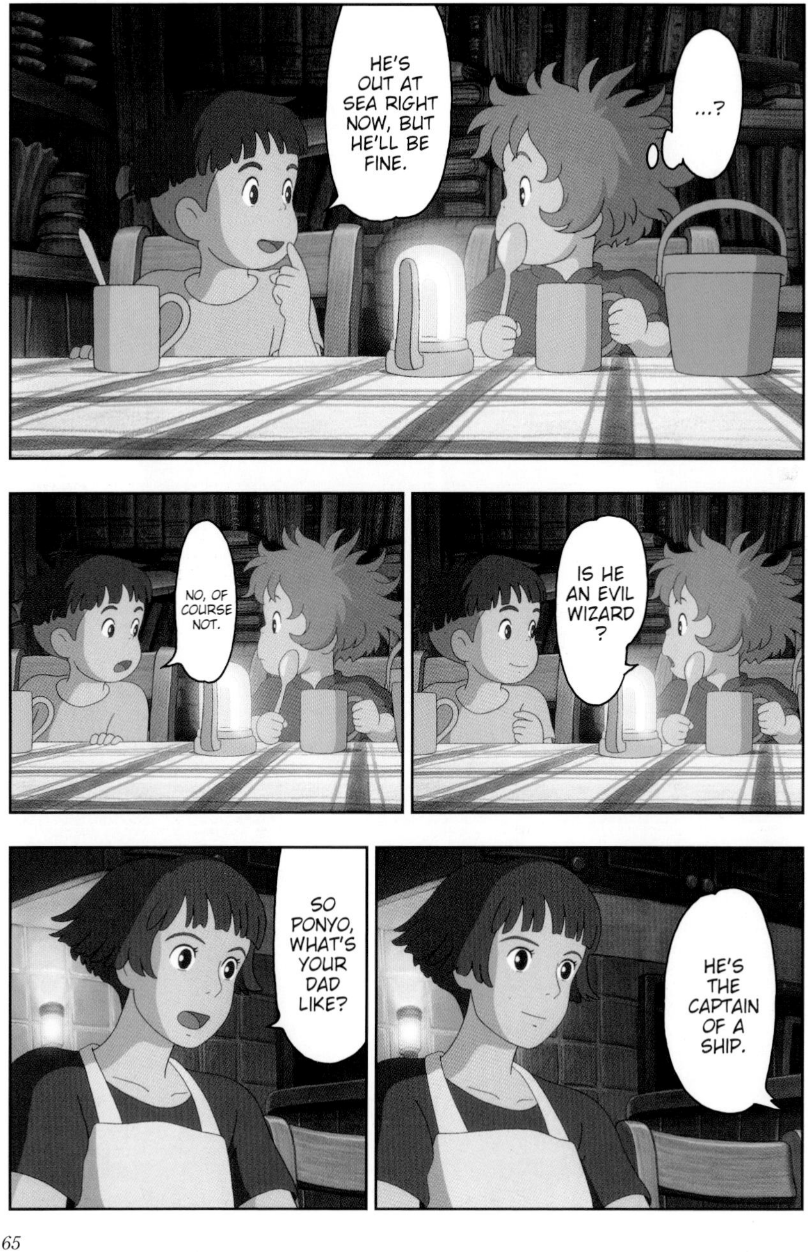
...?
HE'S OUT AT SEA RIGHT NOW, BUT HE'LL BE FINE.
IS HE AN EVIL WIZARD?
NO, OF COURSE NOT.
HE'S THE CAPTAIN OF A SHIP.
SO PONYO, WHAT'S YOUR DAD LIKE?

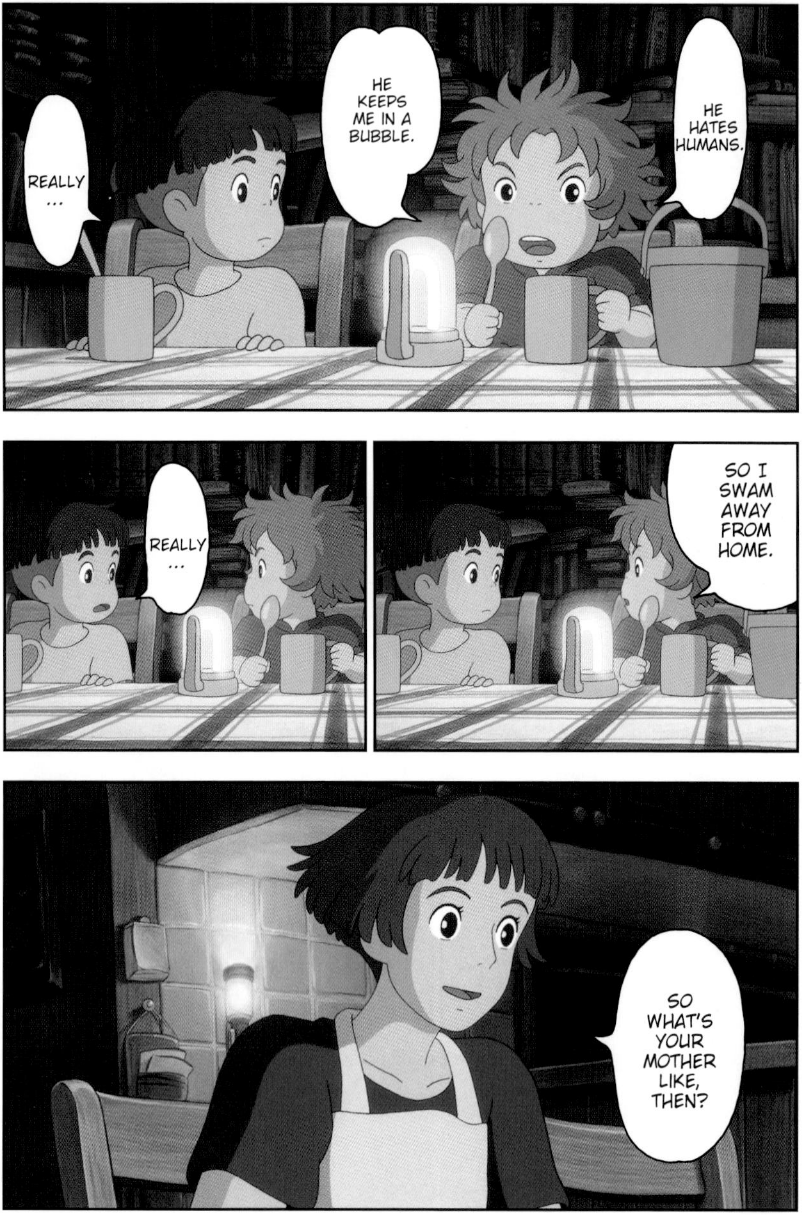
HE HATES HUMANS.
HE KEEPS ME IN A BUBBLE.
REALLY ...
SO I SWAM AWAY FROM HOME.
REALLY ...
SO WHAT'S YOUR MOTHER LIKE, THEN?

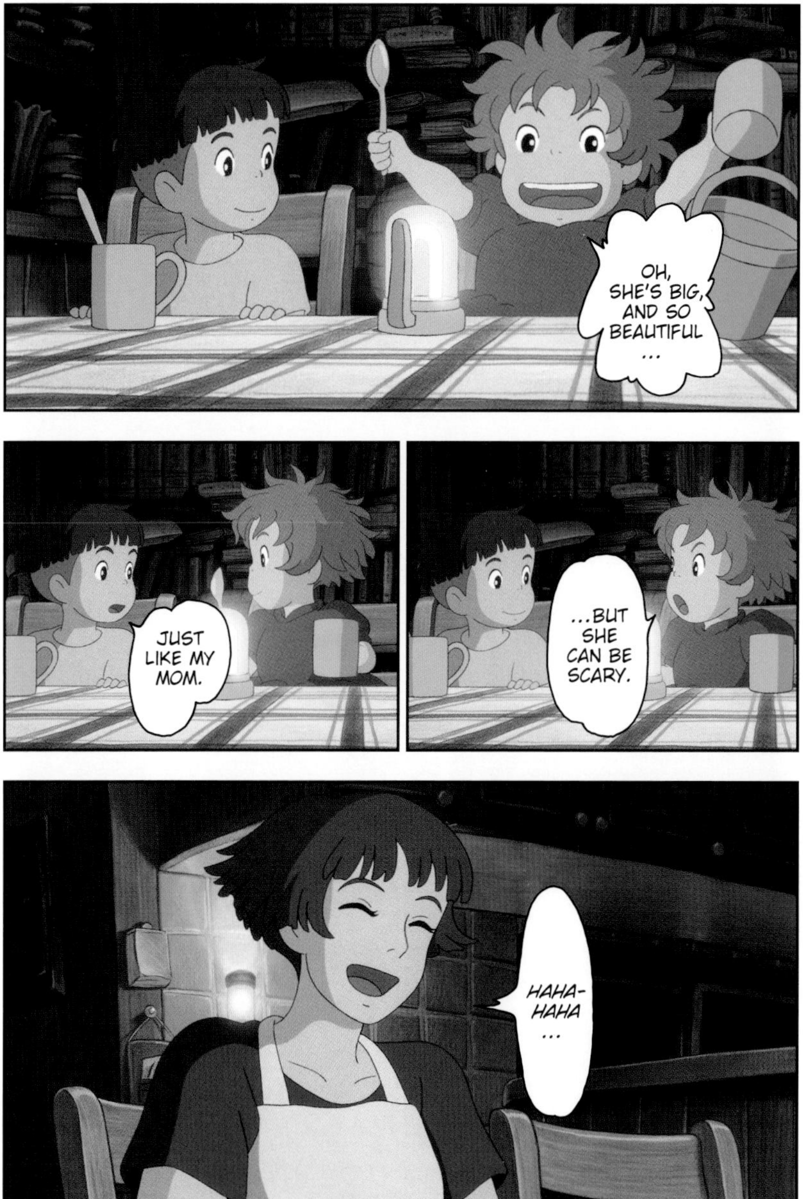
OH, SHE'S BIG, AND SO BEAUTIFUL ...
JUST LIKE MY MOM.
...BUT SHE CAN BE SCARY.
HAHA- HAHA ...

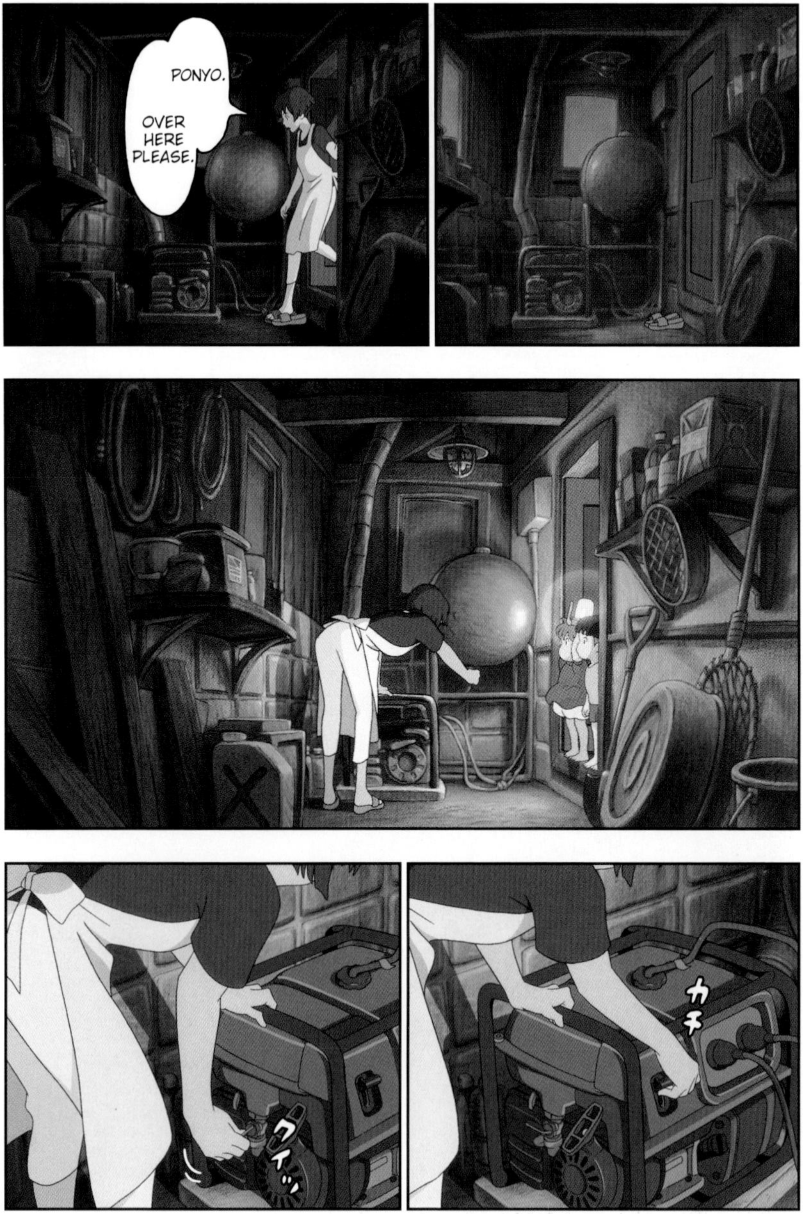
PONYO.
OVER HERE PLEASE.
カチ
クイッ

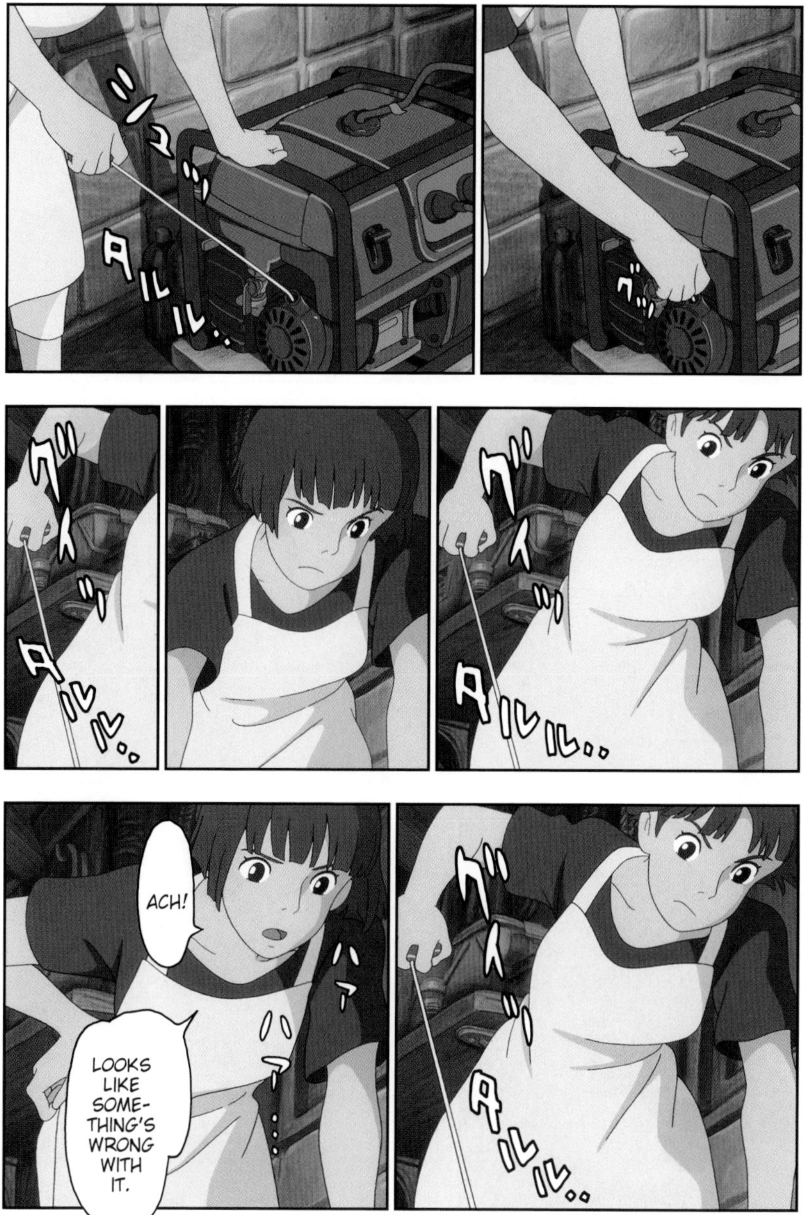
ACH!
LOOKS LIKE SOME-THING'S WRONG WITH IT.

IT IS CLOGGED.

MAYBE IT'S CLOGGED.

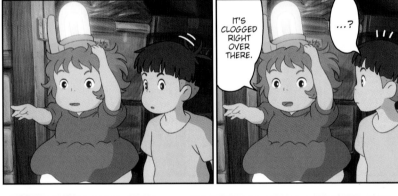

IT'S CLOGGED RIGHT OVER THERE.

...?

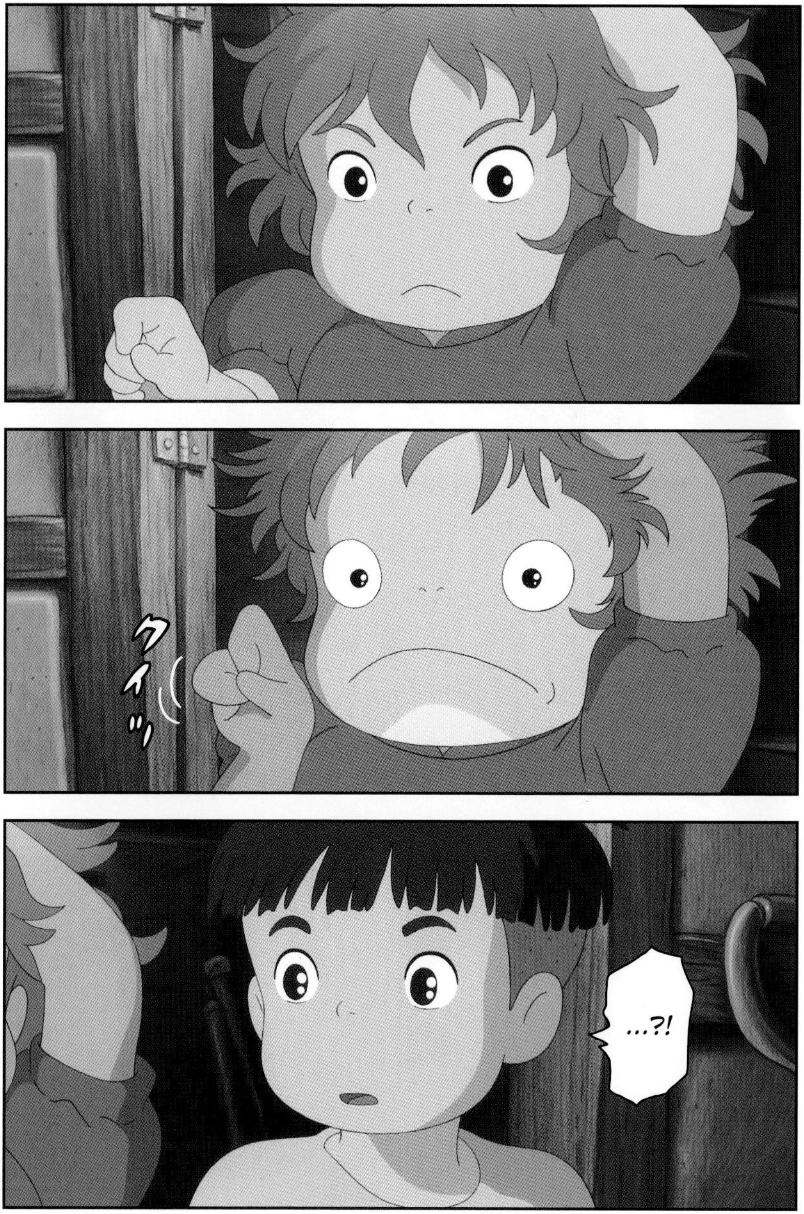
クイッ
...?!

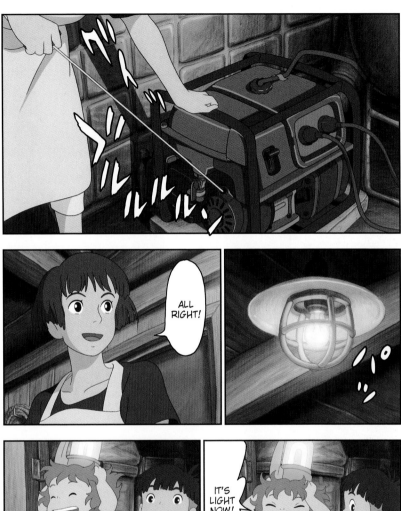

ALL RIGHT!

PONYO, YOU'RE EN-CHANTED.

IT'S LIGHT NOW!

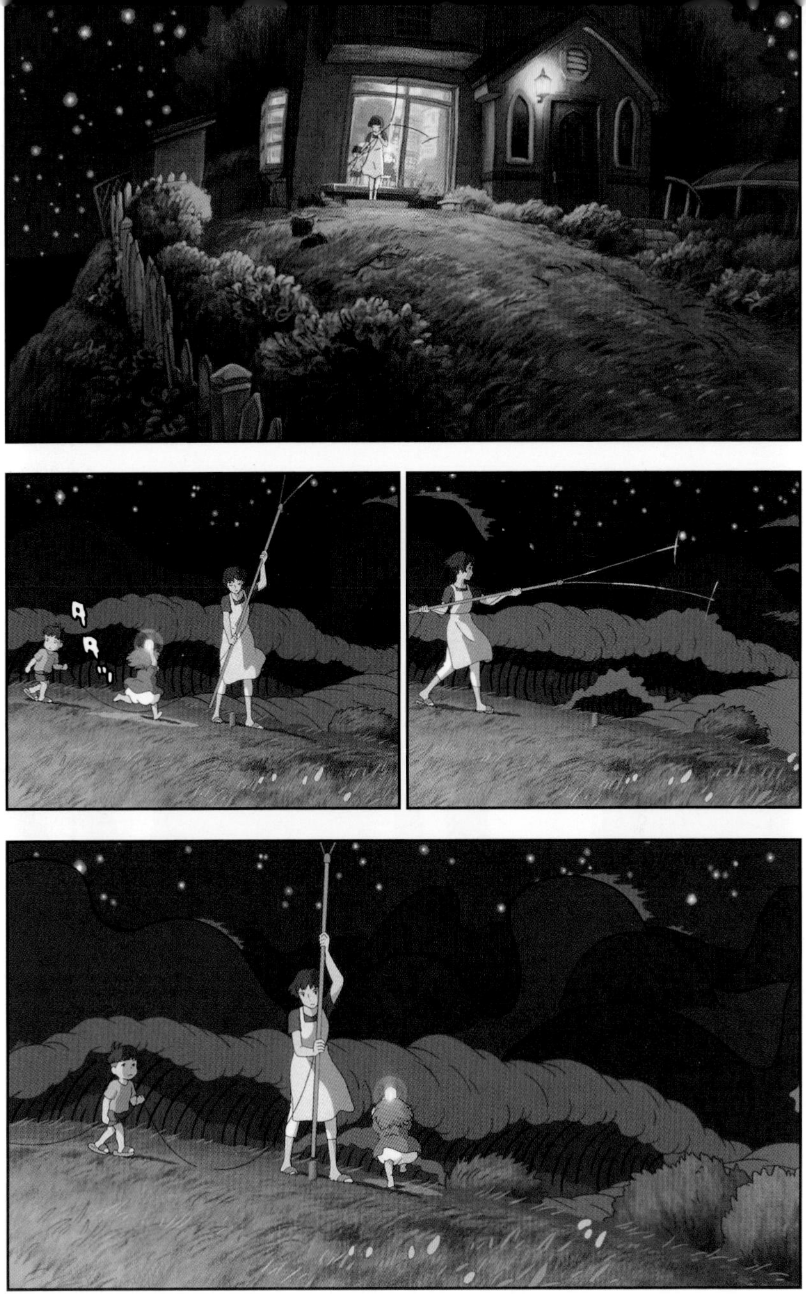
タタッ

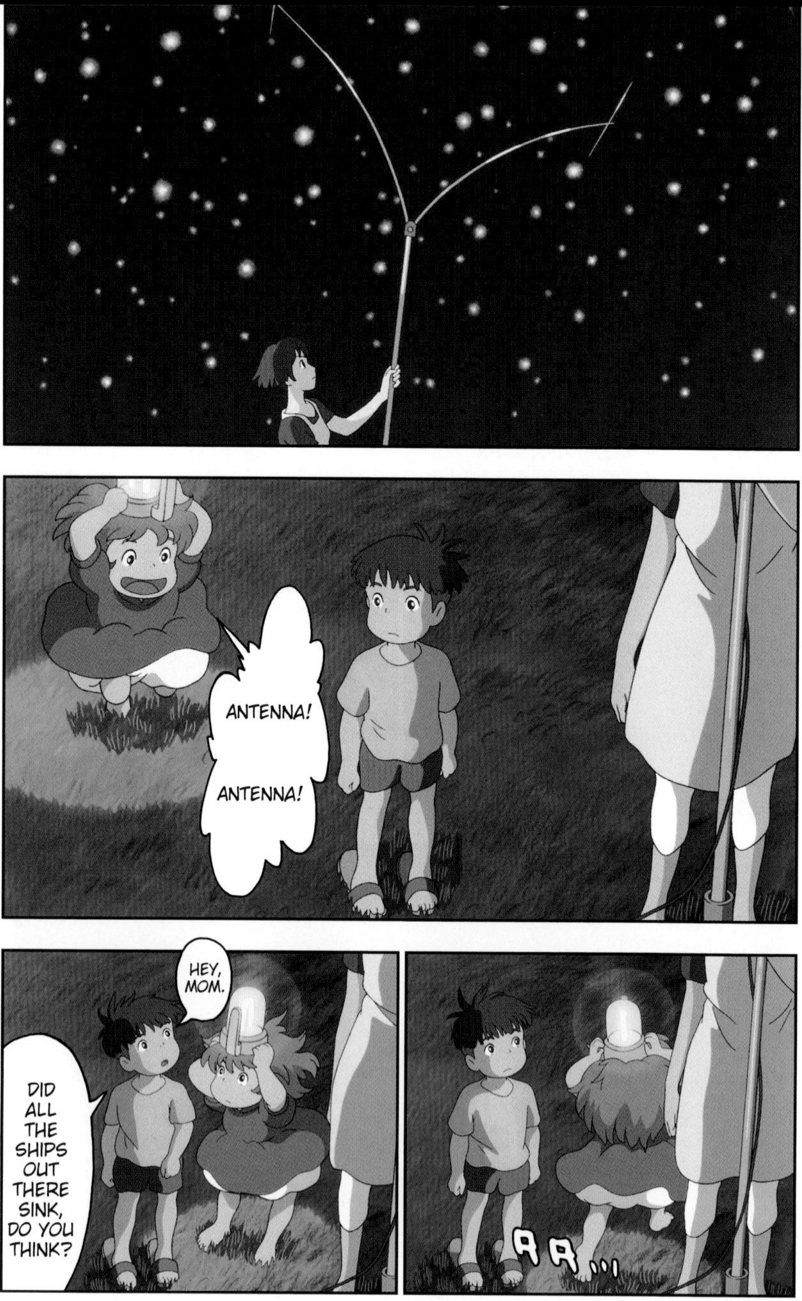
ANTENNA! ANTENNA!
HEY, MOM.
DID ALL THE SHIPS OUT THERE SINK, DO YOU THINK?

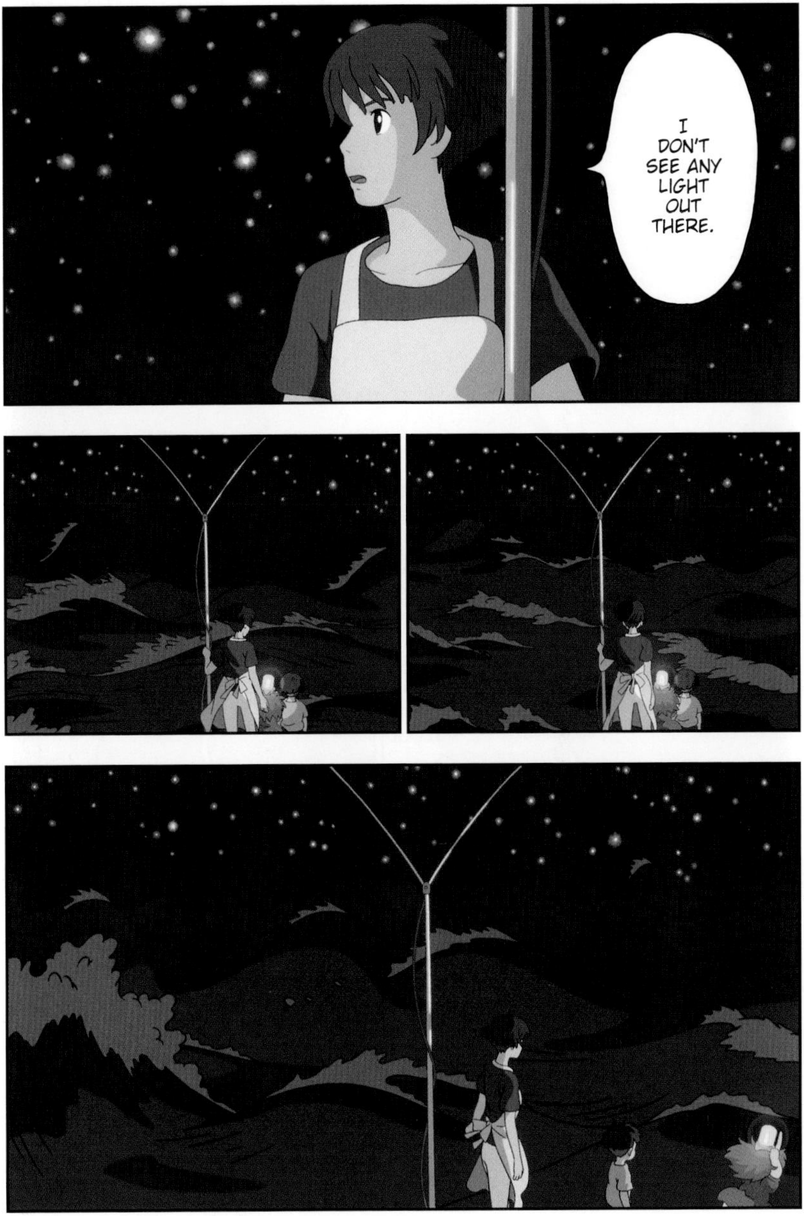
I DON'T SEE ANY LIGHT OUT THERE.

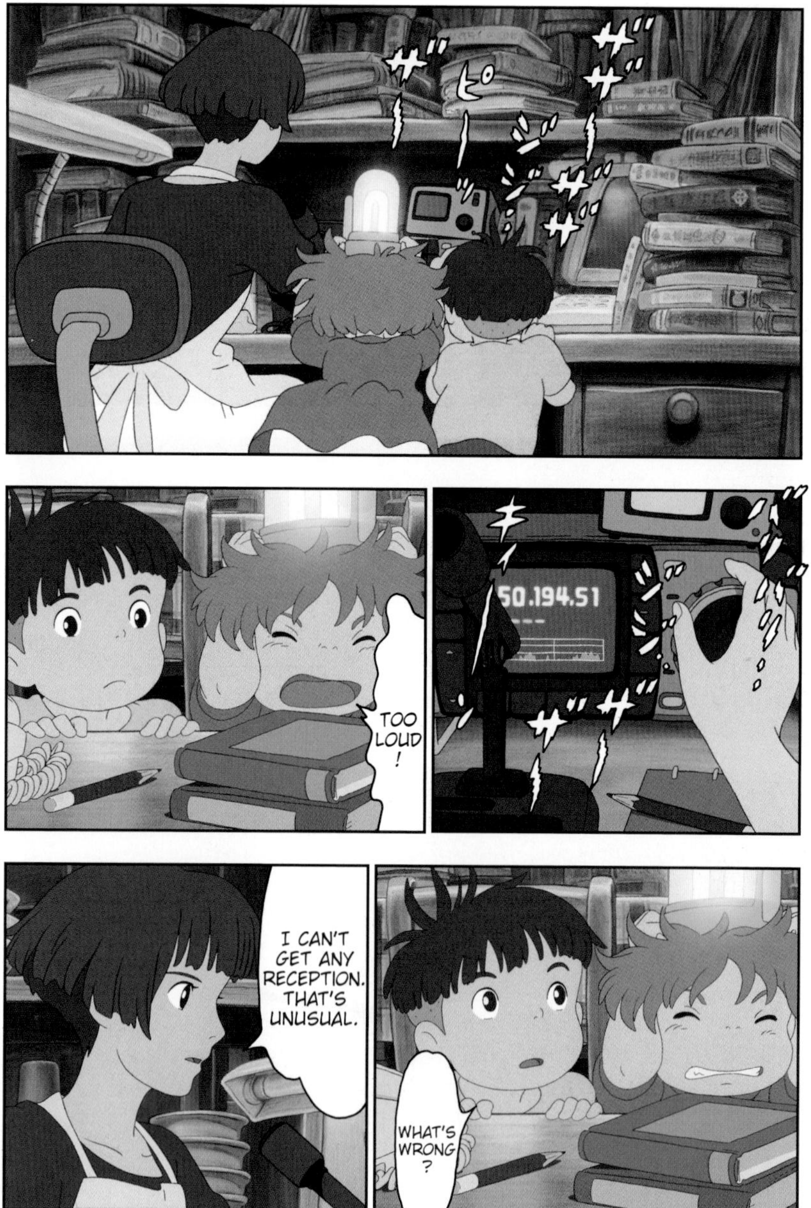
50.194.51
TOO LOUD!
WHAT'S WRONG?
I CAN'T GET ANY RECEPTION. THAT'S UNUSUAL.

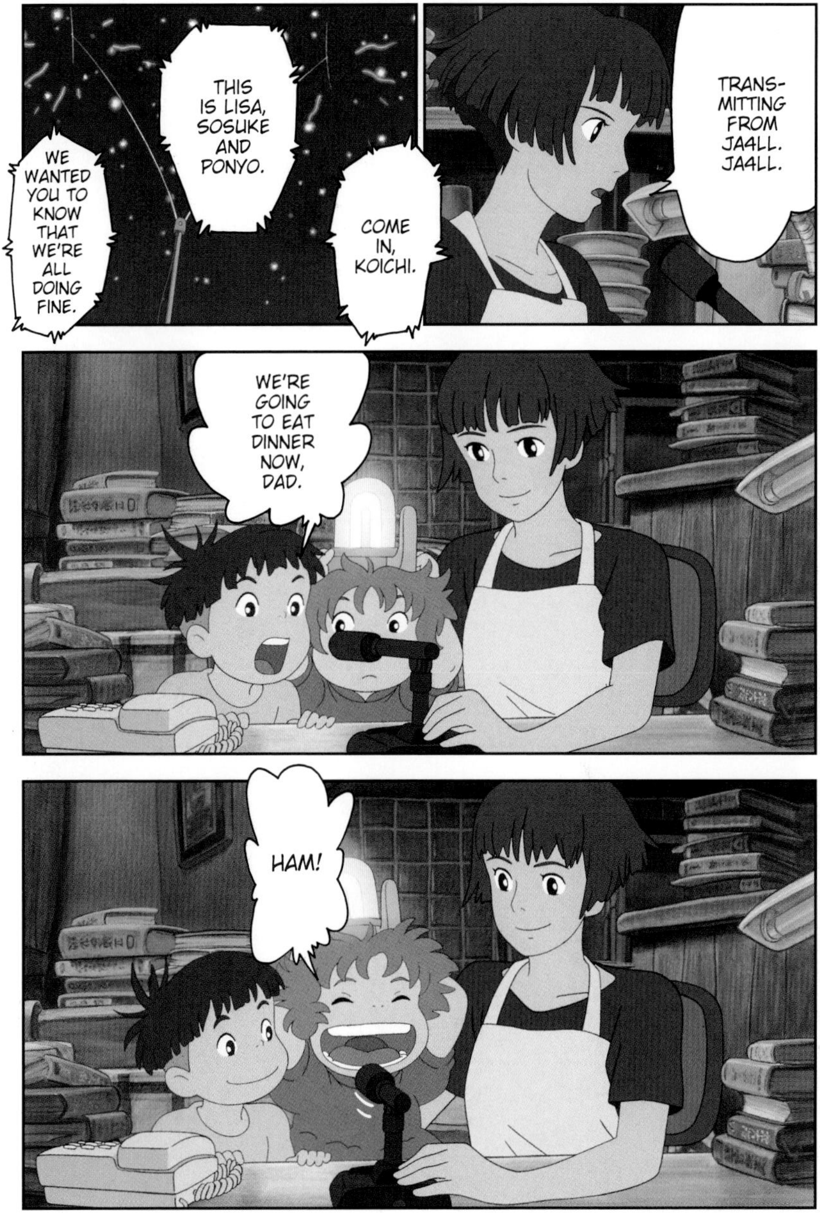
TRANS-MITTING FROM JA4LL. JA4LL.
COME IN, KOICHI.
THIS IS LISA, SOSUKE AND PONYO.
WE WANTED YOU TO KNOW THAT WE'RE ALL DOING FINE.
WE'RE GOING TO EAT DINNER NOW, DAD.
HAM!

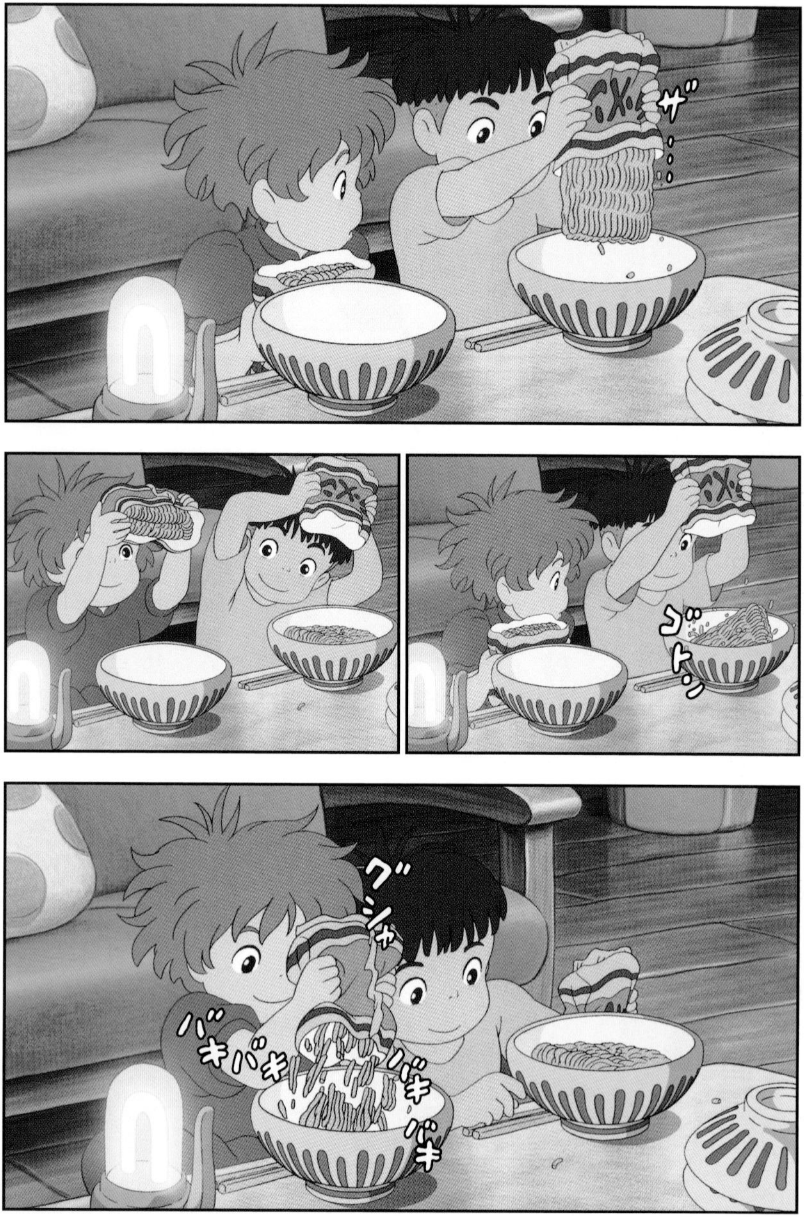
ザ…
ゴトン
グシャ
バキバキ
バキバキ

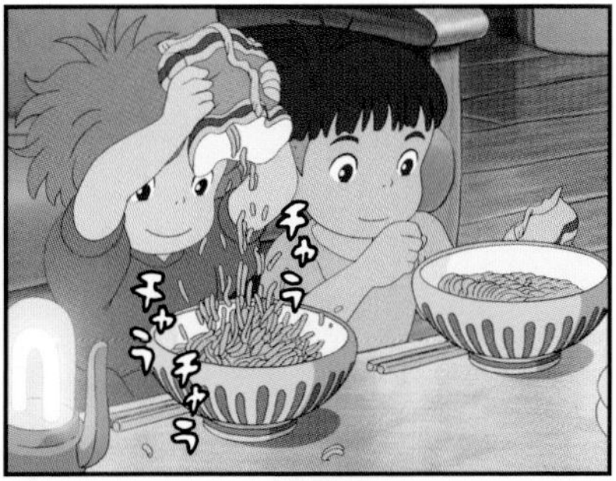
チャラ
チャラ
チャラ

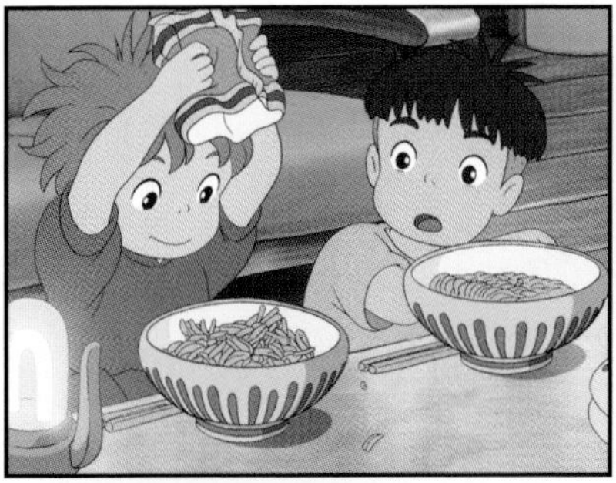

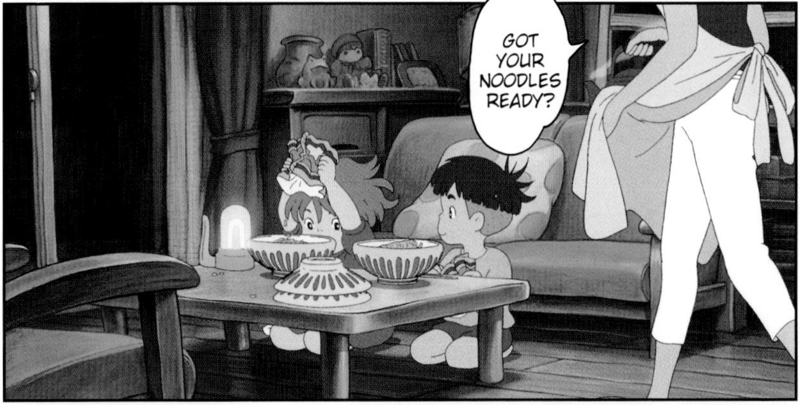
GOT YOUR NOODLES READY?

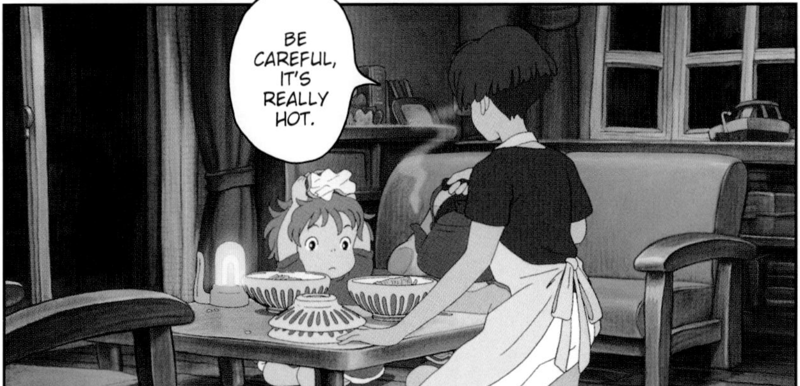
BE CAREFUL, IT'S REALLY HOT.

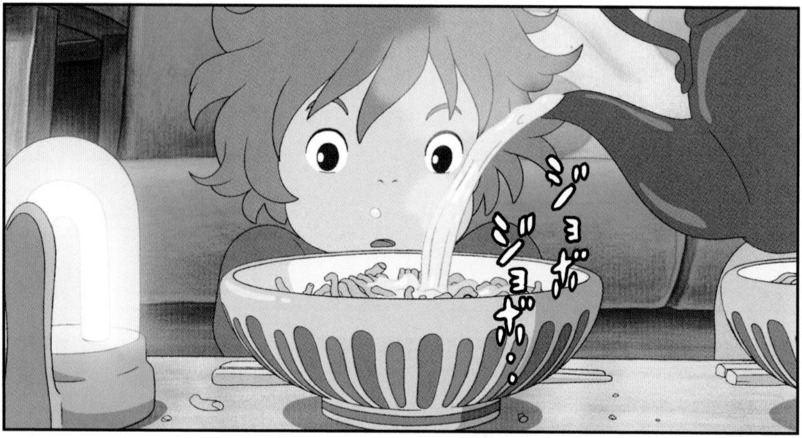
ジョボ
ジョボ…
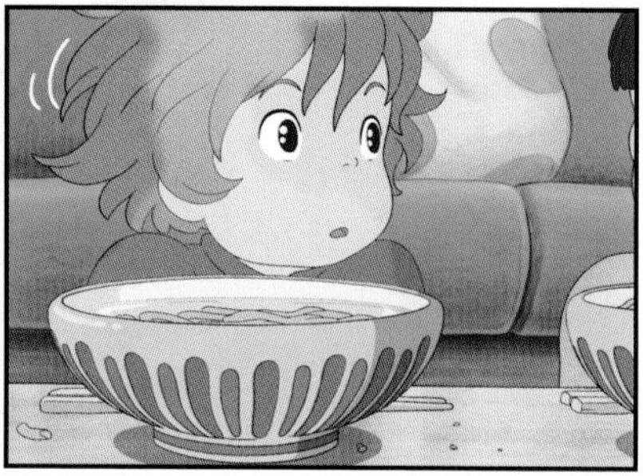
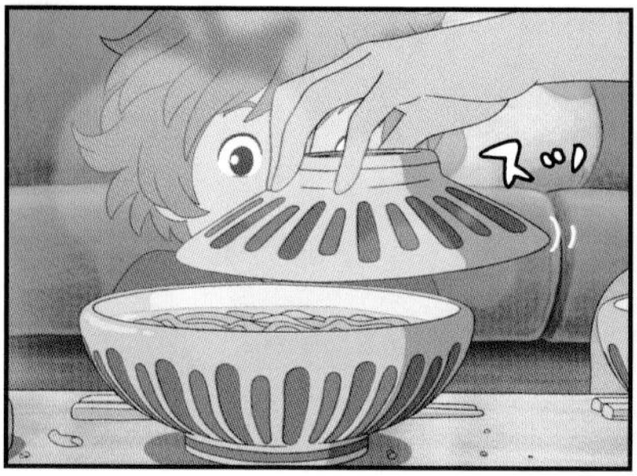
スッ
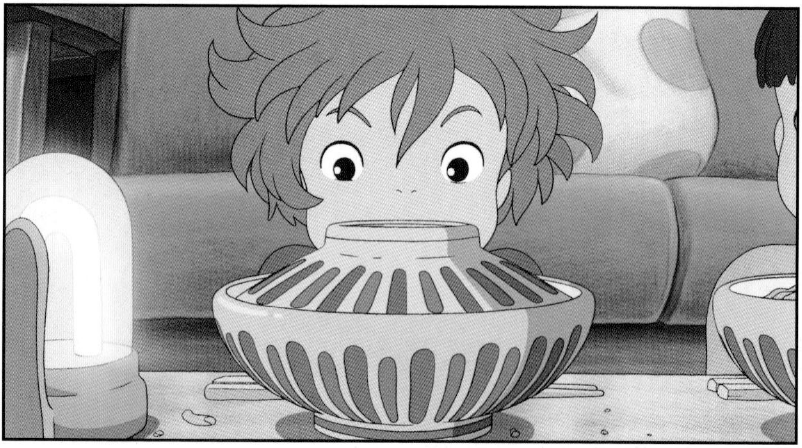

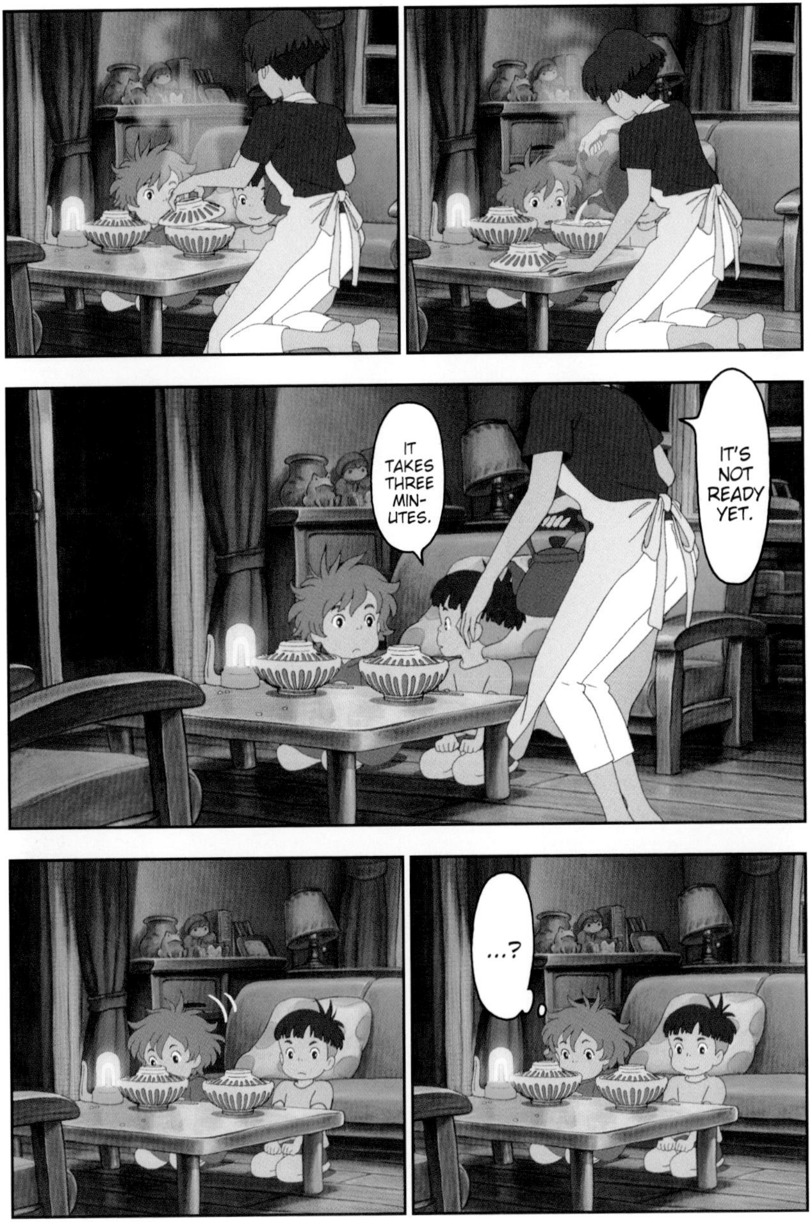
IT'S NOT READY YET.
IT TAKES THREE MIN-UTES.
...?

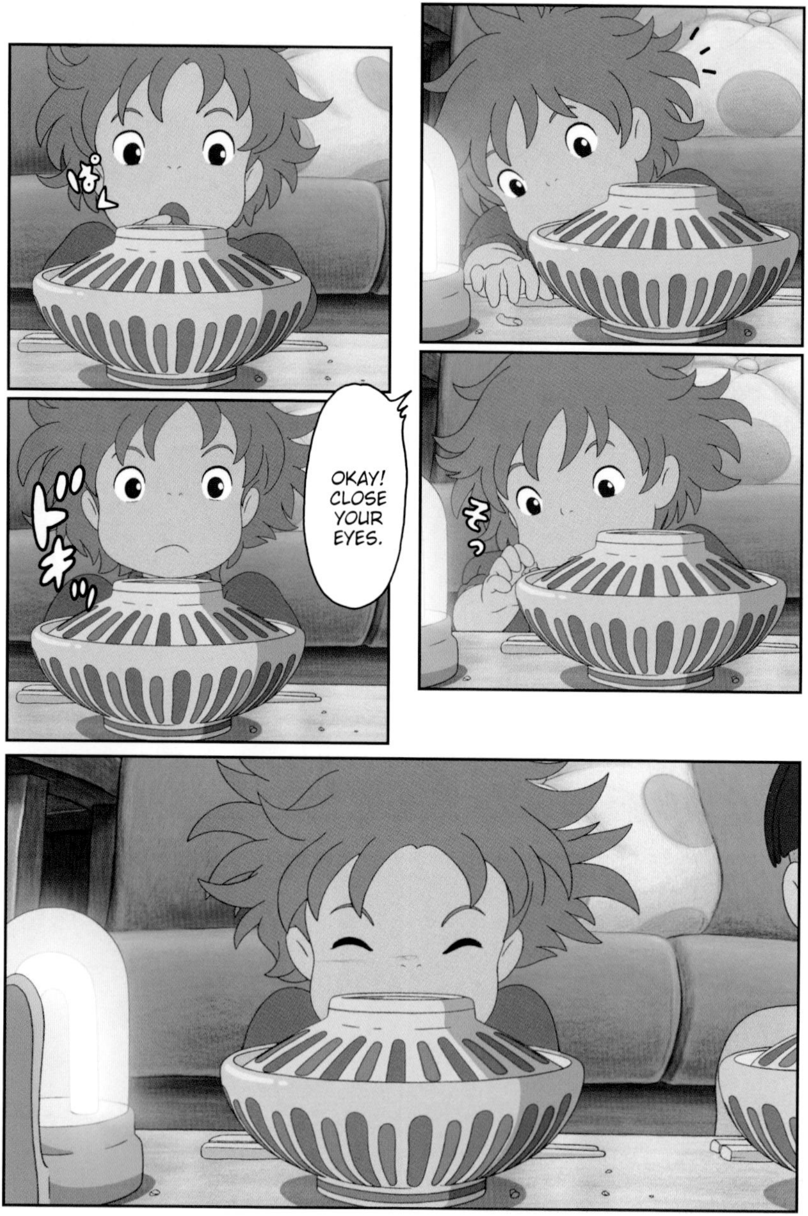
そっ
OKAY! CLOSE YOUR EYES.
ドキッ

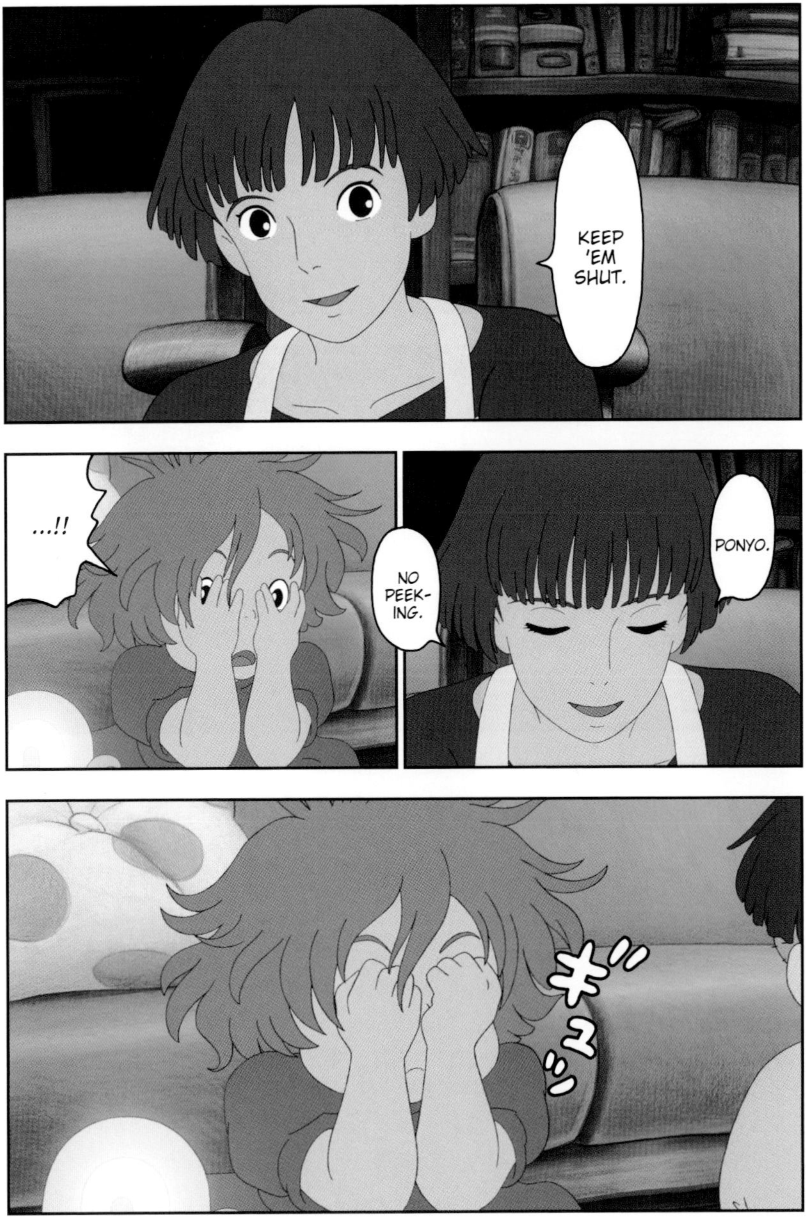
KEEP 'EM SHUT.
PONYO.
NO PEEK-ING.
...!!
ギュッ

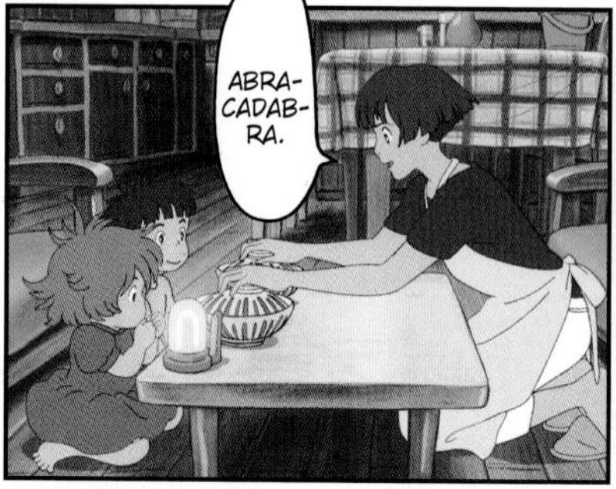
ABRA-
CADAB-
RA.
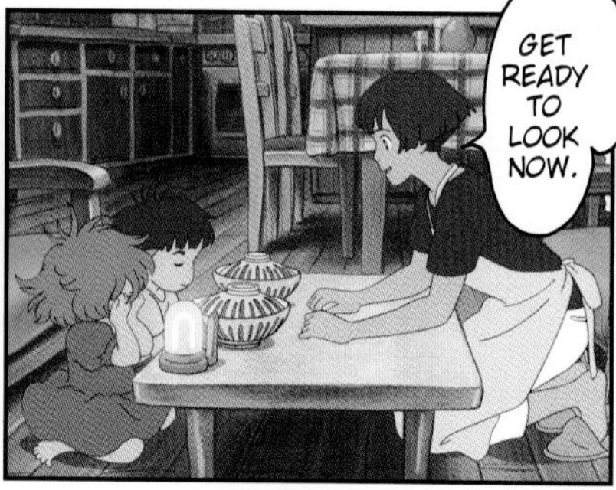
GET
READY
TO
LOOK
NOW.
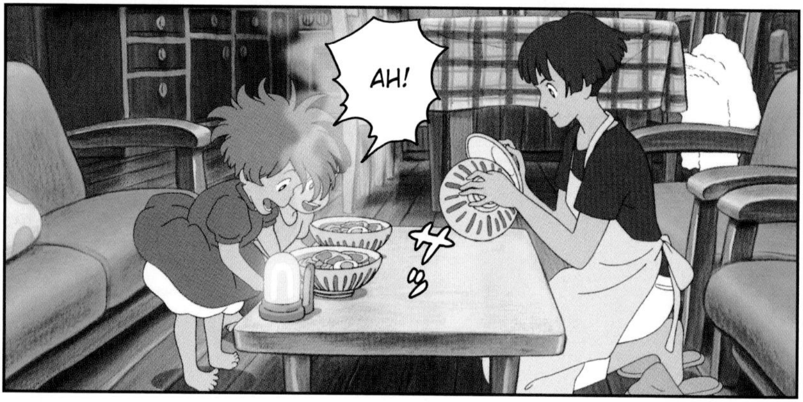
AH!
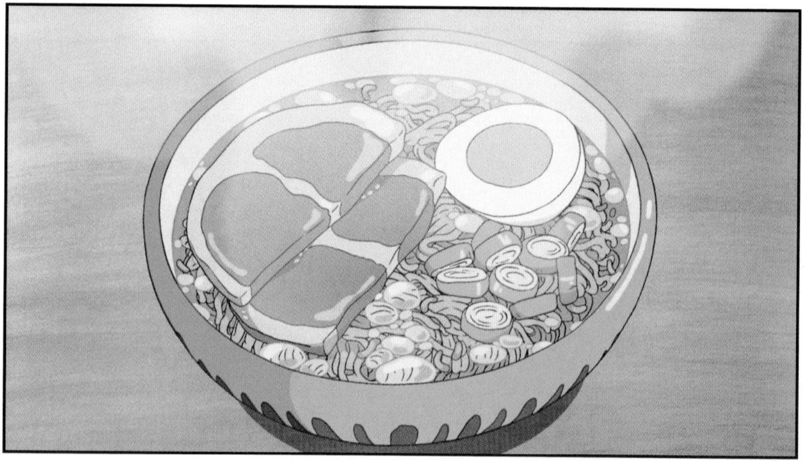

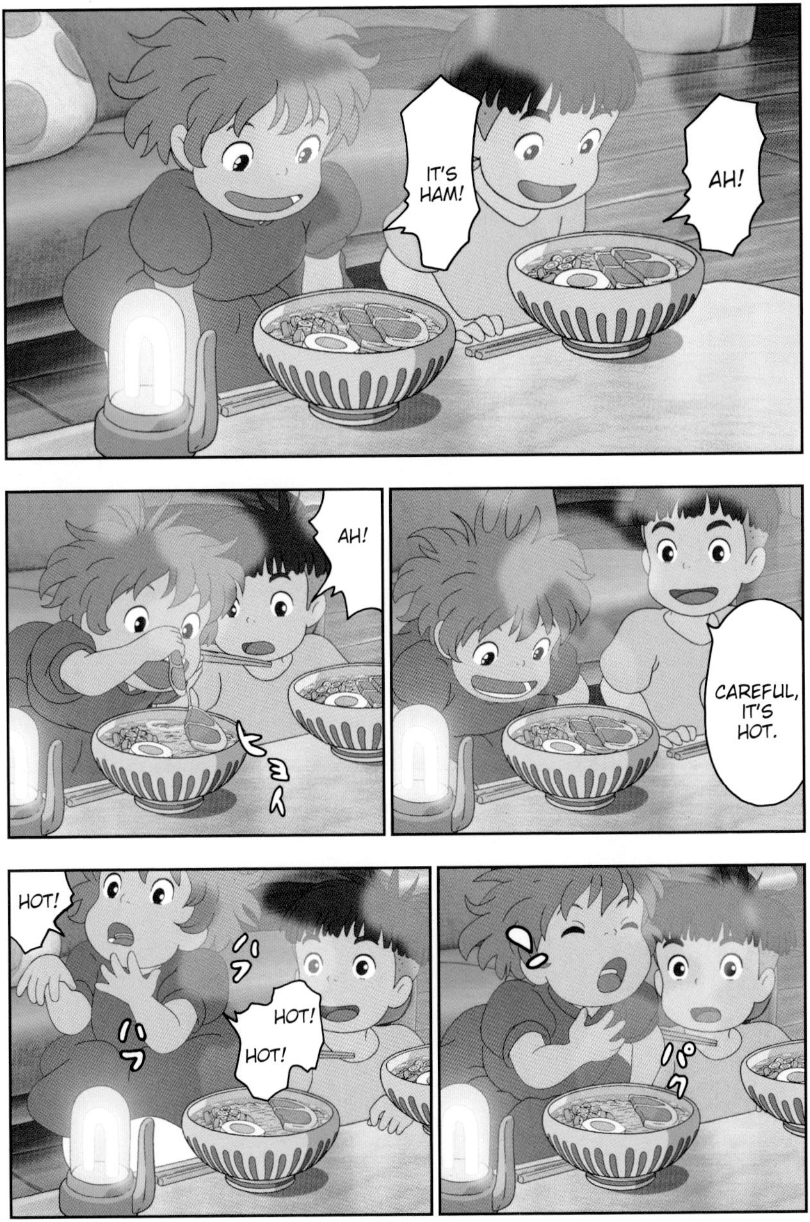
IT'S HAM!
AH!
AH!
ヒョイ
CAREFUL, IT'S HOT.
HOT!
ハフ
ハフ
HOT! HOT!
パク

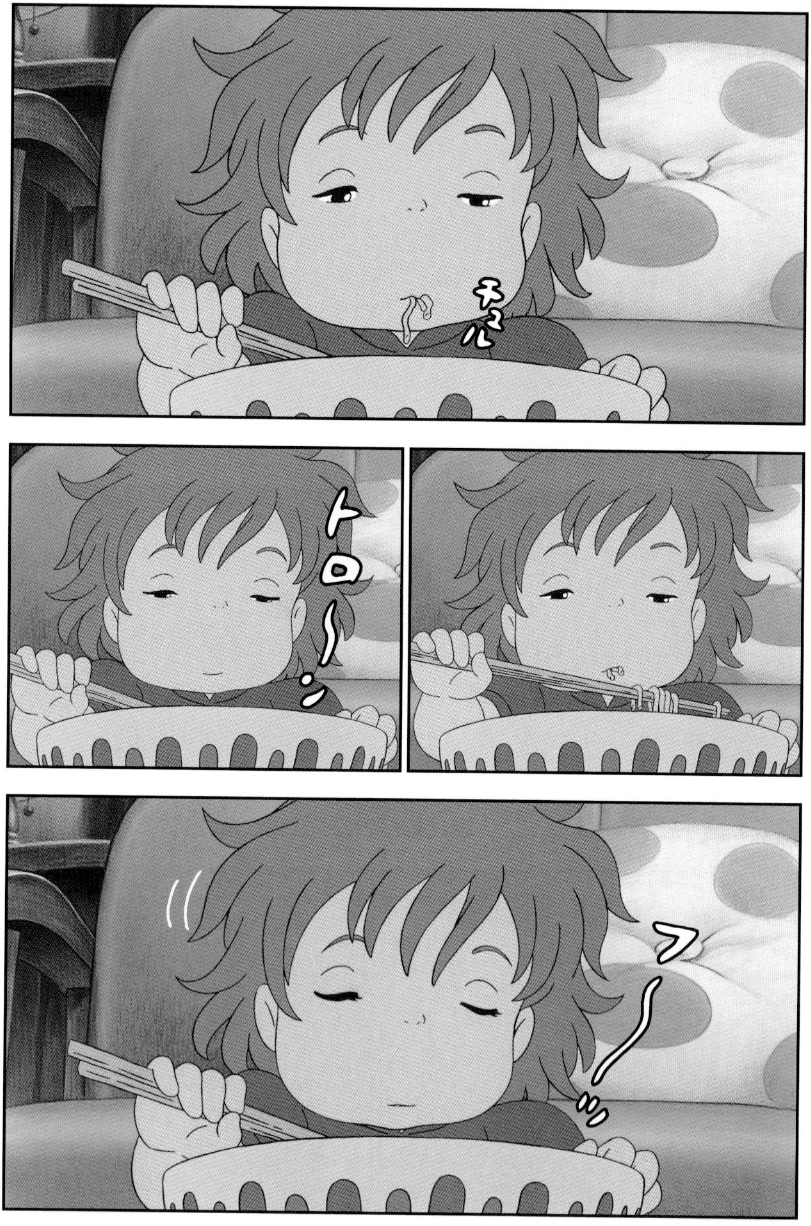
チュル
トロ〜ン
フ〜ッ

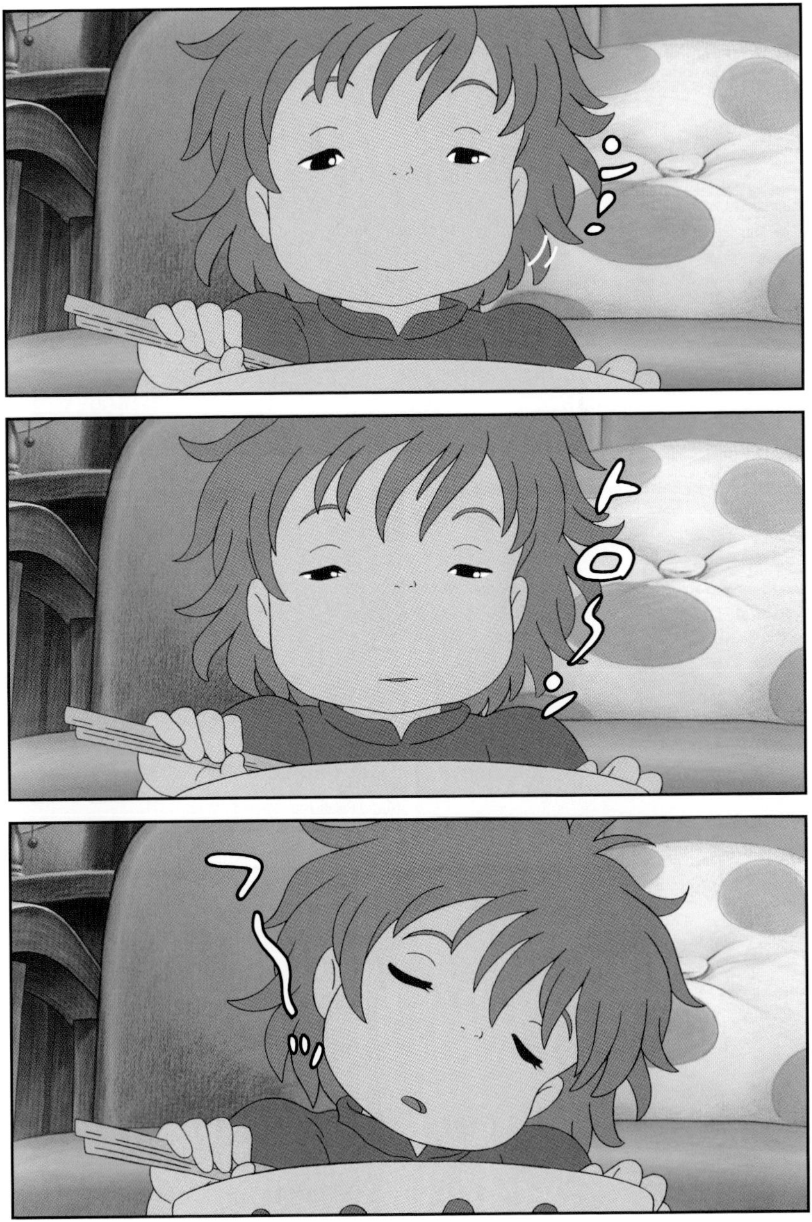
トロ～ン
フ～ッ

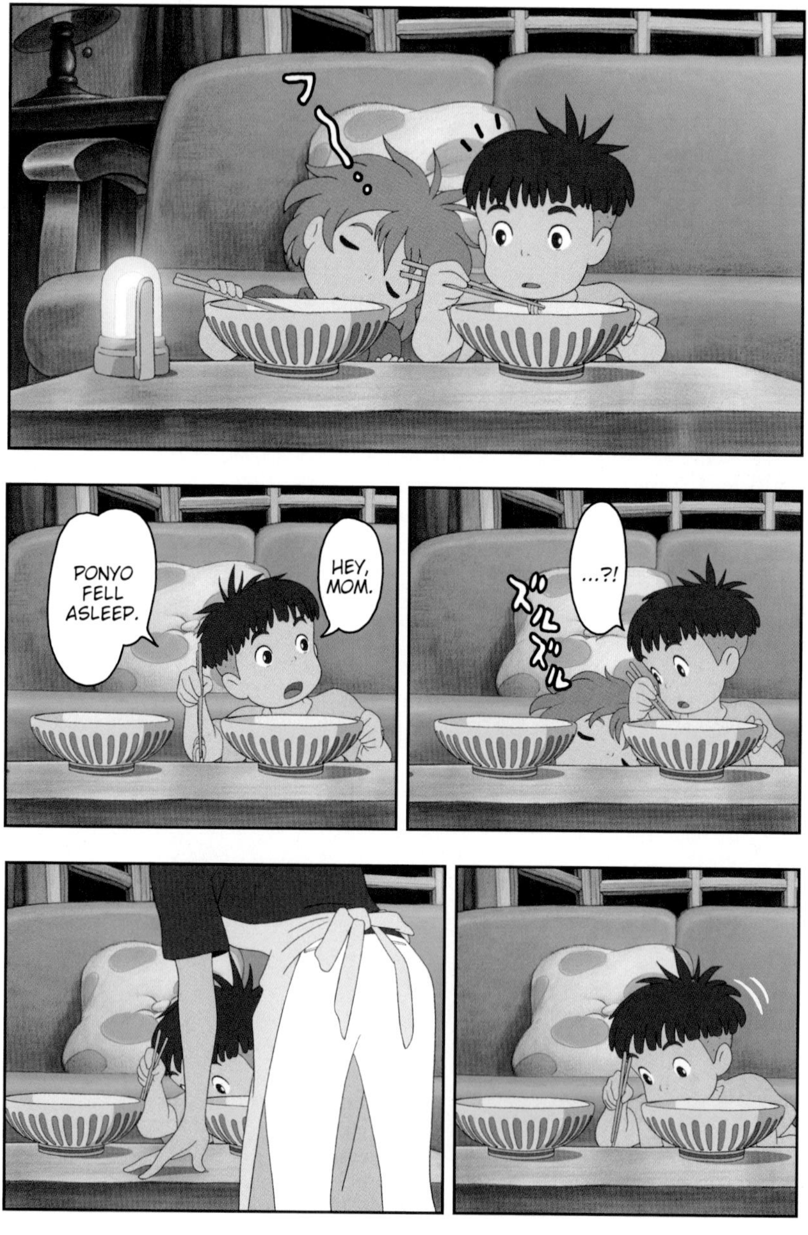
フ〜..
HEY, MOM.
PONYO FELL ASLEEP.
...?!
ズルズル

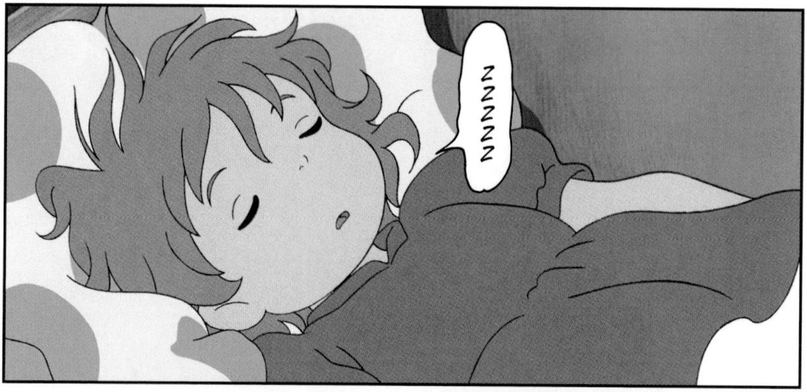
ZZZZZ

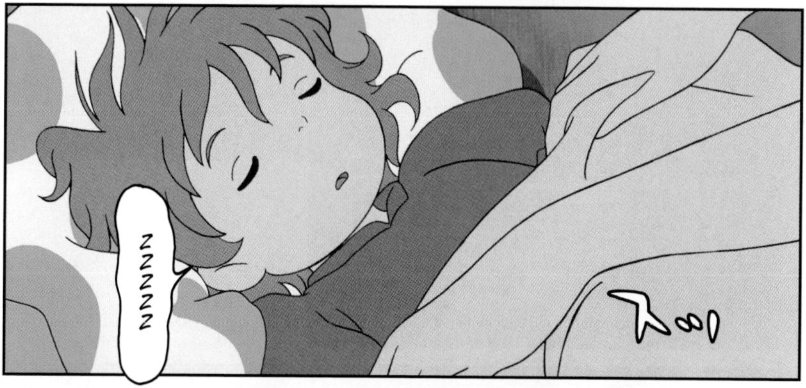
ZZZZZ

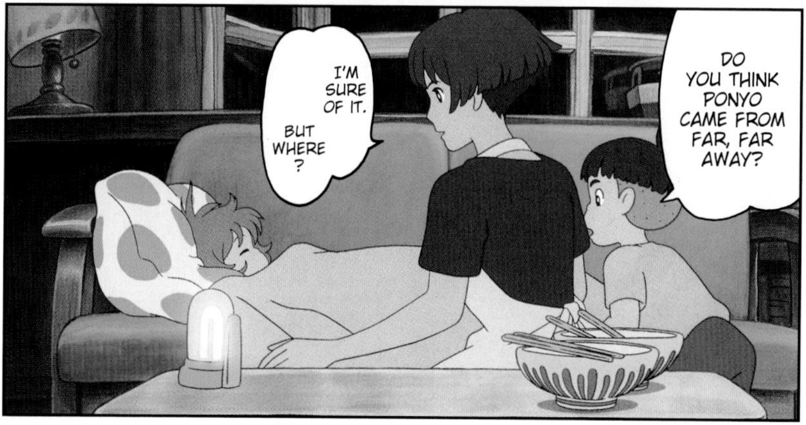
DO YOU THINK PONYO CAME FROM FAR, FAR AWAY?
I'M SURE OF IT.
BUT WHERE?

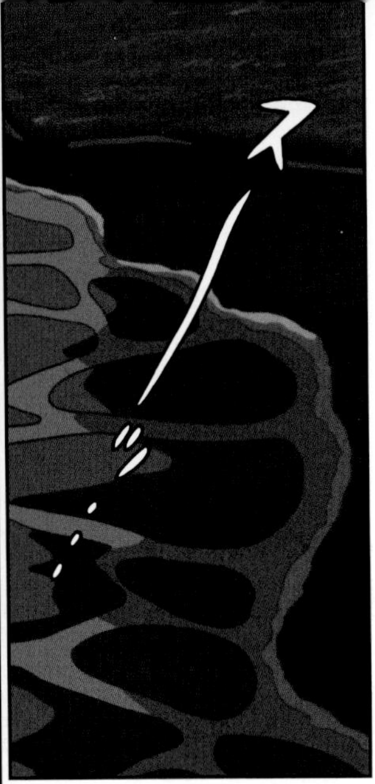
スー
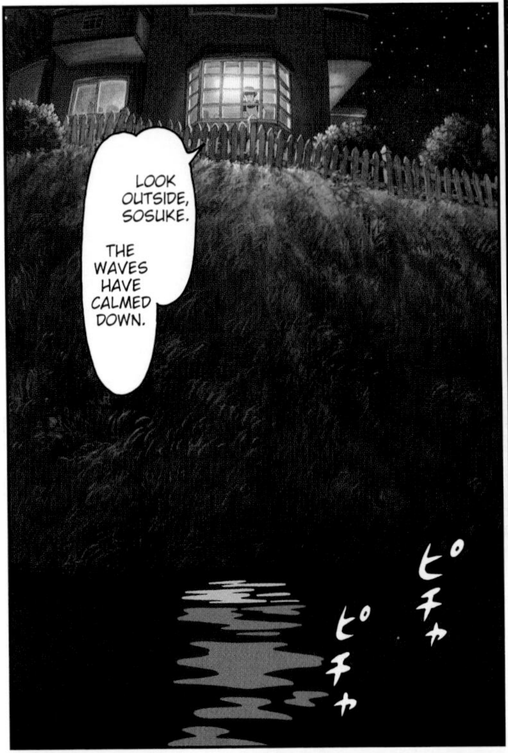
LOOK OUTSIDE, SOSUKE.
THE WAVES HAVE CALMED DOWN.
ピチャ ピチャ
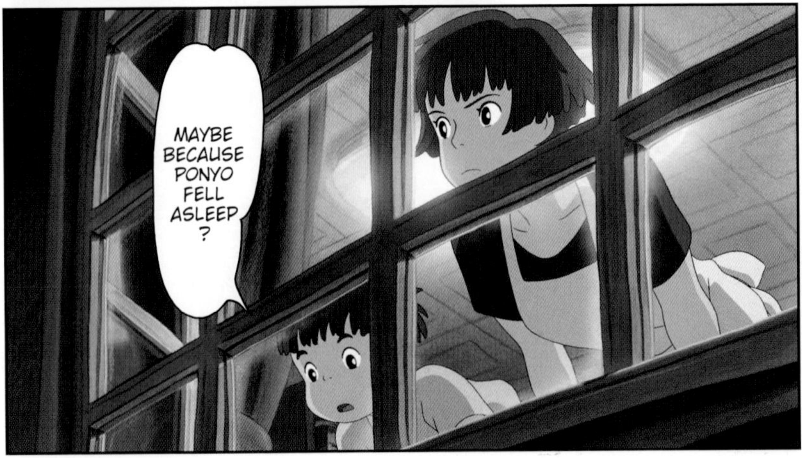
MAYBE BECAUSE PONYO FELL ASLEEP?

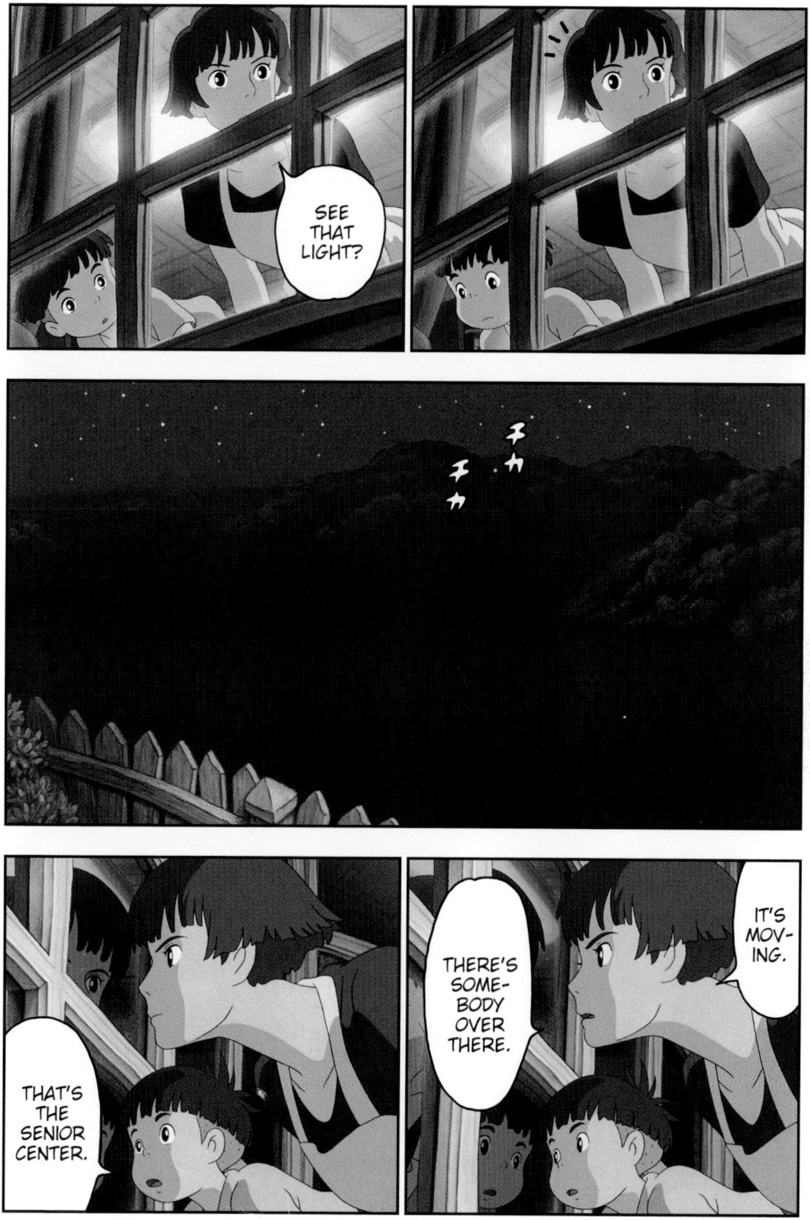
SEE THAT LIGHT?
チカ
チカ
IT'S MOVING.
THERE'S SOMEBODY OVER THERE.
THAT'S THE SENIOR CENTER.

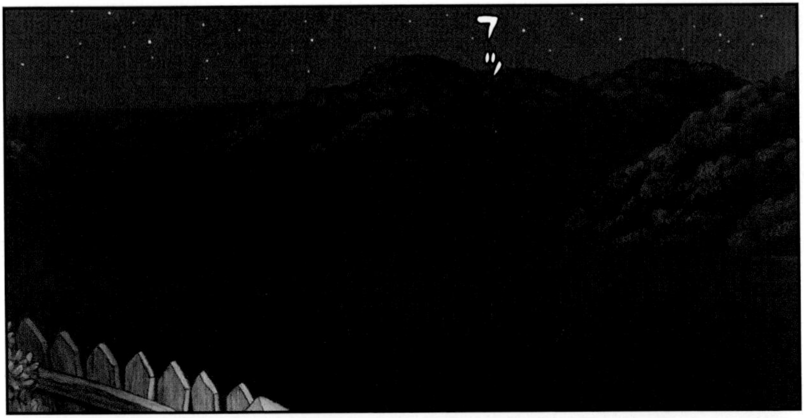
フッ

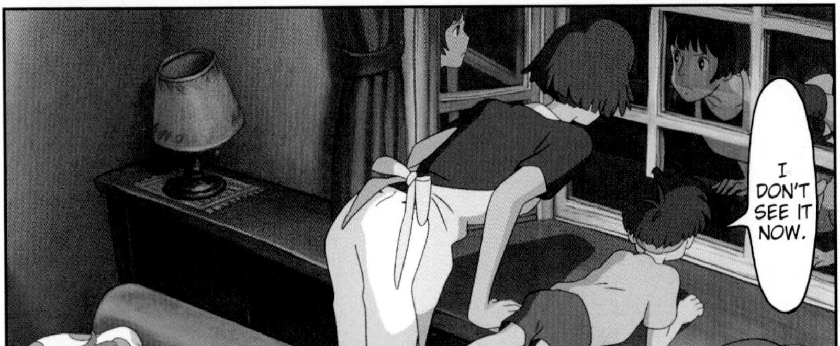
I DON'T SEE IT NOW.

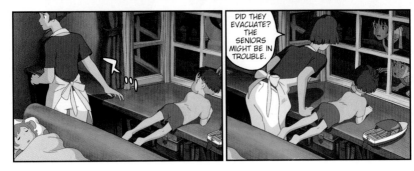

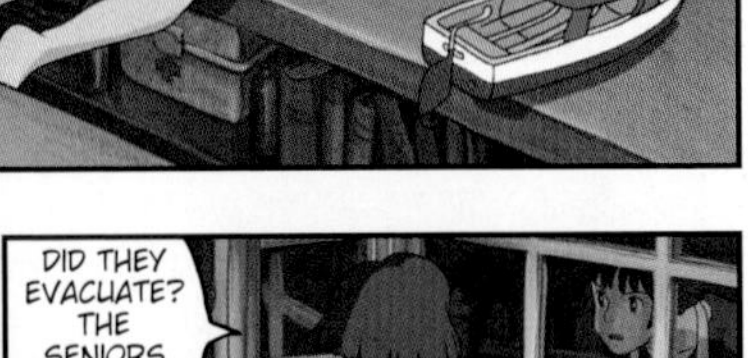
DID THEY EVACUATE? THE SENIORS MIGHT BE IN TROUBLE.

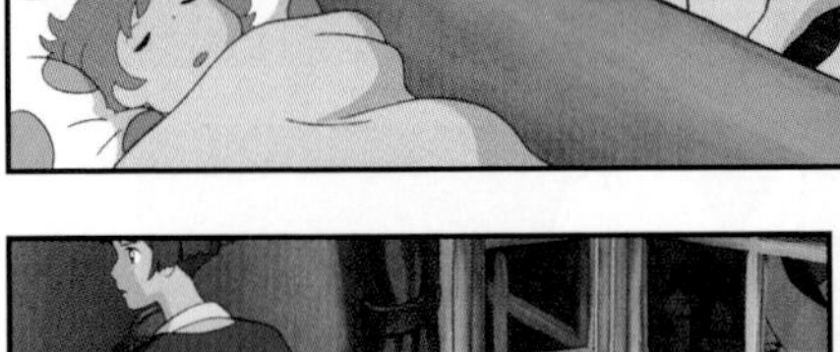

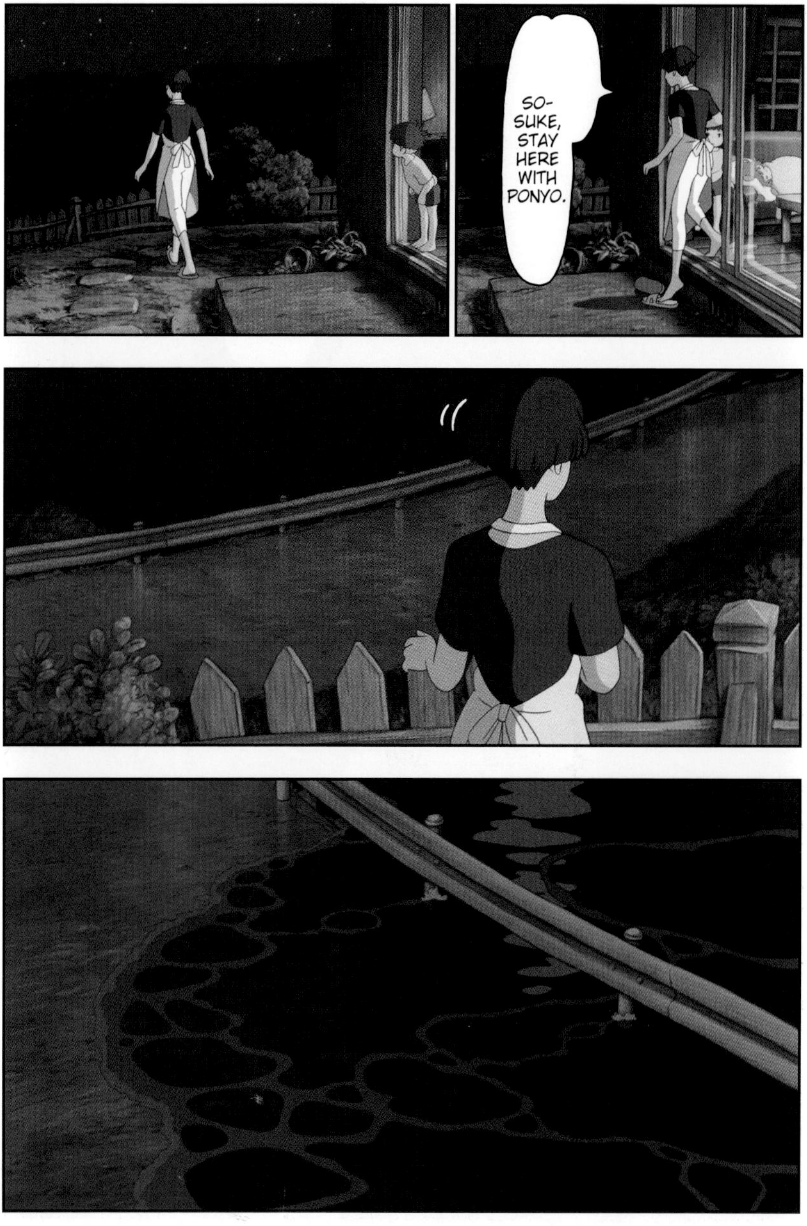
SO-SUKE, STAY HERE WITH PONYO.

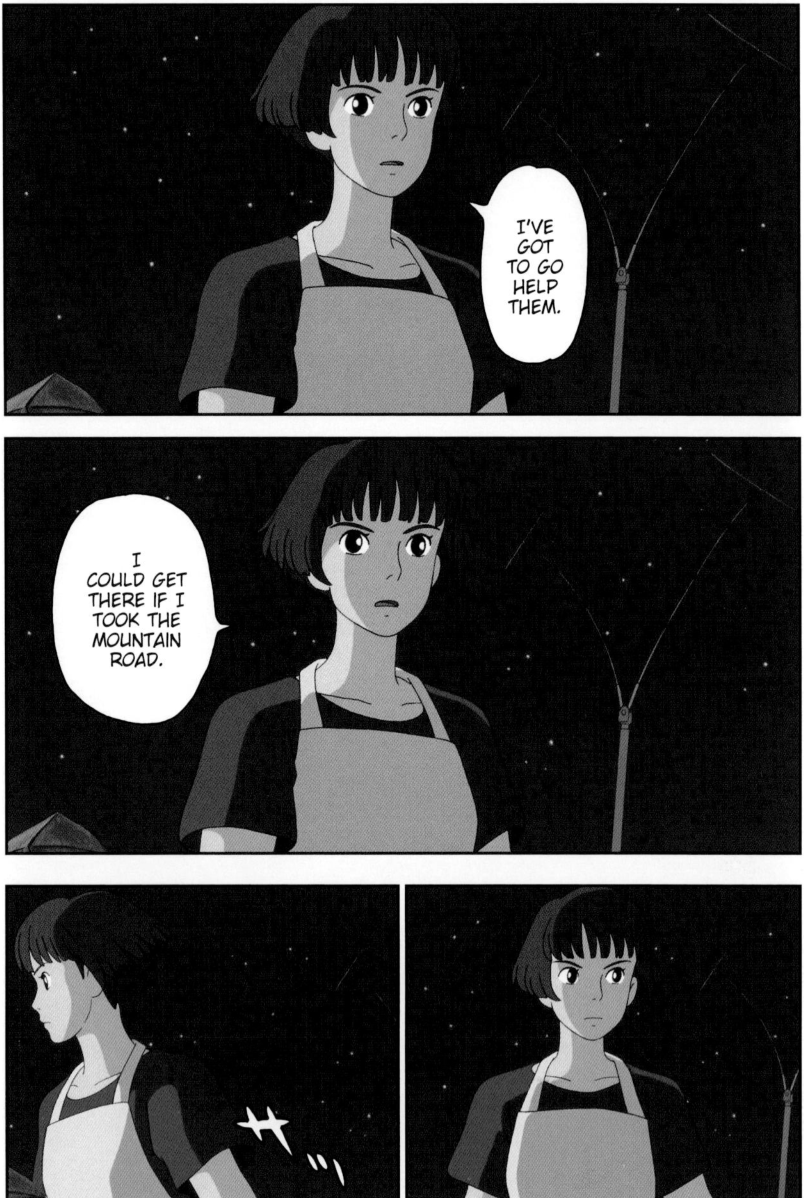
I'VE GOT TO GO HELP THEM.
I COULD GET THERE IF I TOOK THE MOUNTAIN ROAD.
ハッ

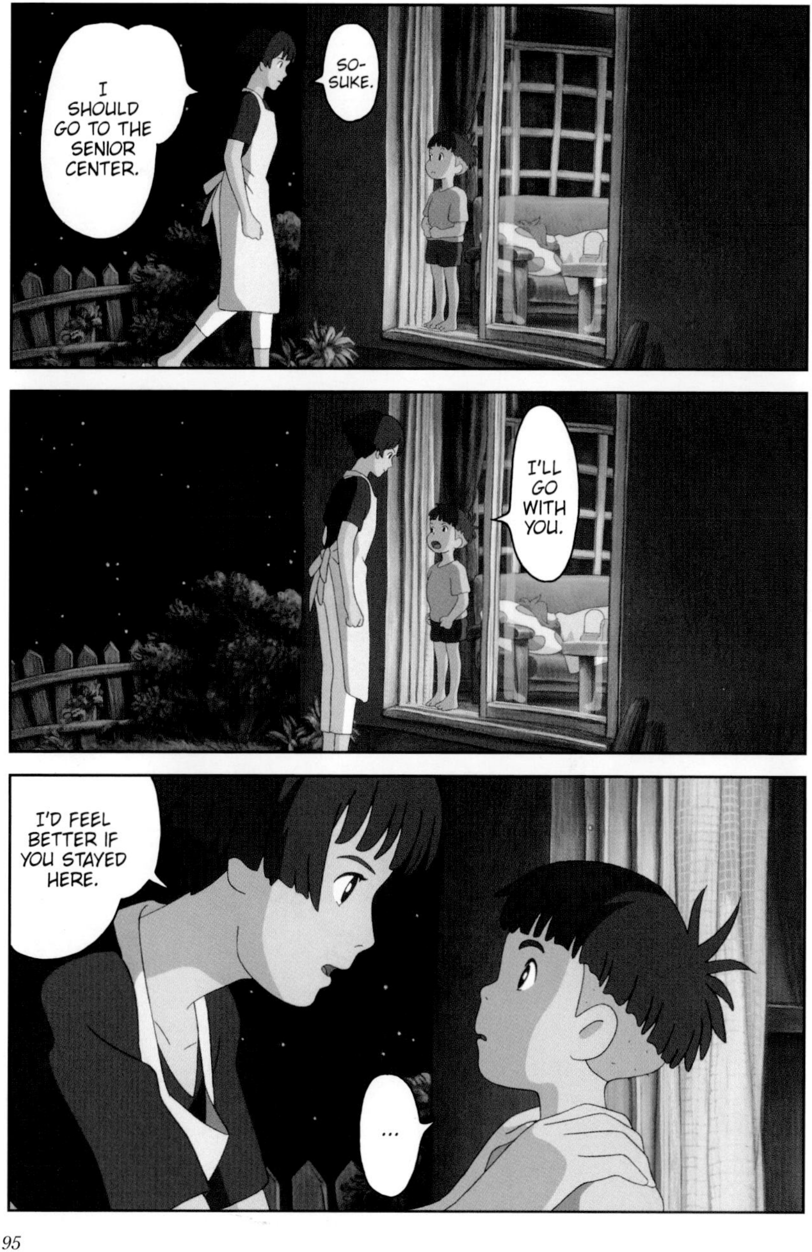
SO-SUKE.
I SHOULD GO TO THE SENIOR CENTER.
I'LL GO WITH YOU.
I'D FEEL BETTER IF YOU STAYED HERE.
...

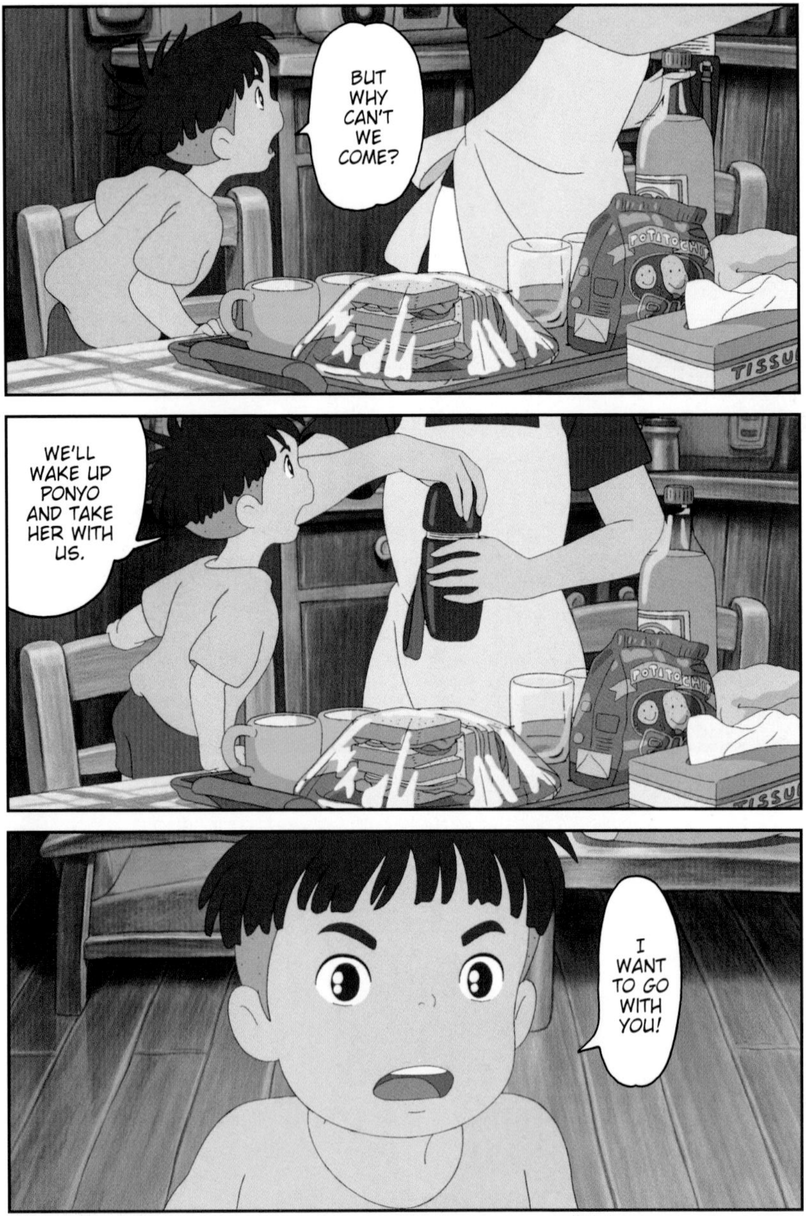
BUT WHY CAN'T WE COME?
WE'LL WAKE UP PONYO AND TAKE HER WITH US.
I WANT TO GO WITH YOU!

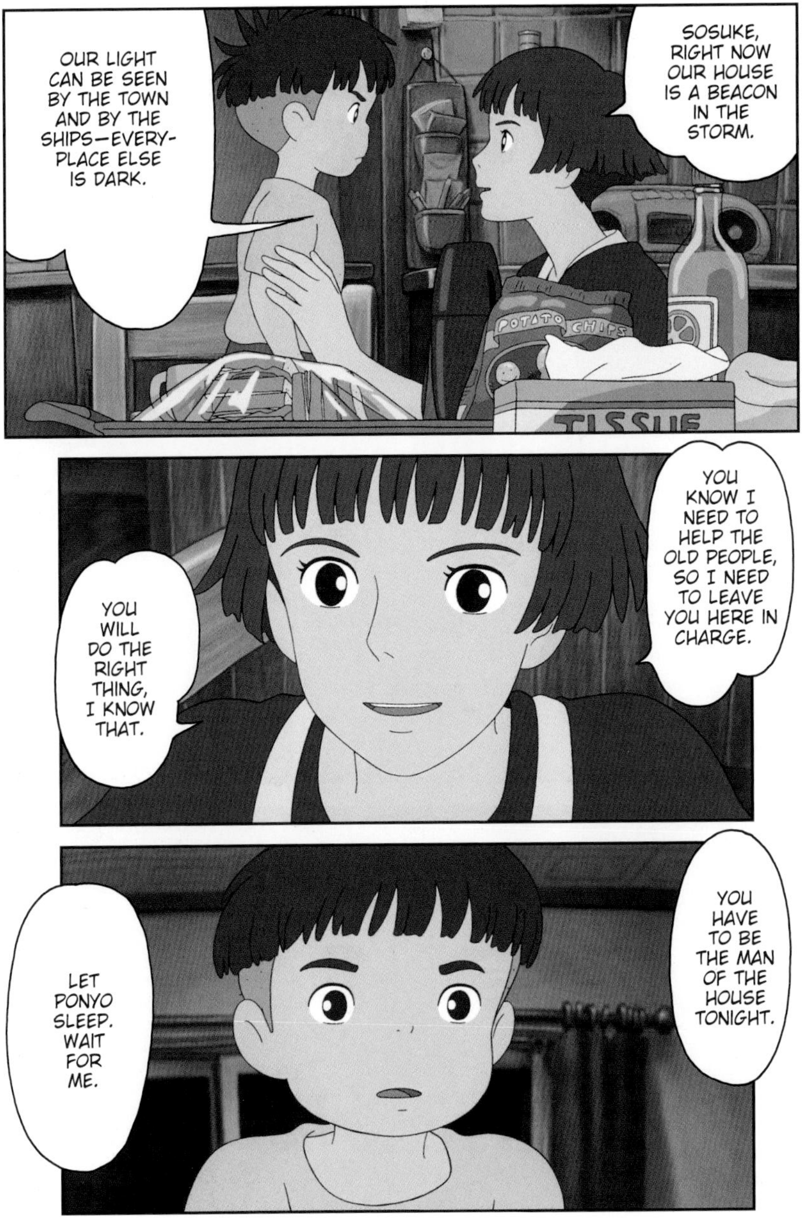
SOSUKE, RIGHT NOW OUR HOUSE IS A BEACON IN THE STORM.
OUR LIGHT CAN BE SEEN BY THE TOWN AND BY THE SHIPS—EVERY-PLACE ELSE IS DARK.
POTATO CHIPS
YOU KNOW I NEED TO HELP THE OLD PEOPLE, SO I NEED TO LEAVE YOU HERE IN CHARGE.
YOU WILL DO THE RIGHT THING, I KNOW THAT.
YOU HAVE TO BE THE MAN OF THE HOUSE TONIGHT.
LET PONYO SLEEP. WAIT FOR ME.

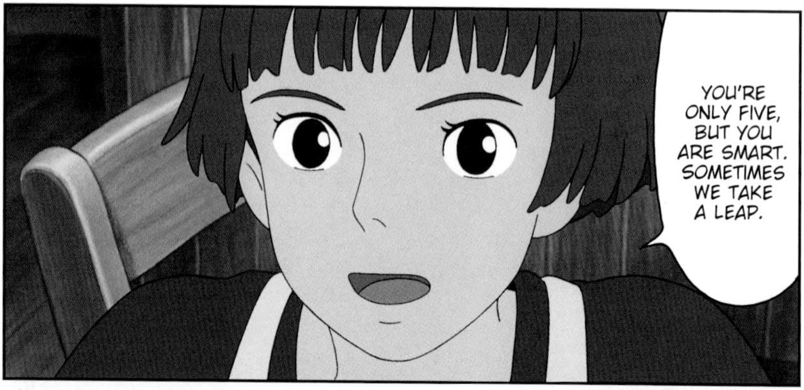
YOU'RE ONLY FIVE, BUT YOU ARE SMART. SOMETIMES WE TAKE A LEAP.
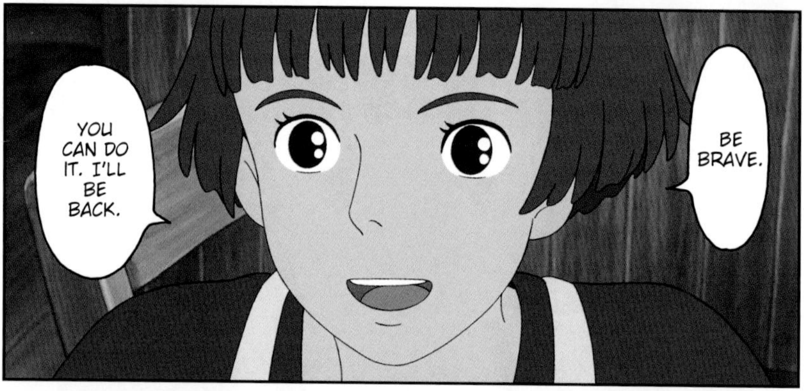
BE BRAVE.
YOU CAN DO IT. I'LL BE BACK.
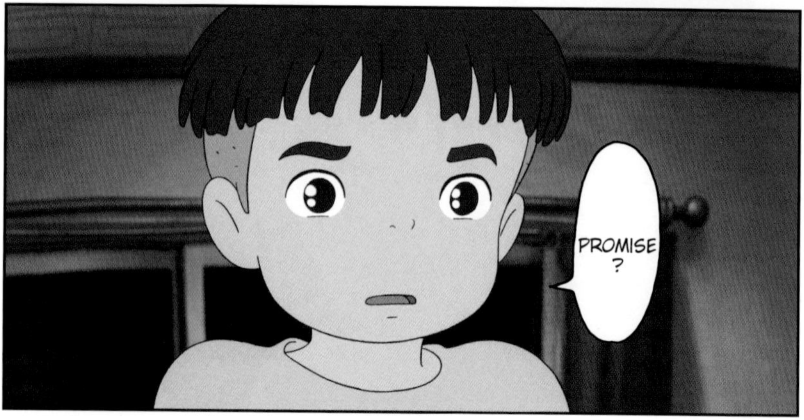
PROMISE?

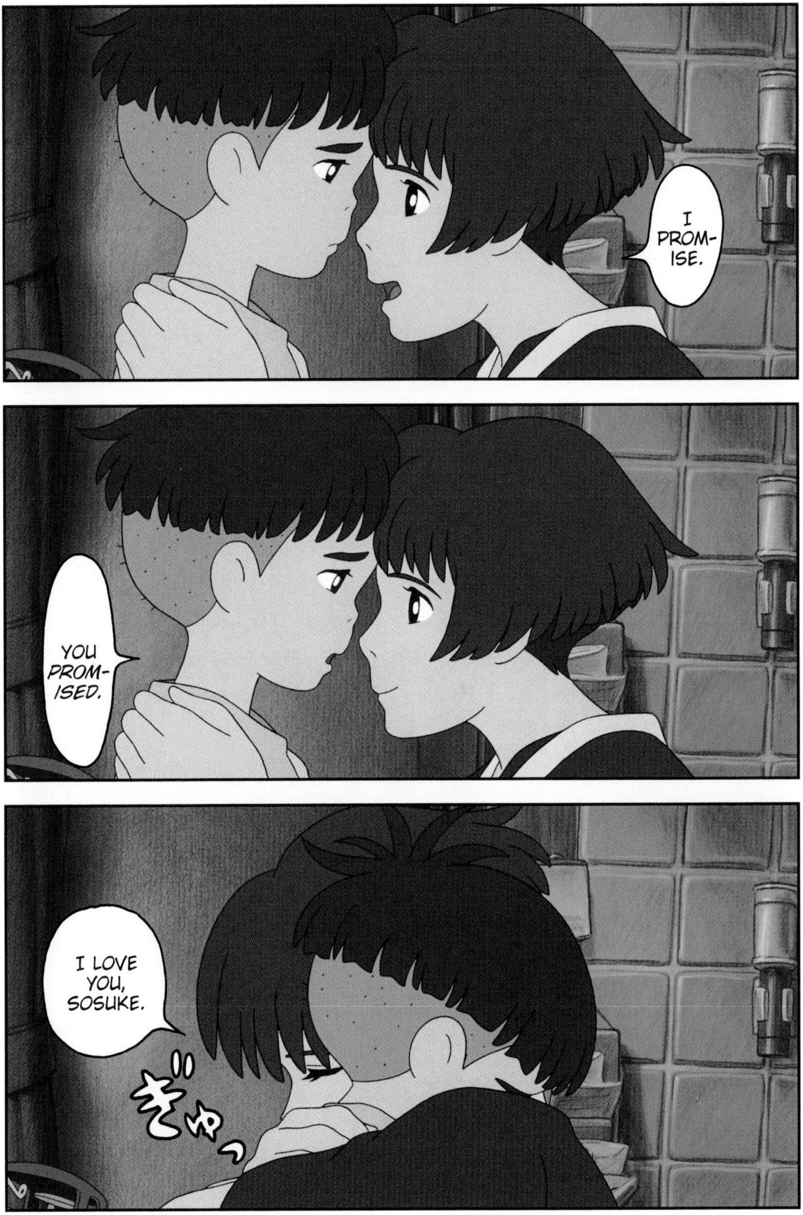
I PROMISE.
YOU PROMISED.
I LOVE YOU, SOSUKE.
ぎゅっ

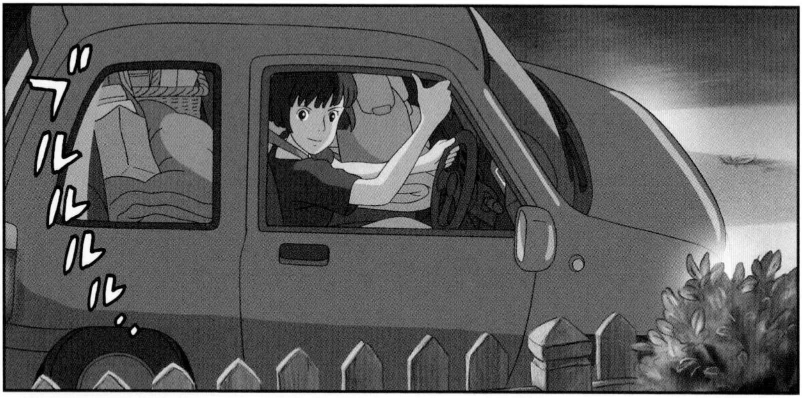
ブルルルル‥
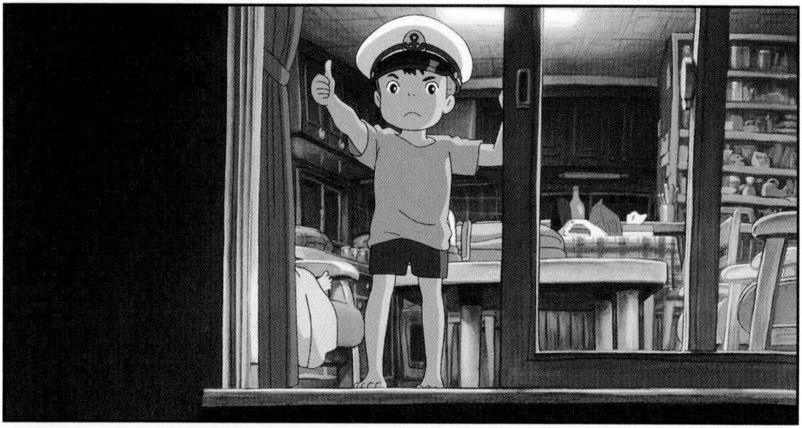
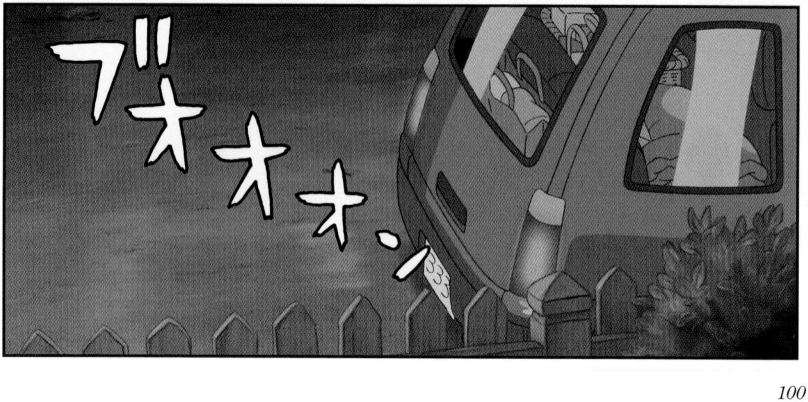
ブオオオ‥ン

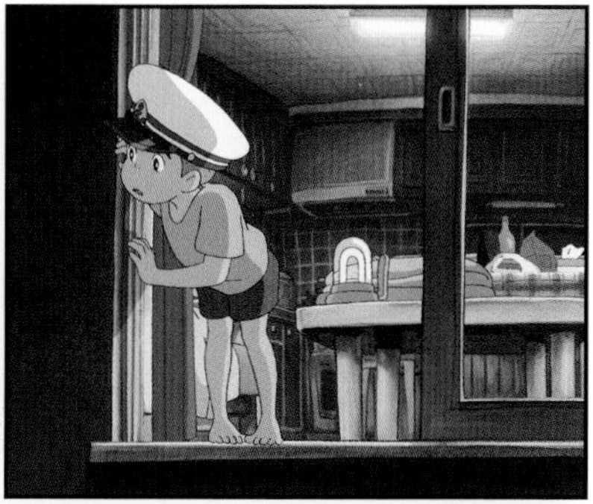

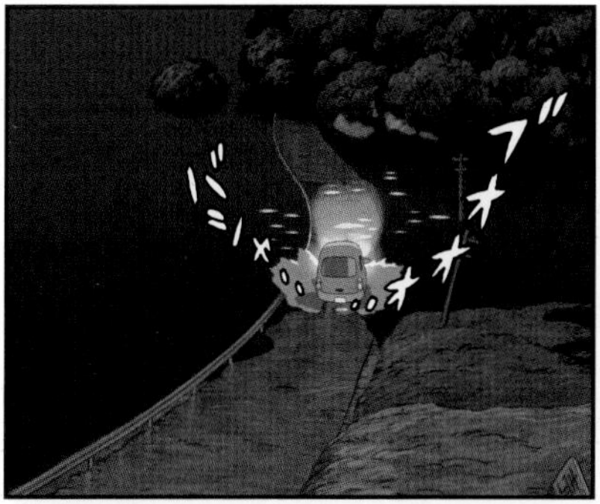
ブオオオ
バシャ

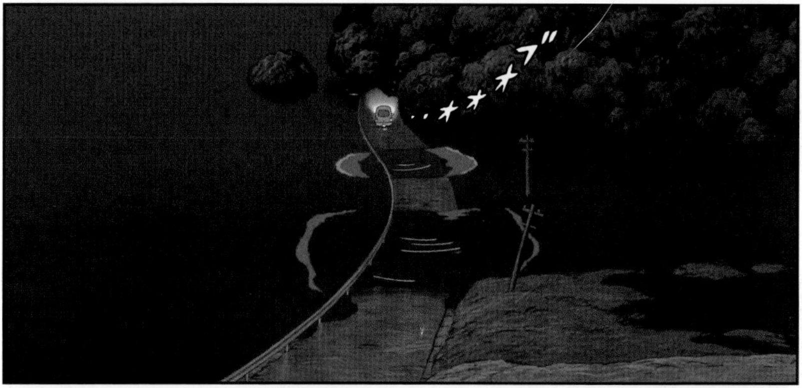
ブオオオ..

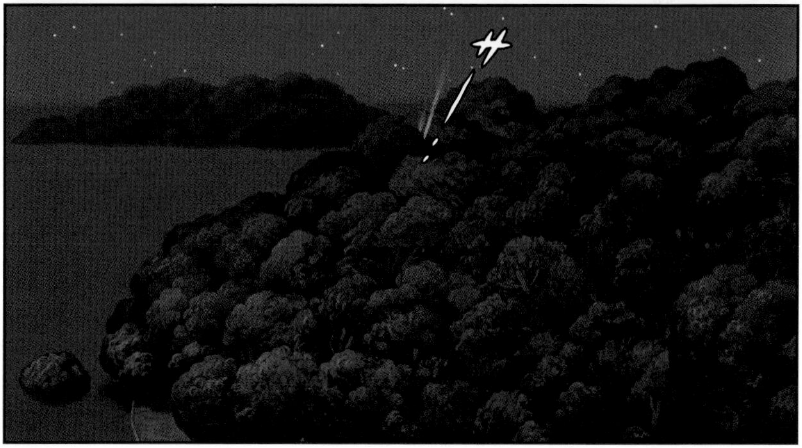
サー

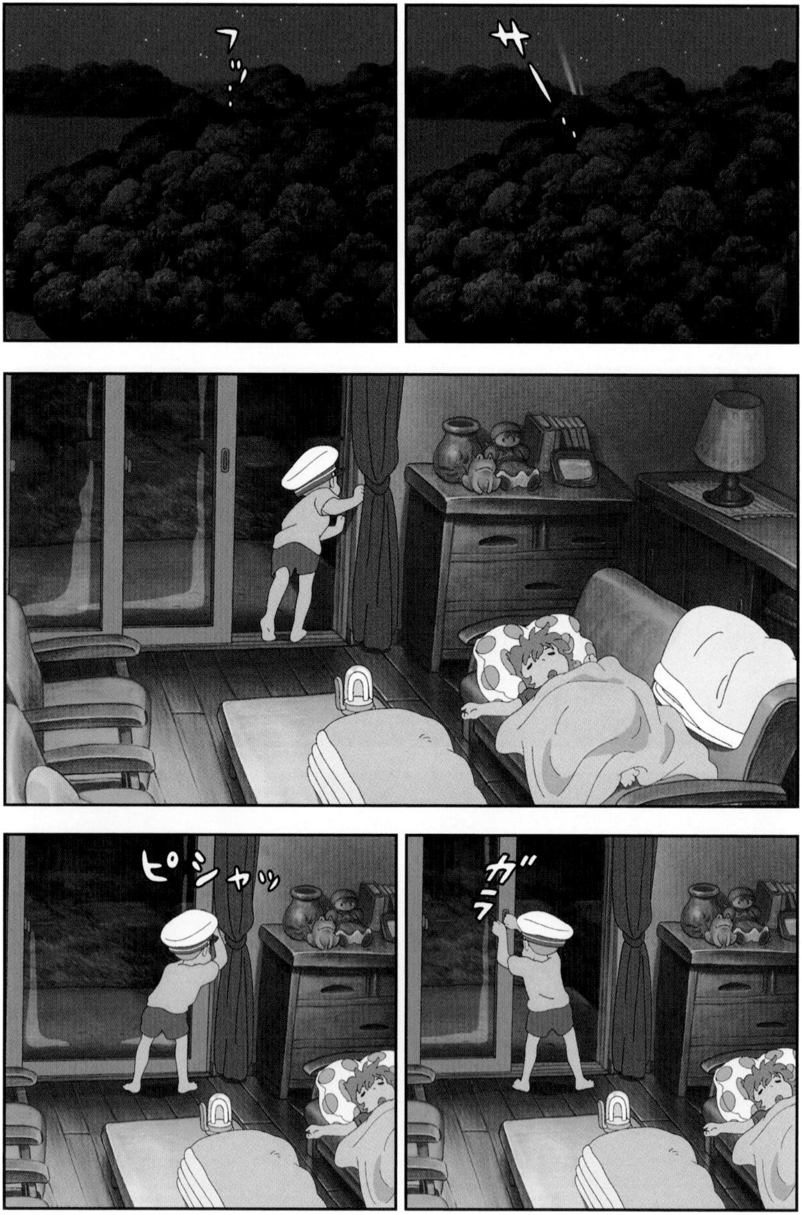
サー
フッ
ガラ
ピシャッ

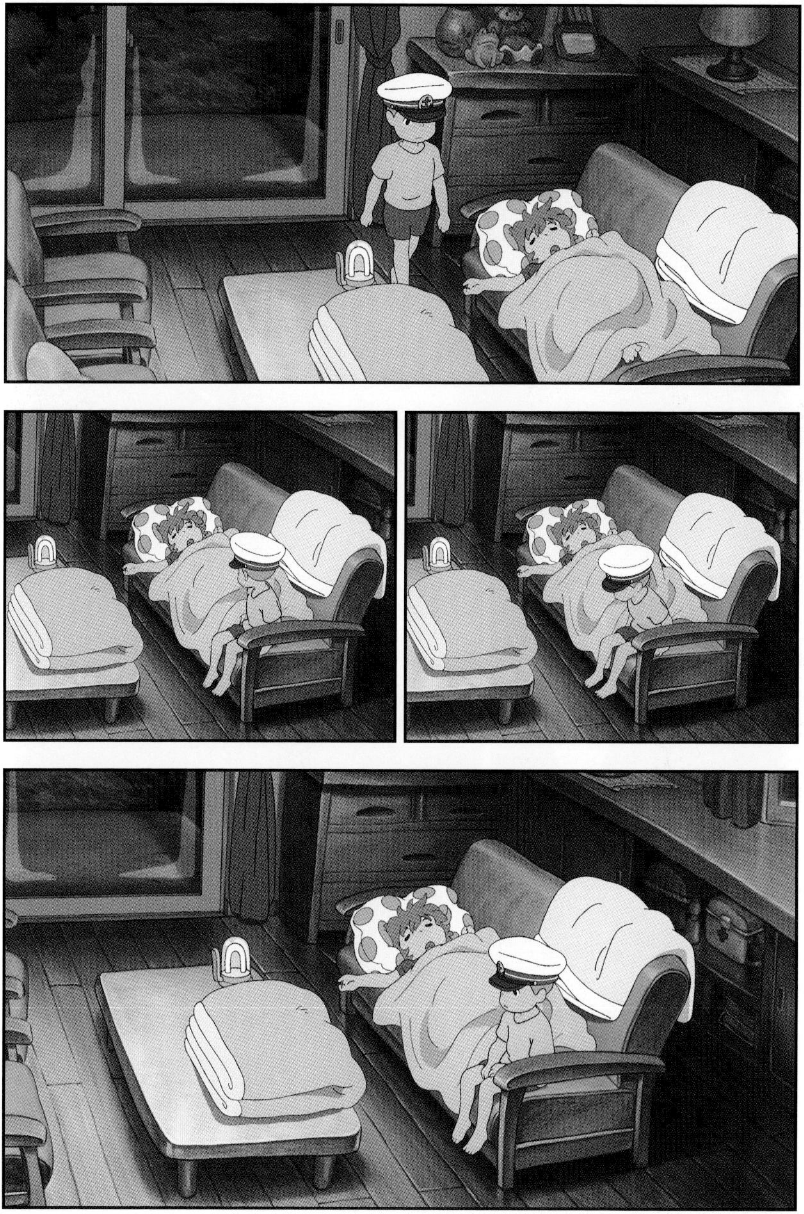

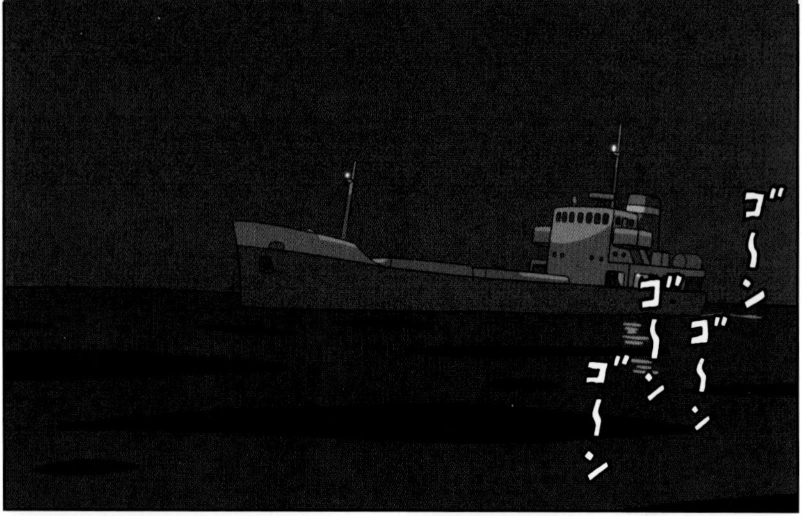
ゴ〜ン
ゴ〜ン
ゴ〜ン
ゴ〜ン
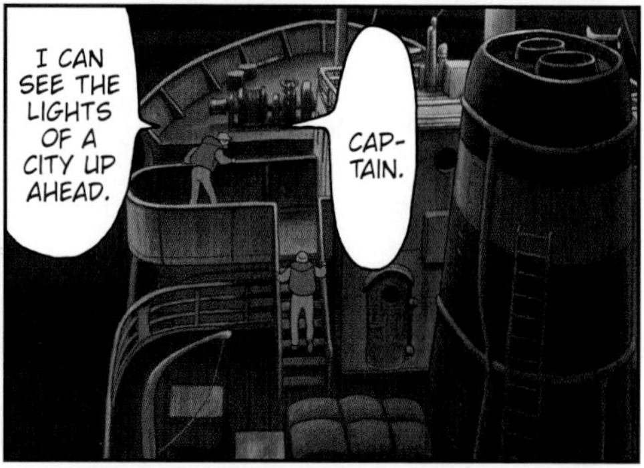
CAP-TAIN.
I CAN SEE THE LIGHTS OF A CITY UP AHEAD.
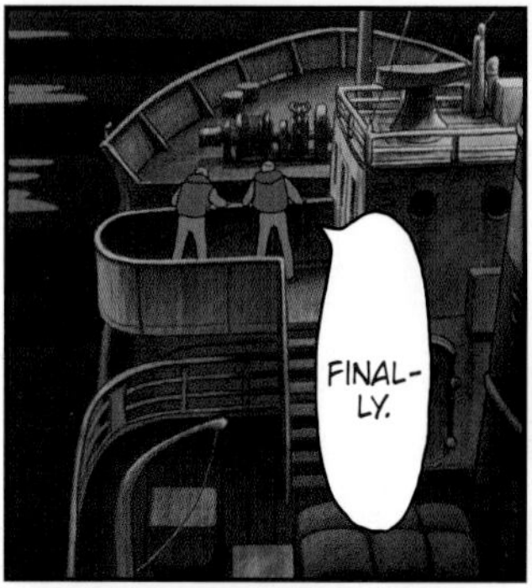
FINAL-LY.
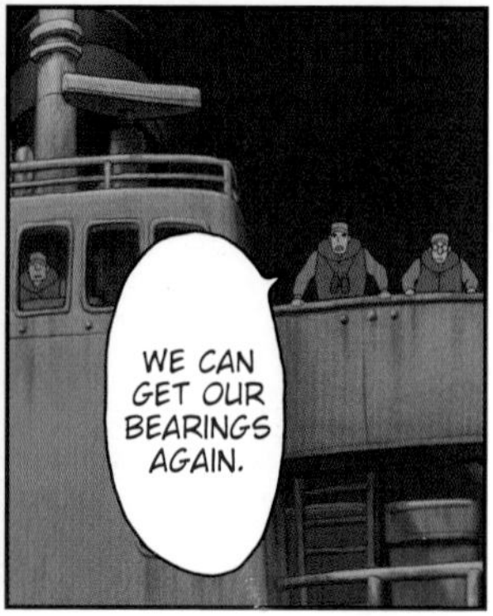
WE CAN GET OUR BEARINGS AGAIN.
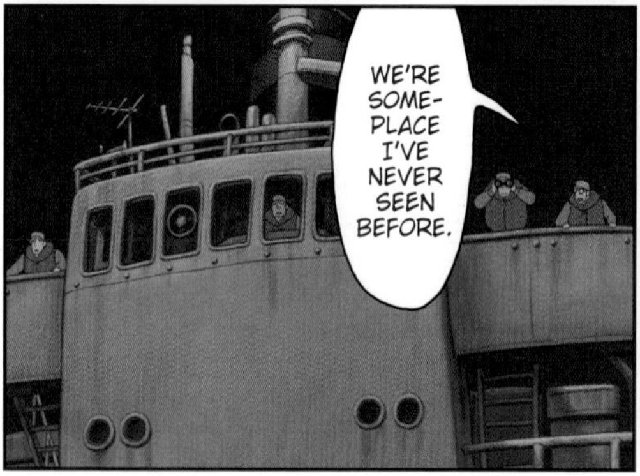
WE'RE SOME-PLACE I'VE NEVER SEEN BEFORE.

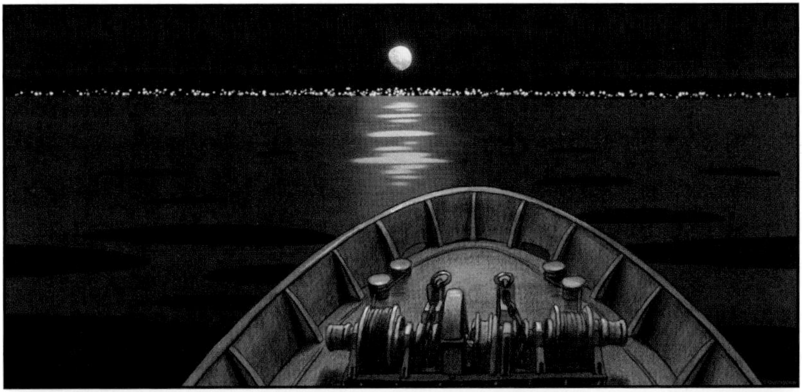

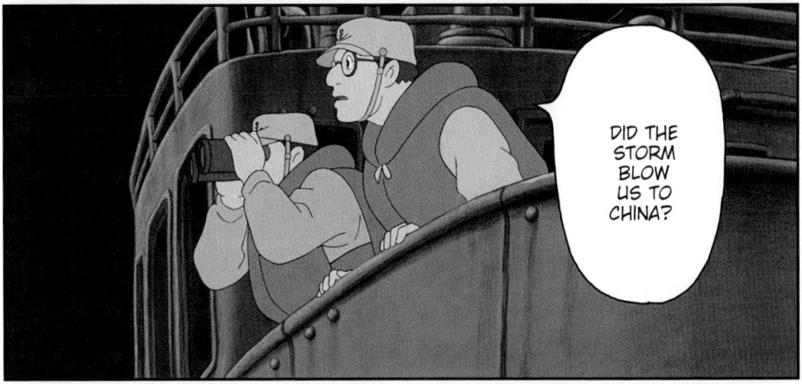
DID THE STORM BLOW US TO CHINA?

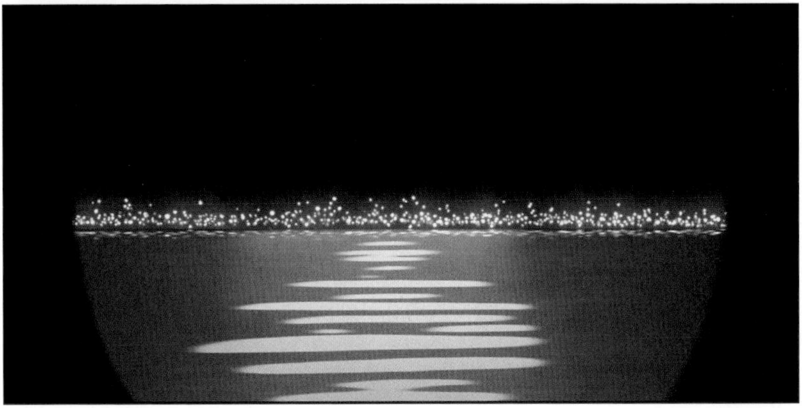

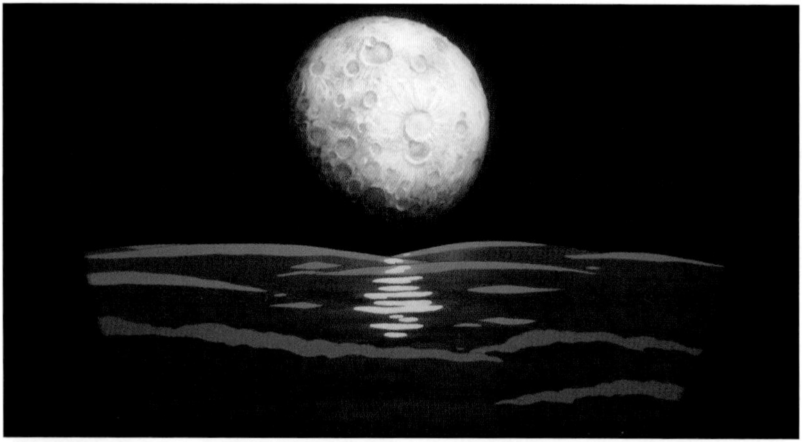

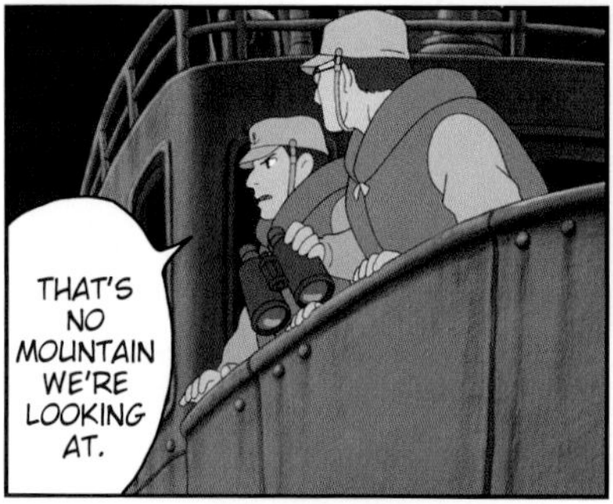
THAT'S NO MOUNTAIN WE'RE LOOKING AT.

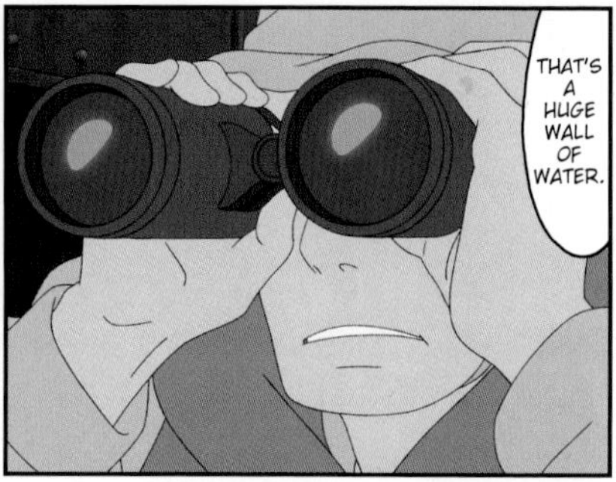
THAT'S A HUGE WALL OF WATER.

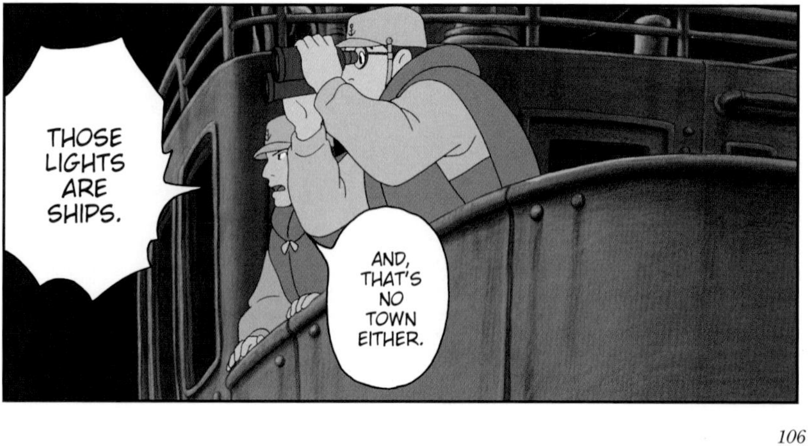
THOSE LIGHTS ARE SHIPS.
AND, THAT'S NO TOWN EITHER.

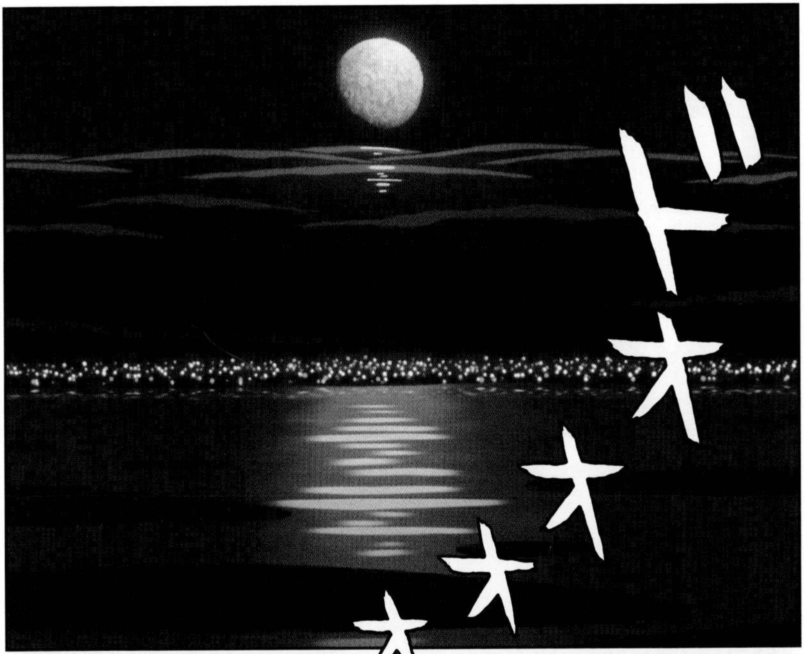
ドォォォォ
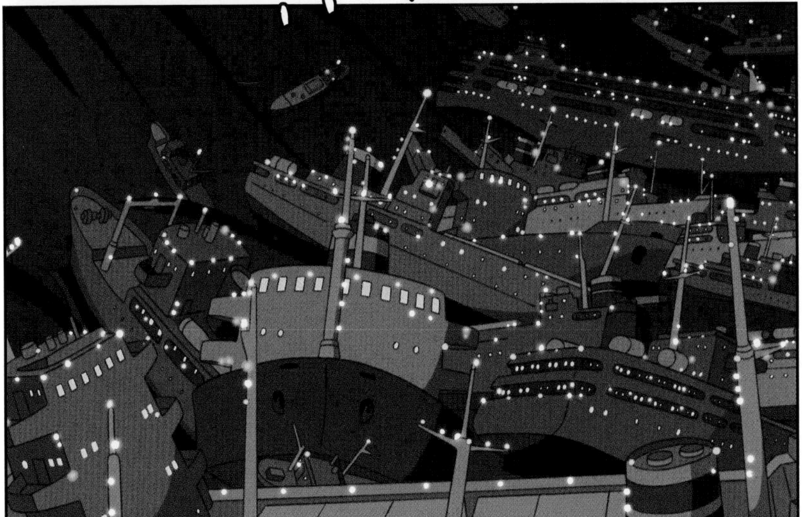

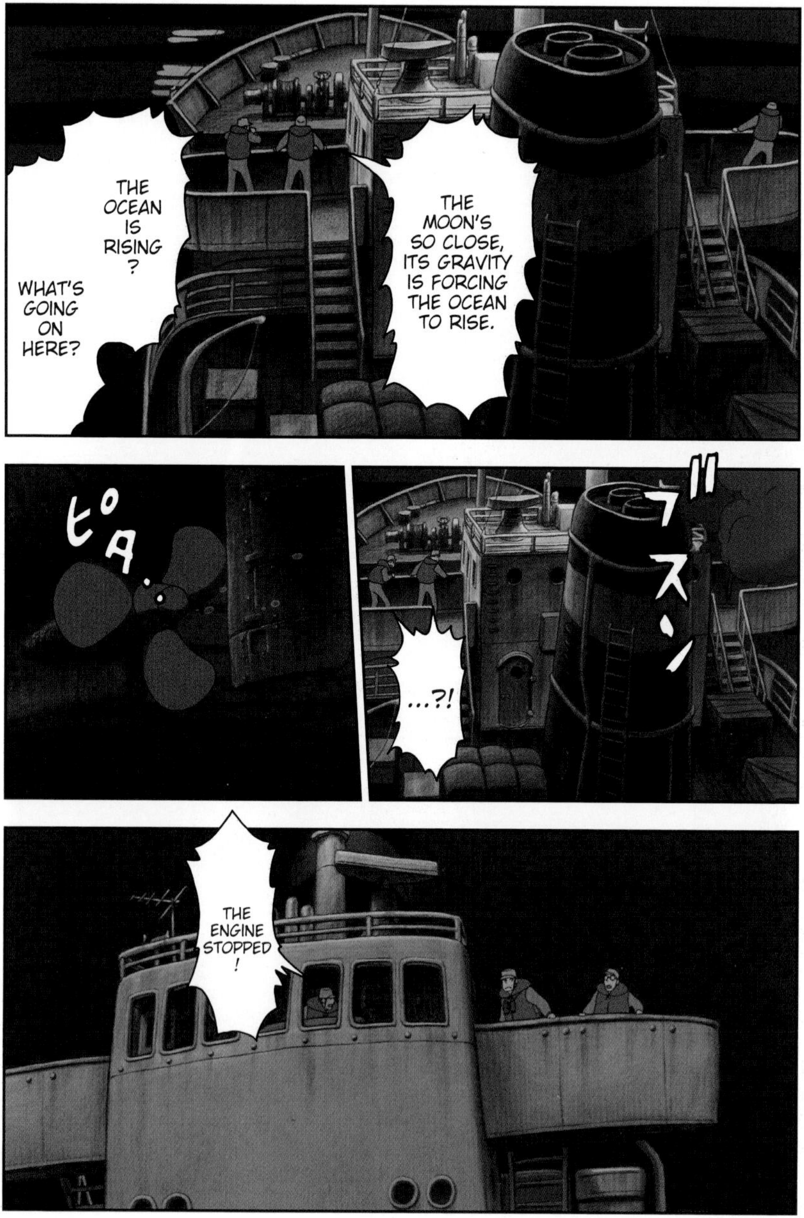
THE OCEAN IS RISING?
WHAT'S GOING ON HERE?
THE MOON'S SO CLOSE, ITS GRAVITY IS FORCING THE OCEAN TO RISE.
ピタ.
ブスン
...?!
THE ENGINE STOPPED!

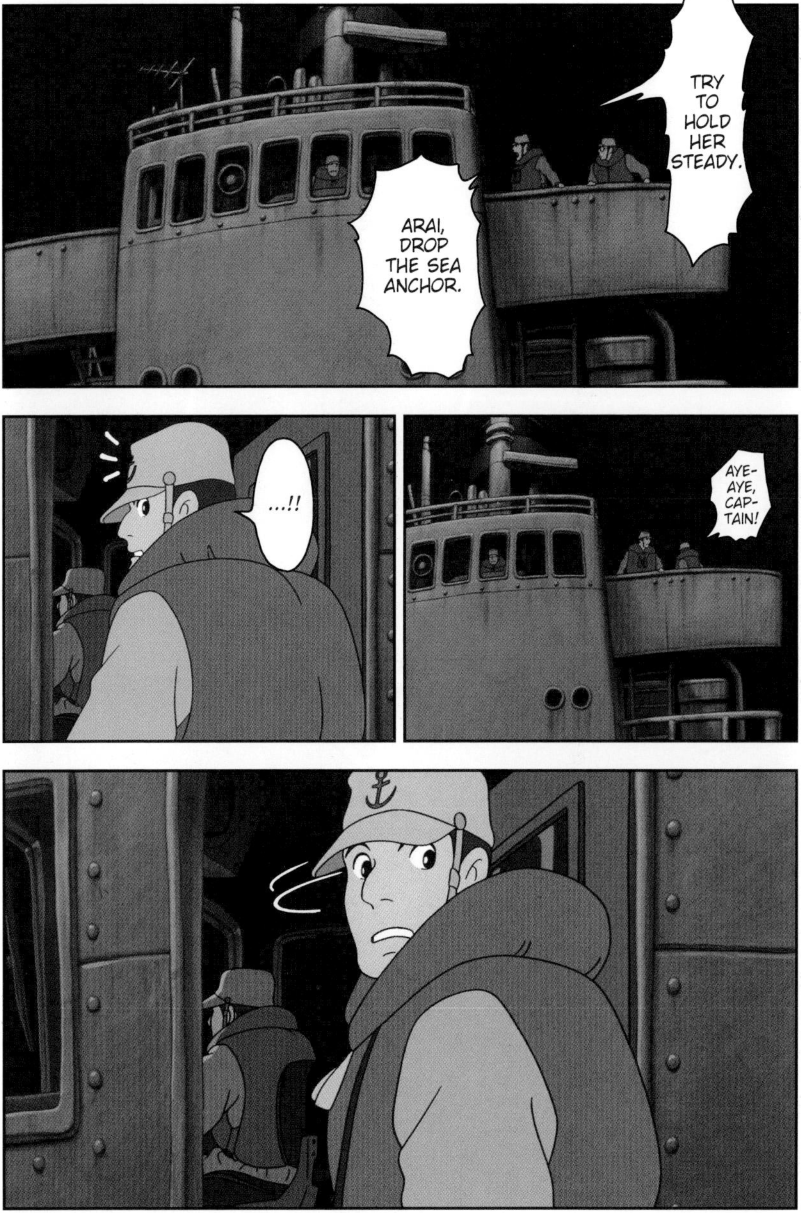
TRY TO HOLD HER STEADY.
ARAI, DROP THE SEA ANCHOR.
AYE-AYE, CAP-TAIN!
...!!

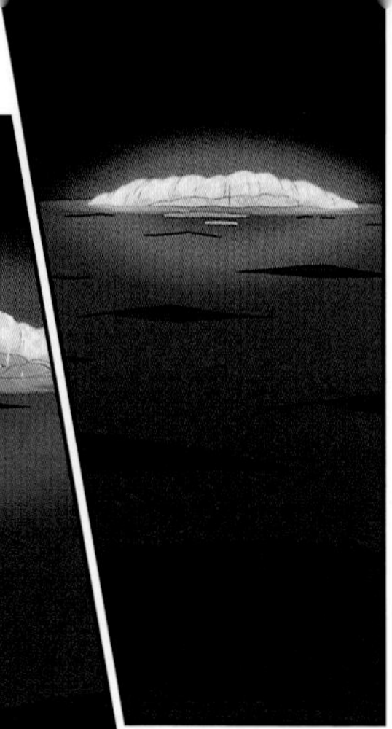
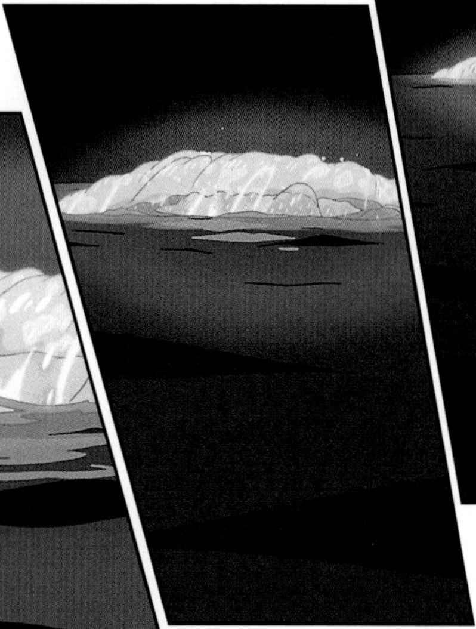
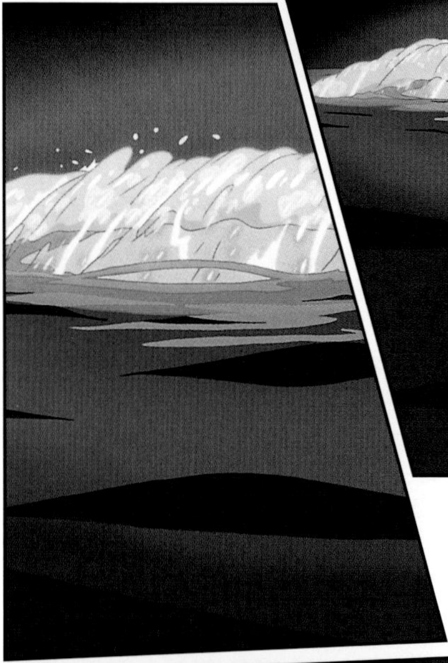
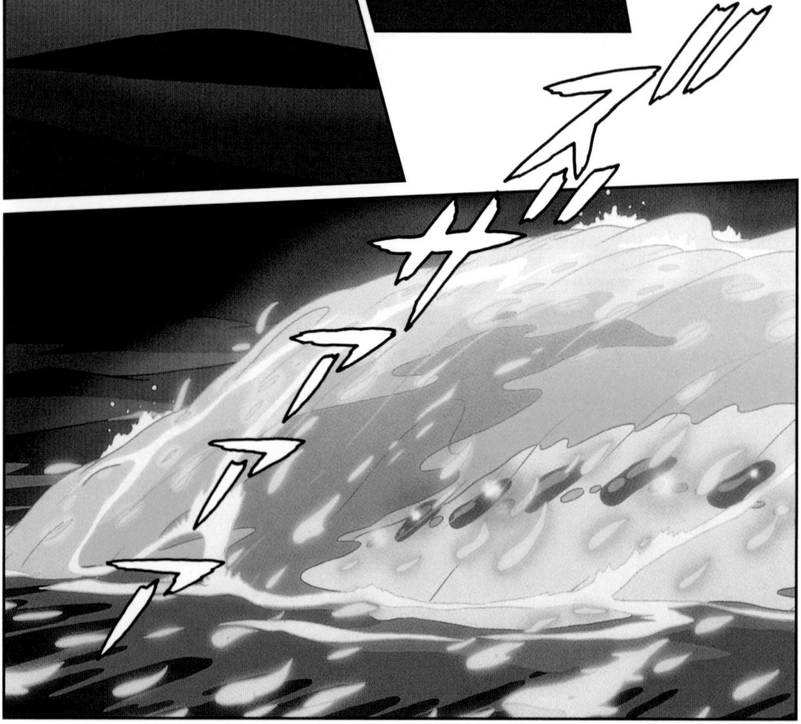
ズザァァァ

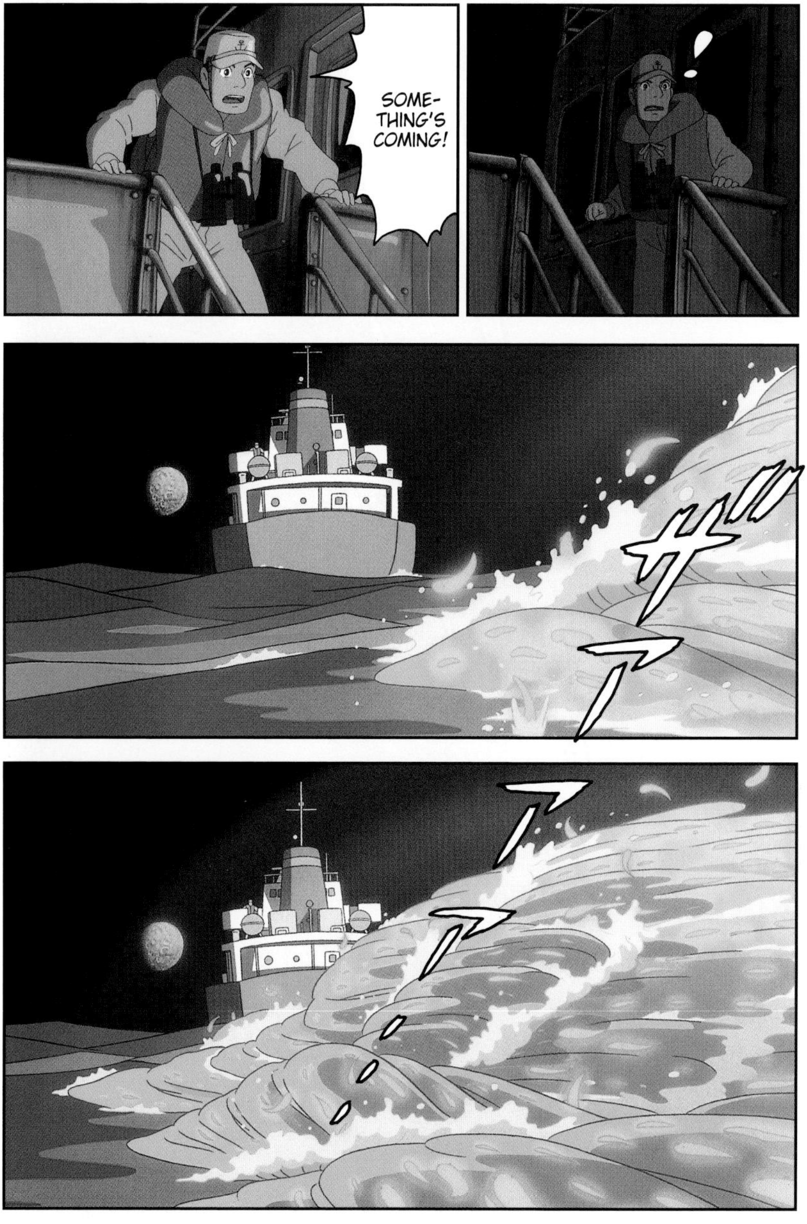
!
SOME-THING'S COMING!
ザァ
アア……

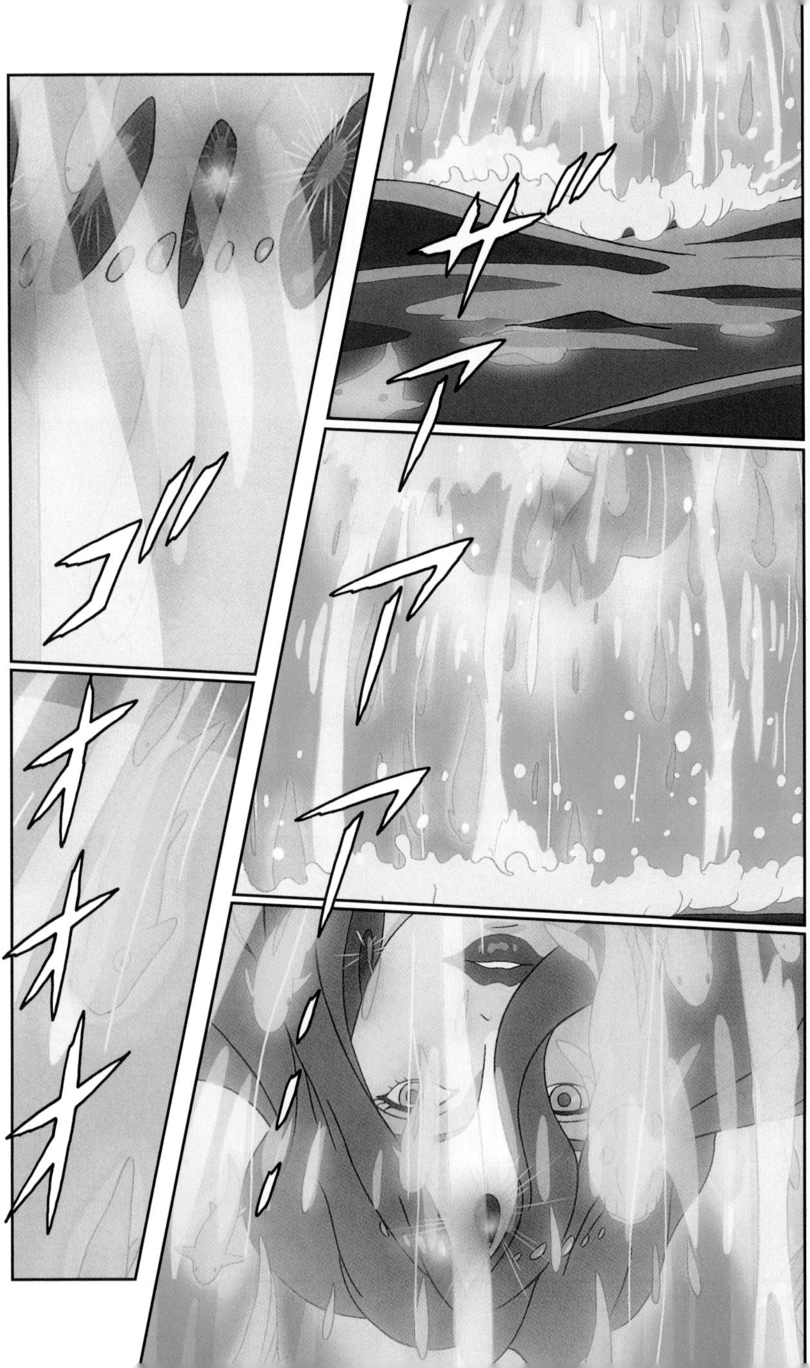
ザアアア…
ゴオオオオ

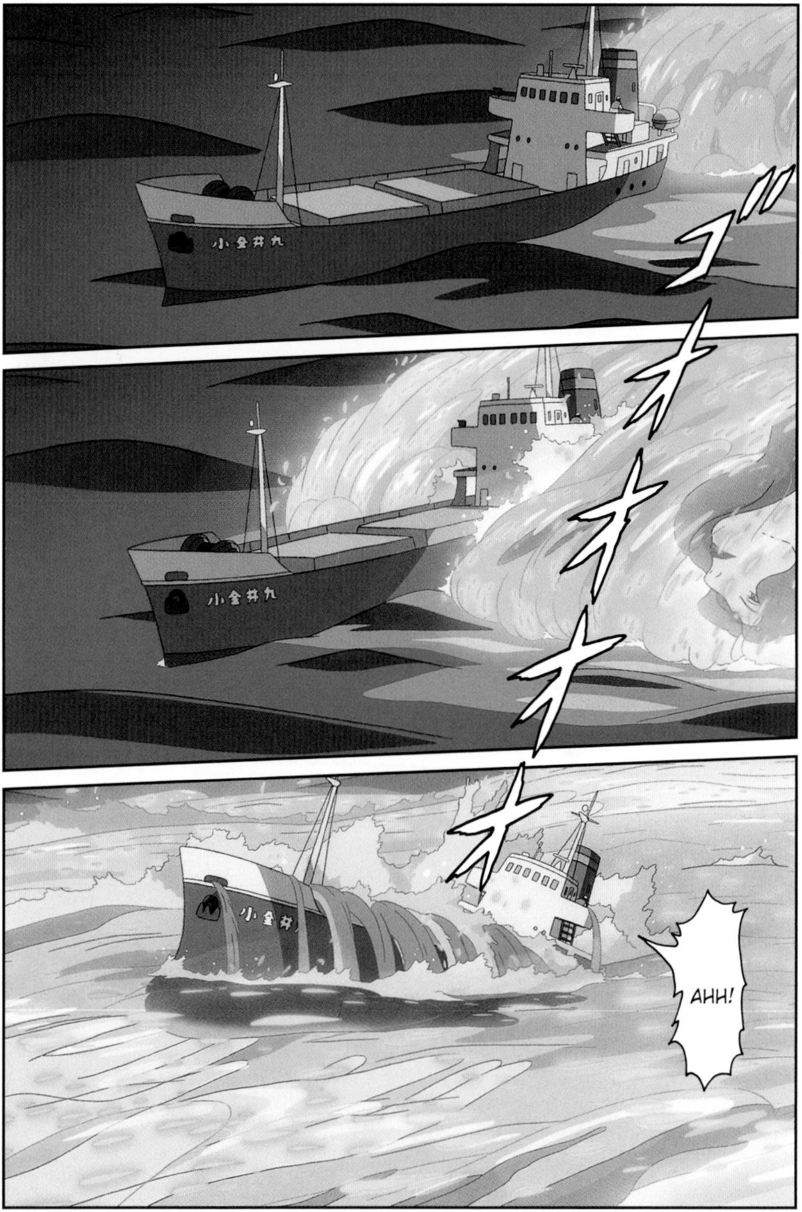
小金井丸
ゴオオオオオ
AHH!

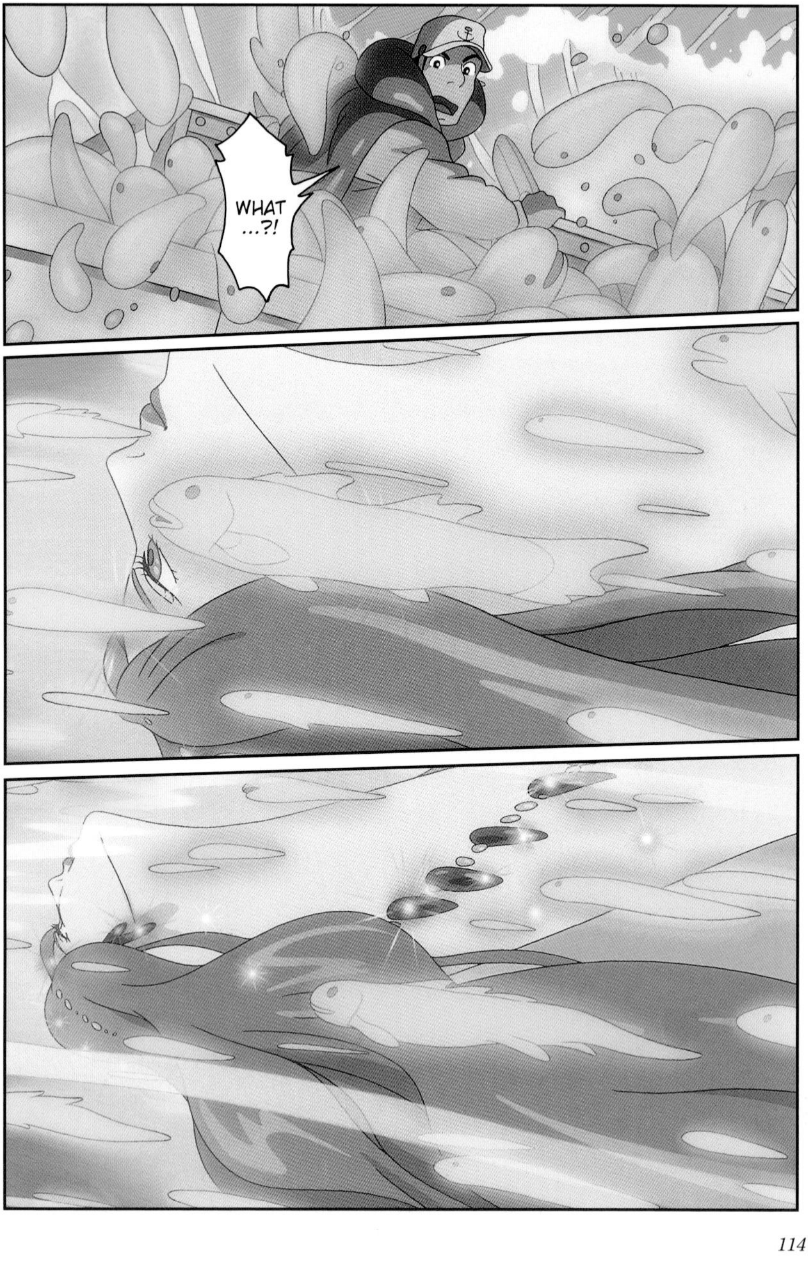
WHAT ...?!

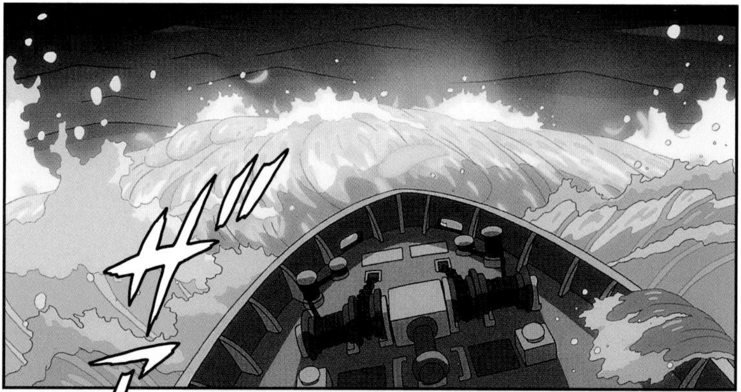
ザァァァ…
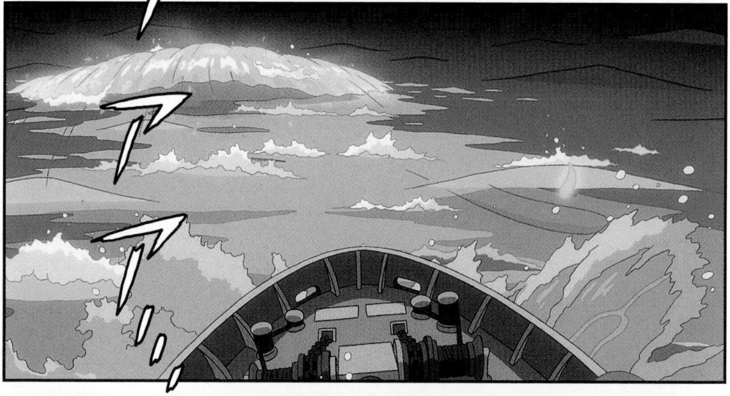
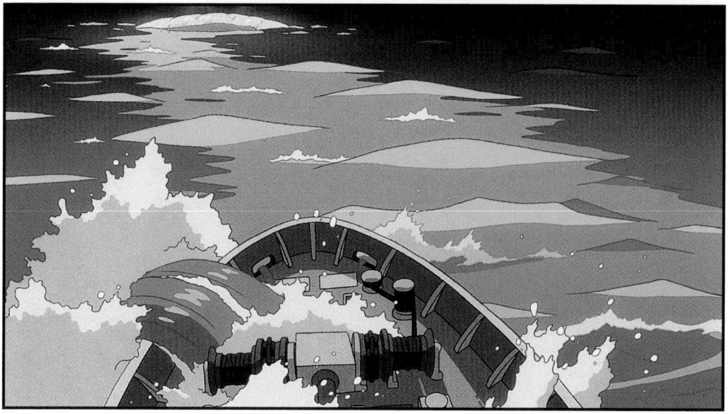

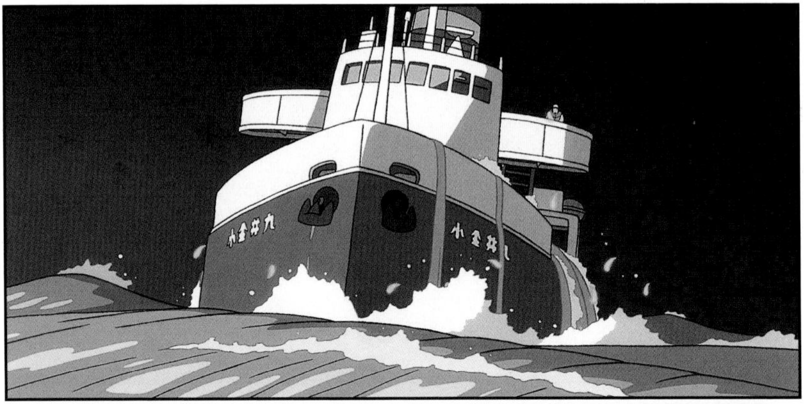

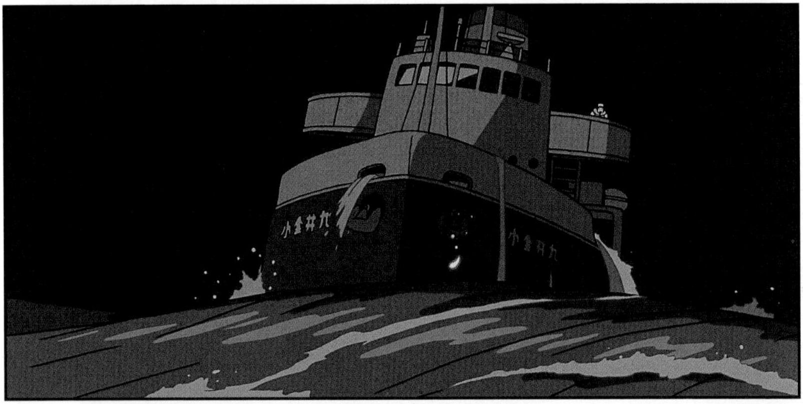

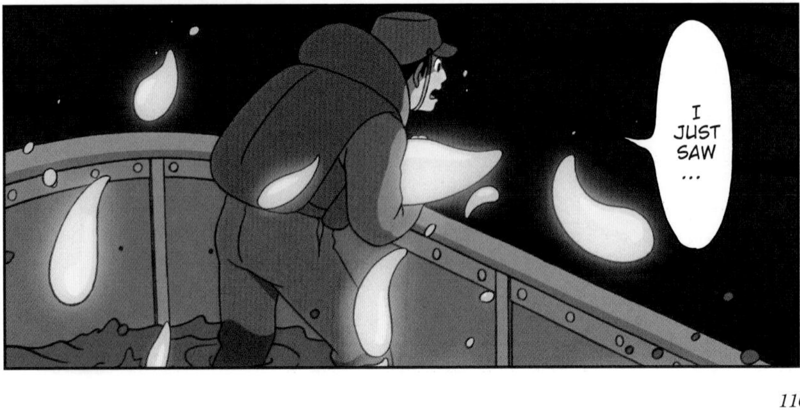
I JUST SAW ...

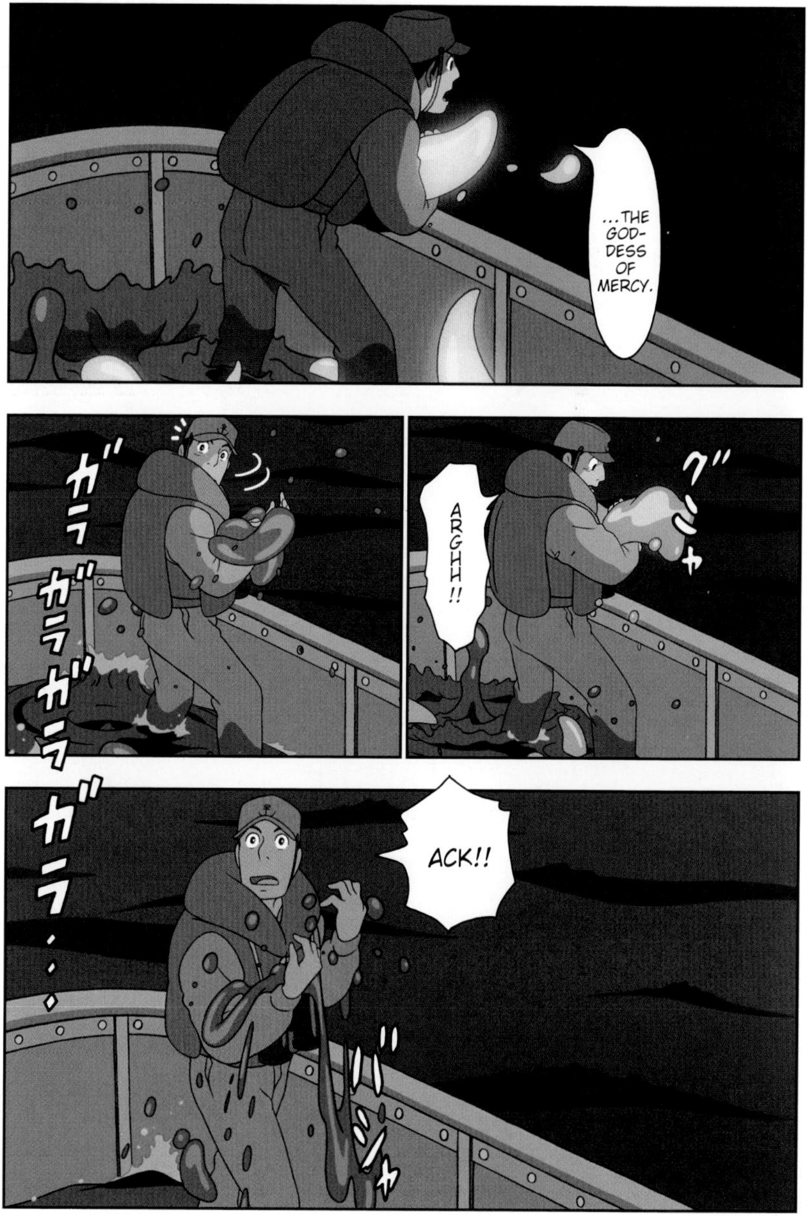
...THE GOD-DESS OF MERCY.
ARGHH!!
ガラガラガラガラガラ…
ACK!!

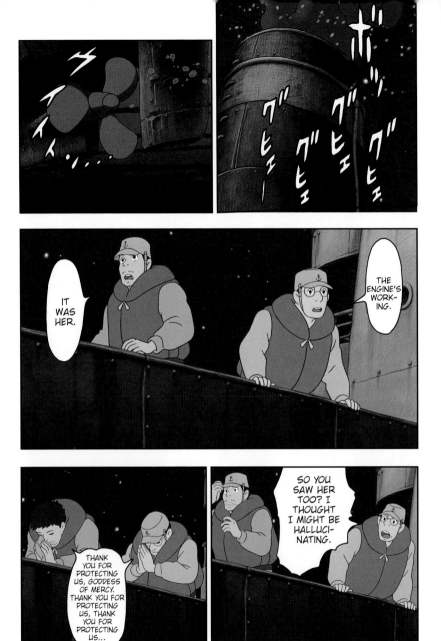

IT WAS HER.

THE ENGINE'S WORK-ING.

THANK YOU FOR PROTECTING US, GODDESS OF MERCY. THANK YOU FOR PROTECTING US, THANK YOU FOR PROTECTING US...

SO YOU SAW HER TOO? I THOUGHT I MIGHT BE HALLUCI-NATING.

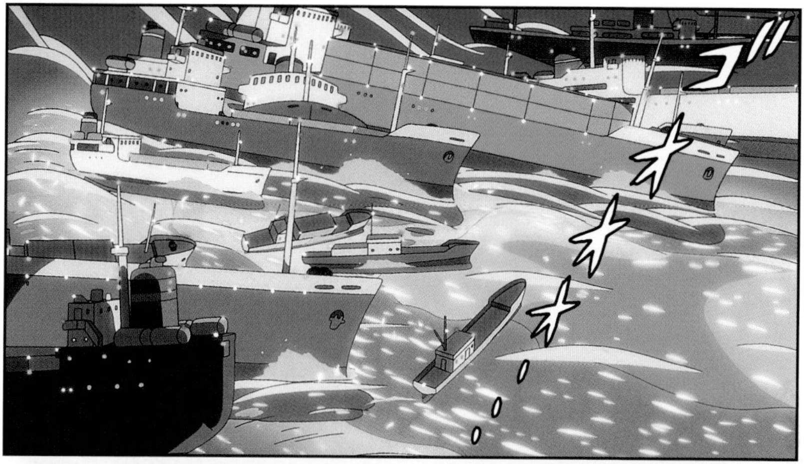
ゴオオオ
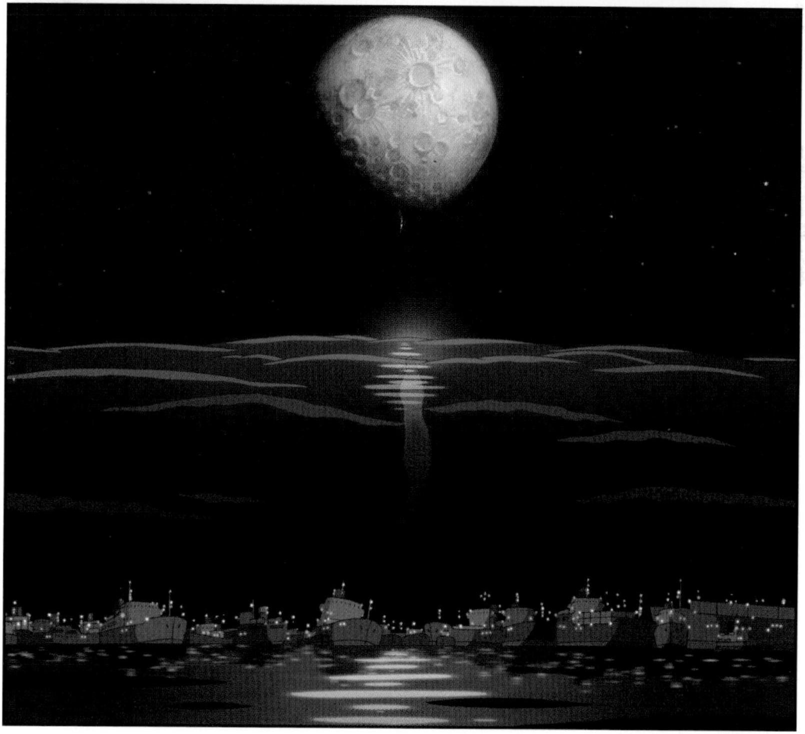

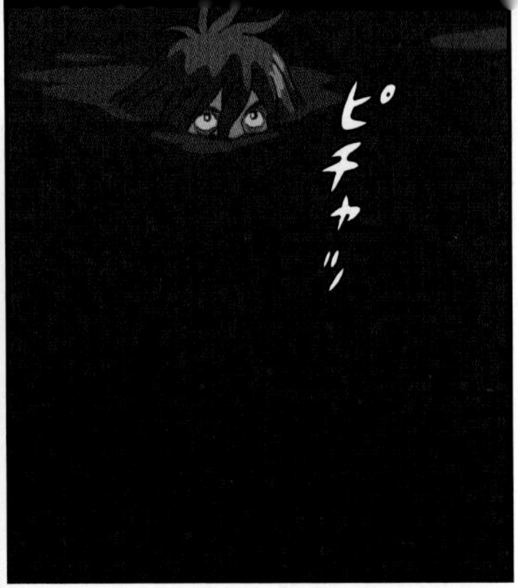
ピチャッ
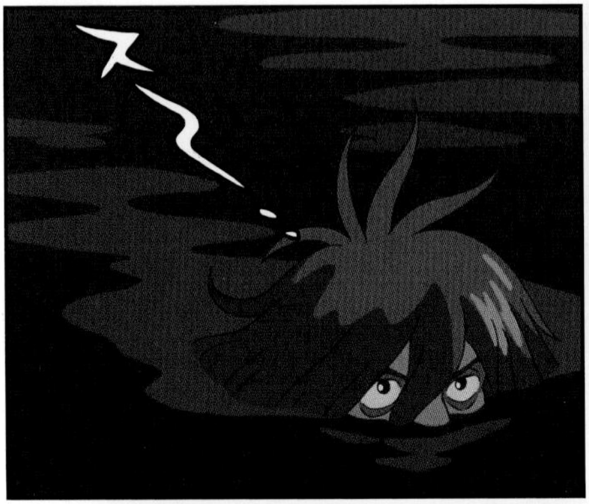
ス〜
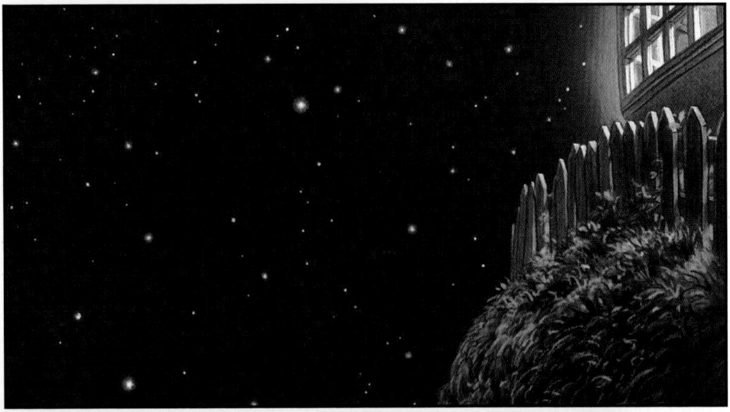
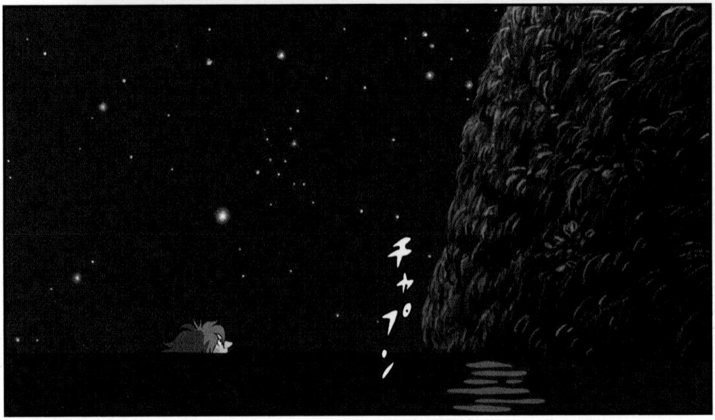
チャプン

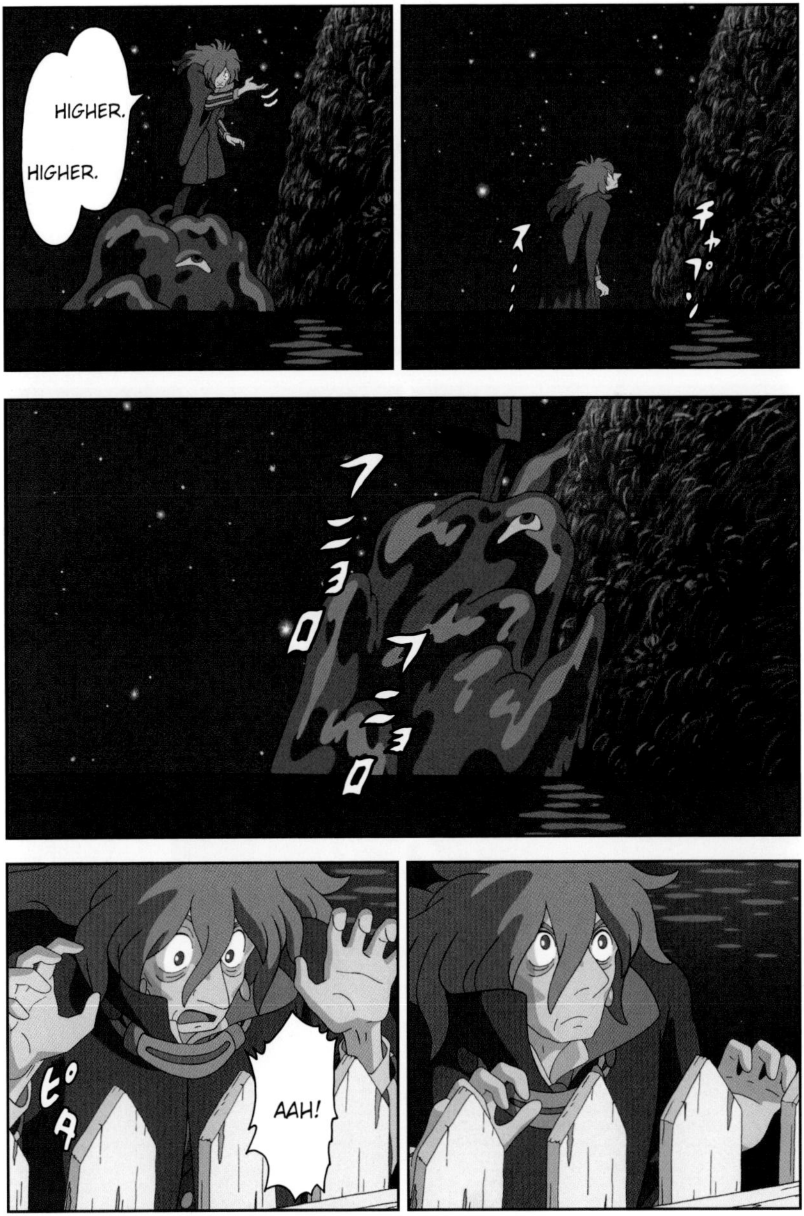
チャプン
ス…
HIGHER.
HIGHER.
フニョロ
フニョロ
ピタ
AAH!

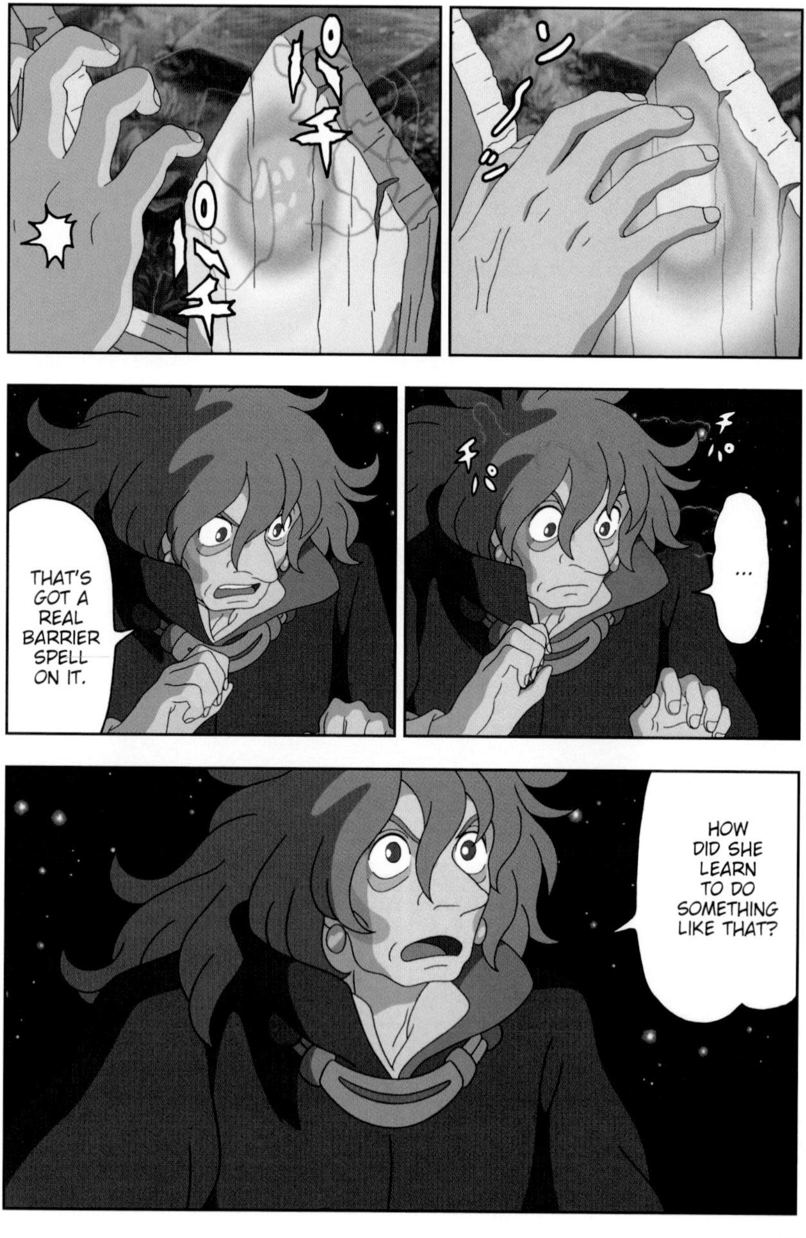
...
THAT'S GOT A REAL BARRIER SPELL ON IT.
HOW DID SHE LEARN TO DO SOMETHING LIKE THAT?

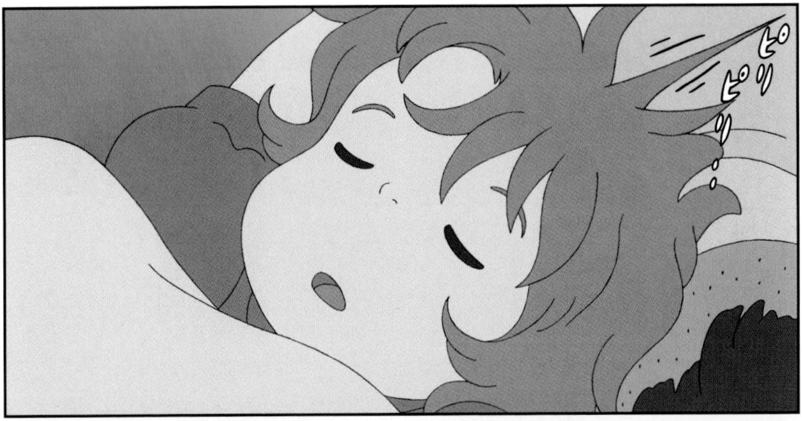
ピリピリ…

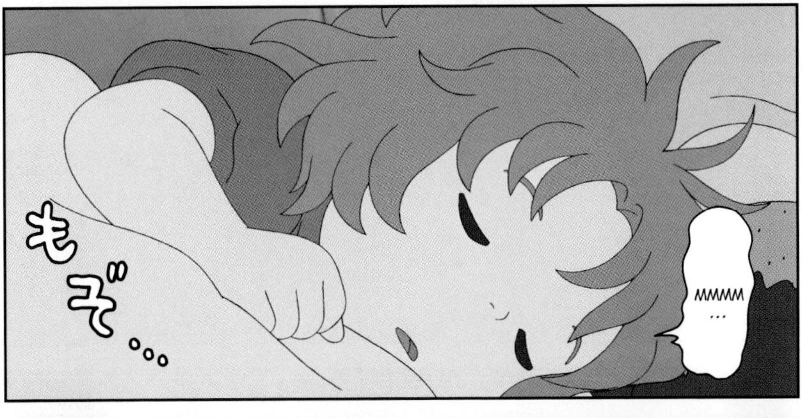
MMMM
...
もぞ…

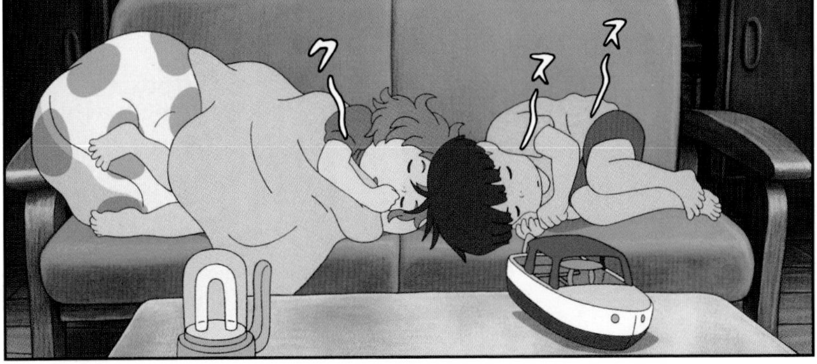
スー
スー
クー

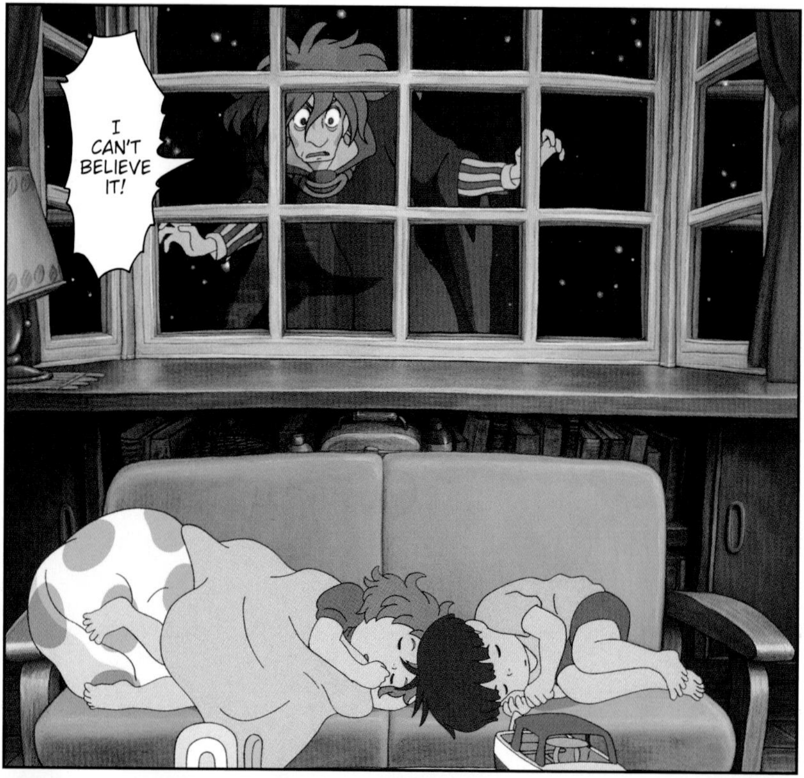
I CAN'T BELIEVE IT!

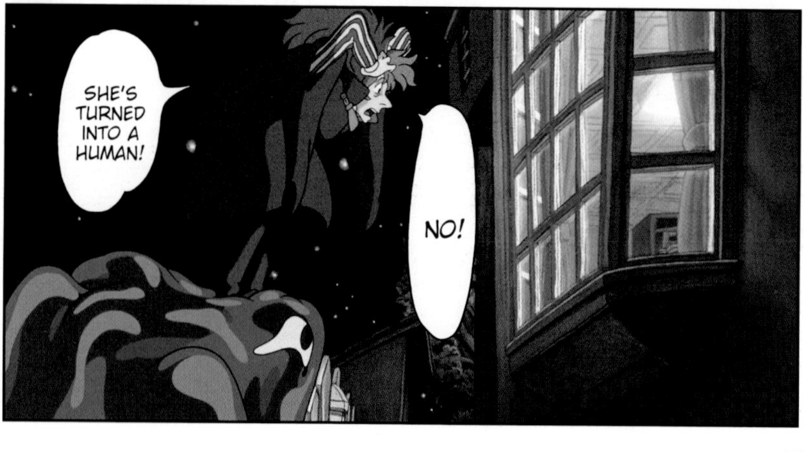
SHE'S TURNED INTO A HUMAN!
NO!

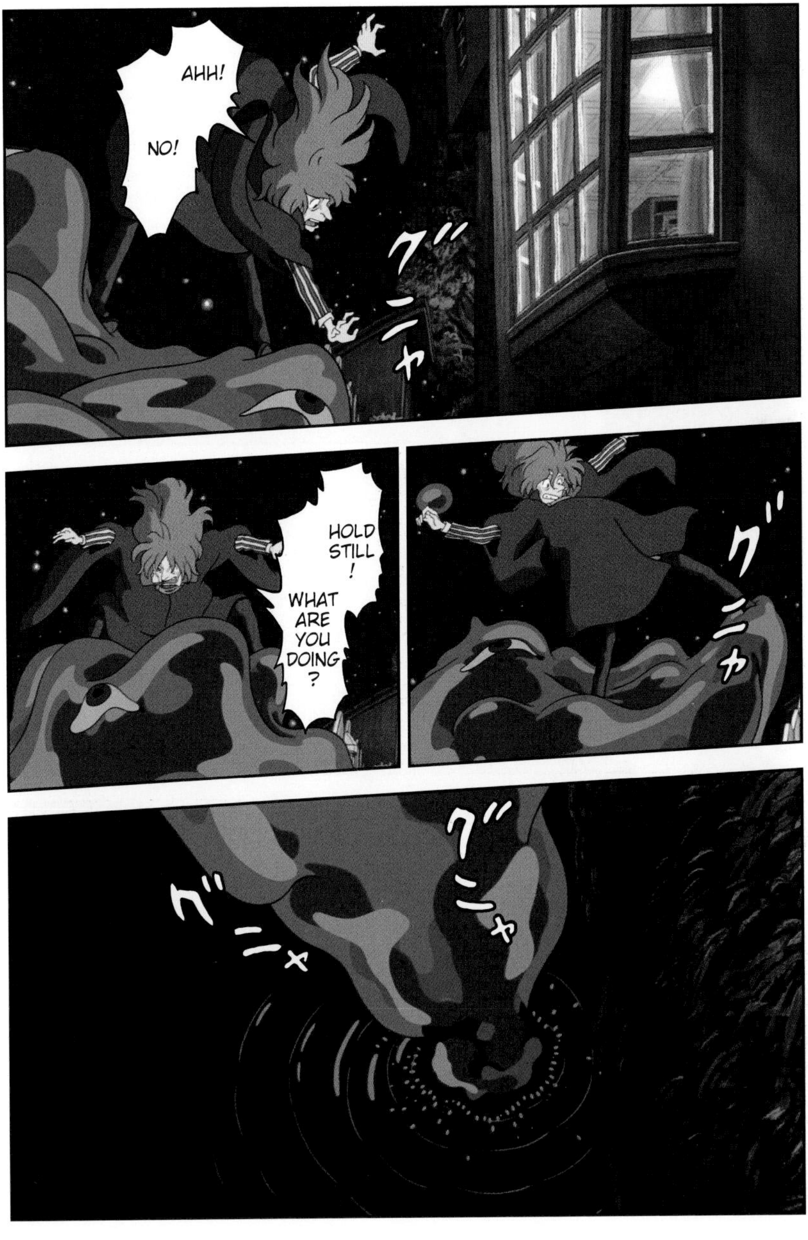
AHH!
NO!
グニャ
グニャ
HOLD STILL!
WHAT ARE YOU DOING?
グニャ
グニャ

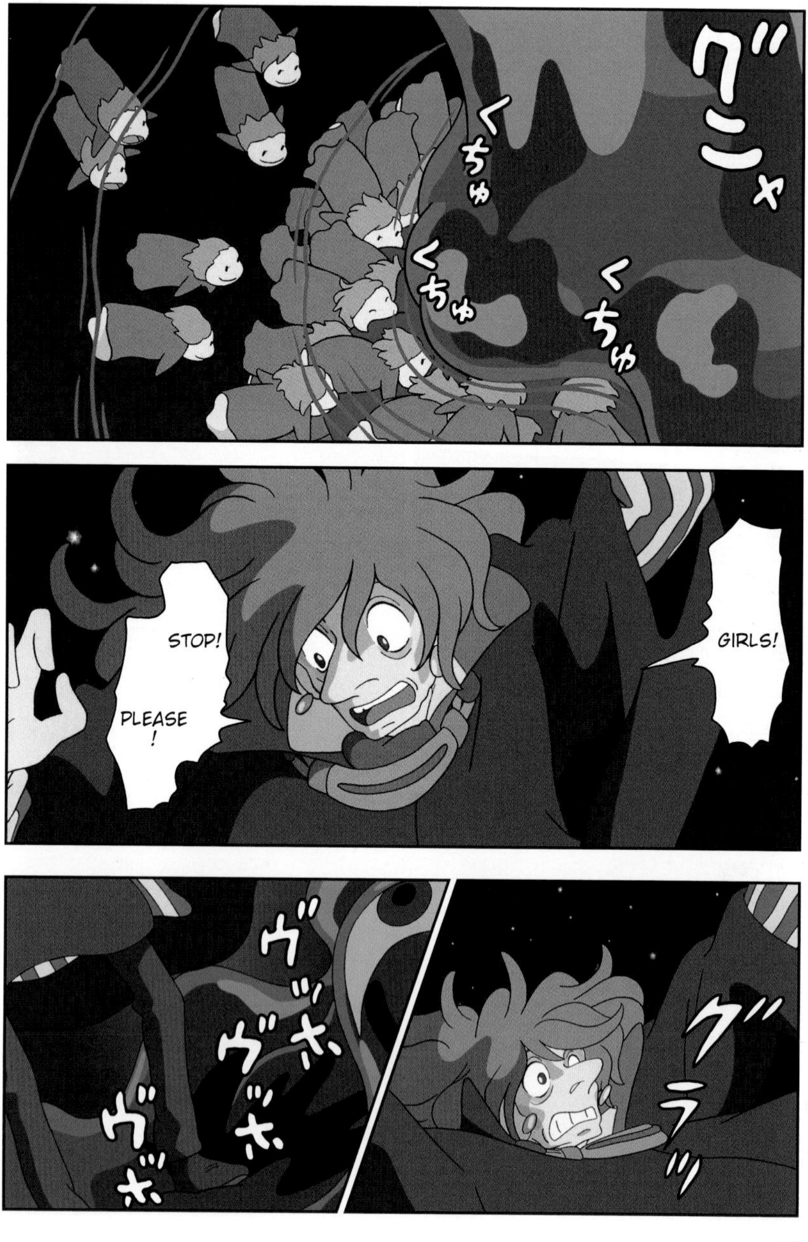
グニャ
くちゅ
くちゅ
くちゅ
GIRLS!
STOP!
PLEASE
!
グラッ
ヴッホ
ヴッホ
ヴッホ

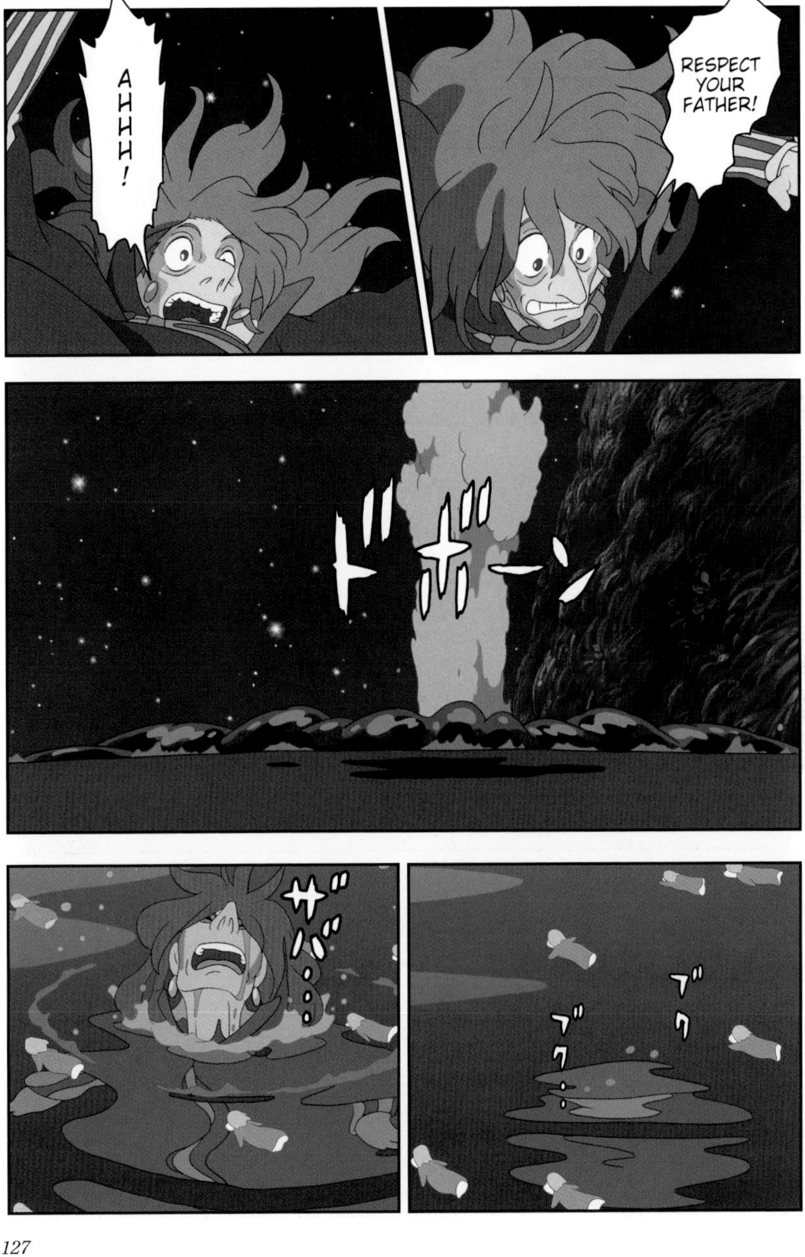

RESPECT YOUR FATHER!
AHHH!
ドボーン
ブクブク…
ザバ…

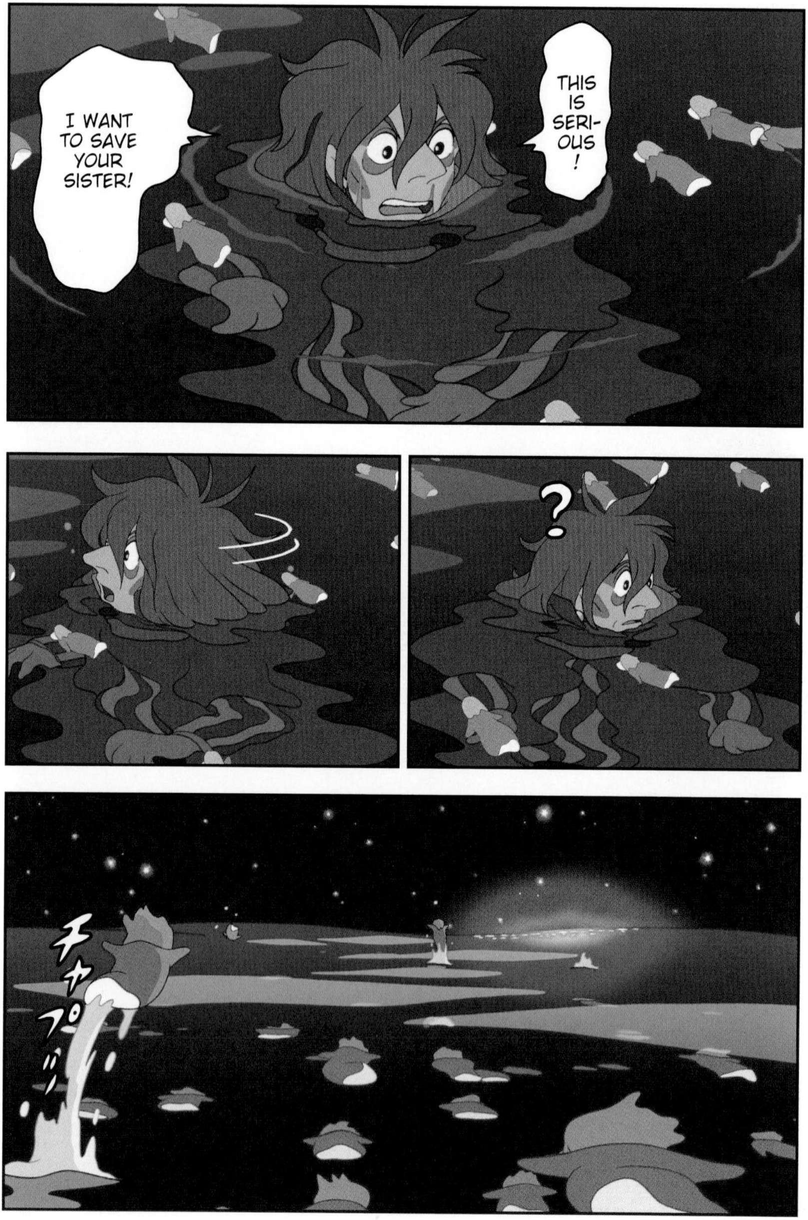
THIS IS SERI-OUS!
I WANT TO SAVE YOUR SISTER!
?
チャプッ

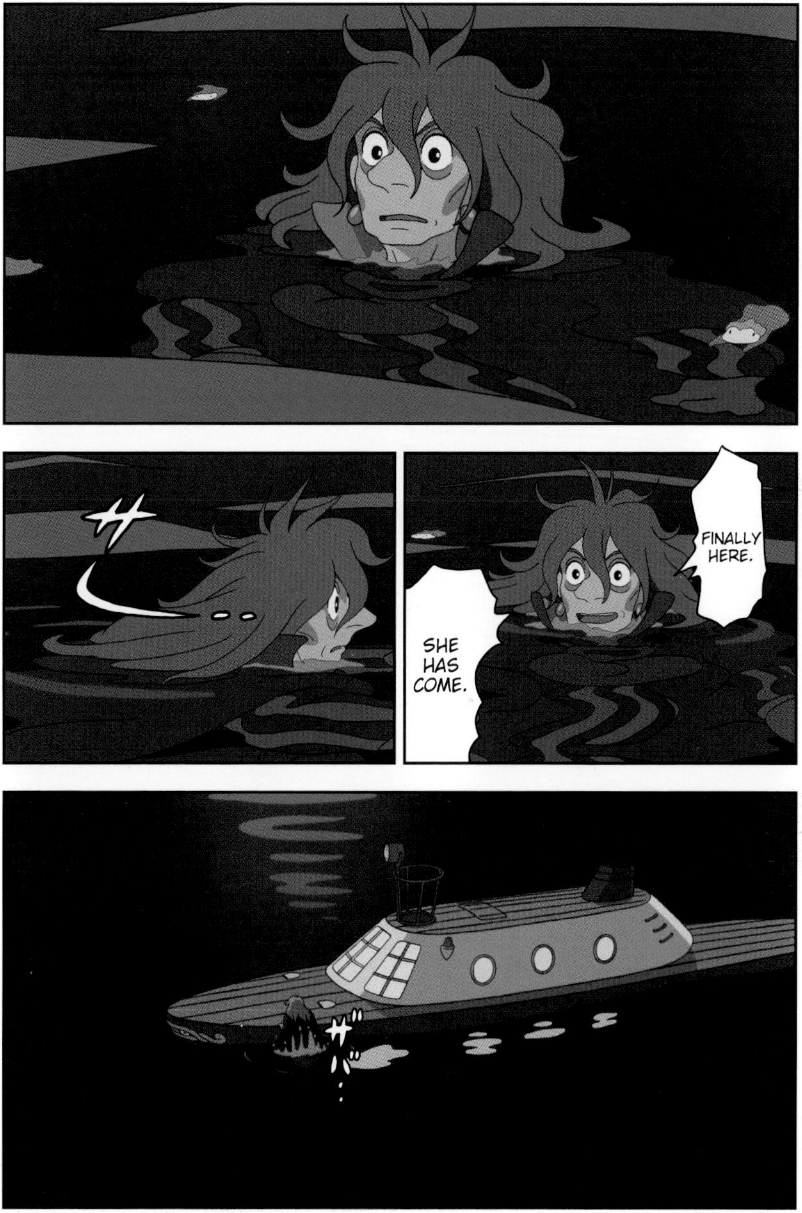
FINALLY HERE.
SHE HAS COME.

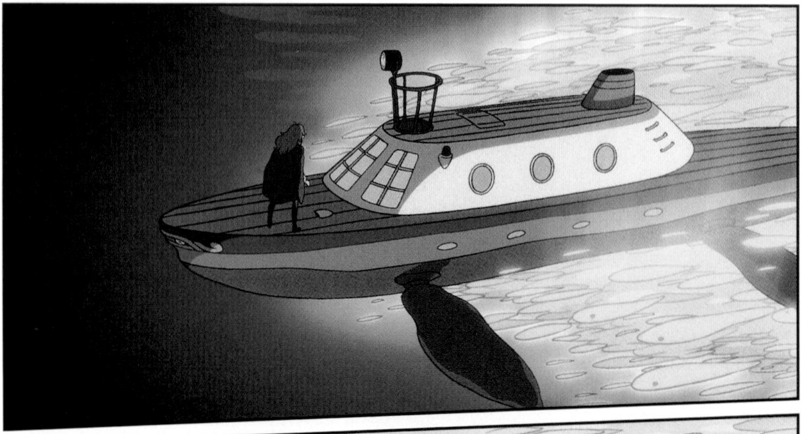

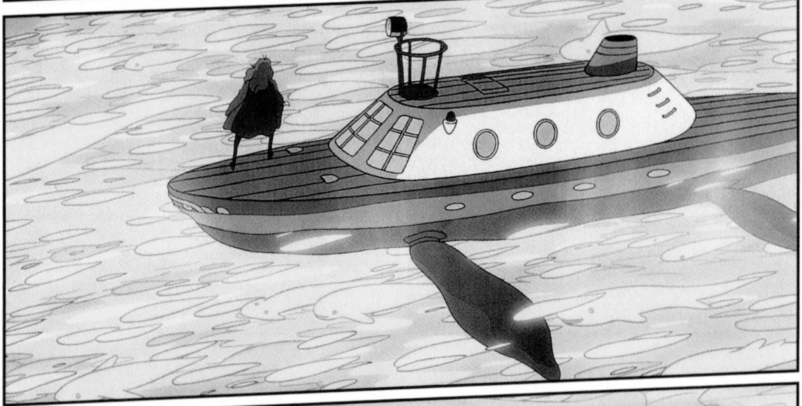

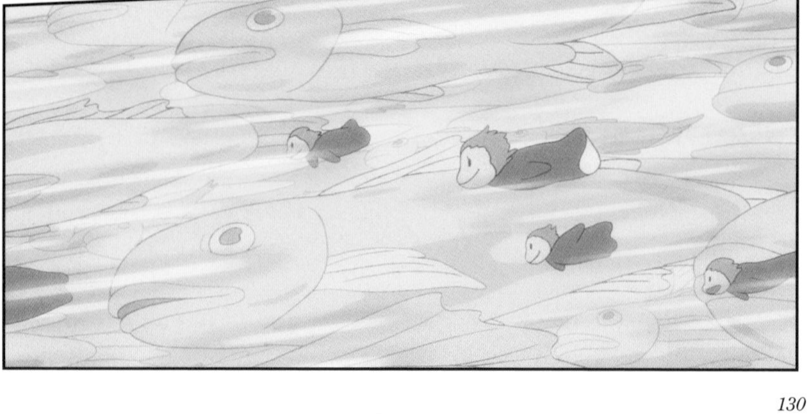

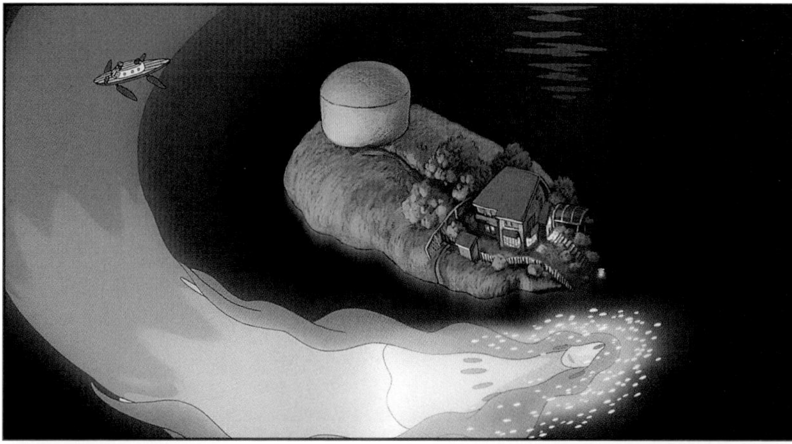
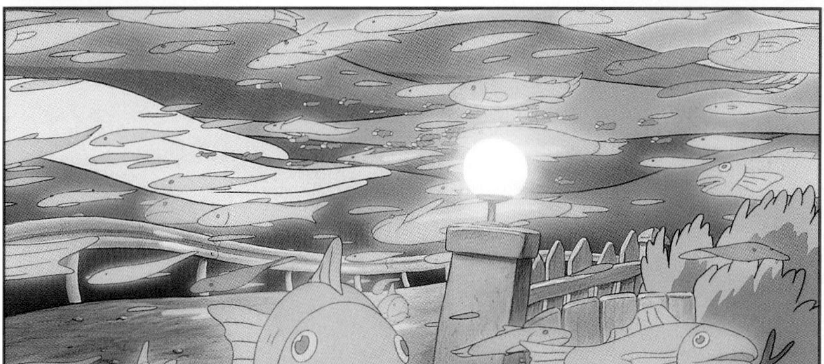
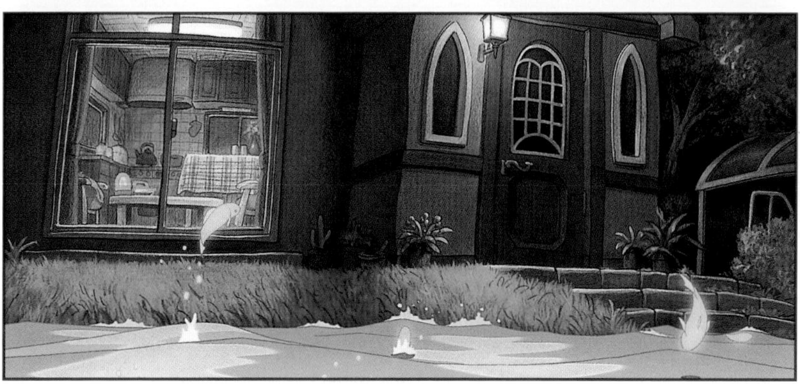

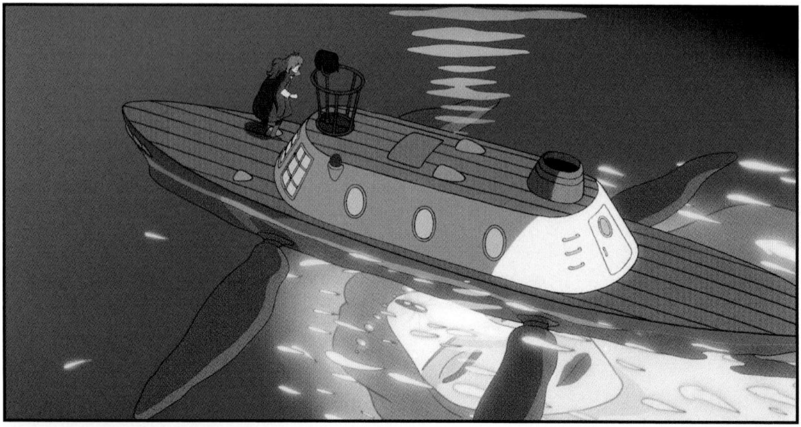

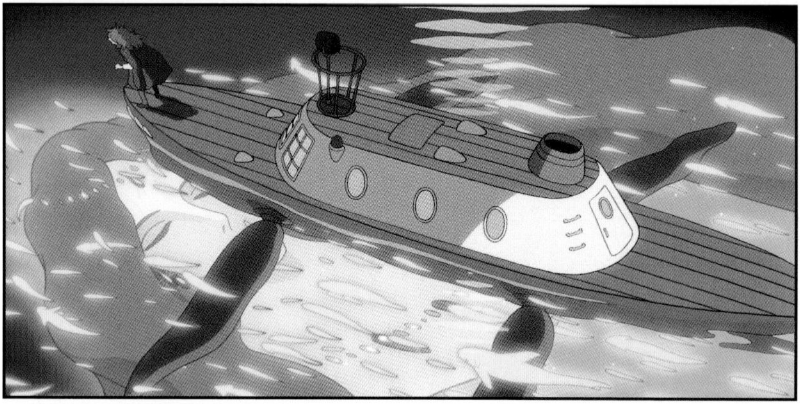

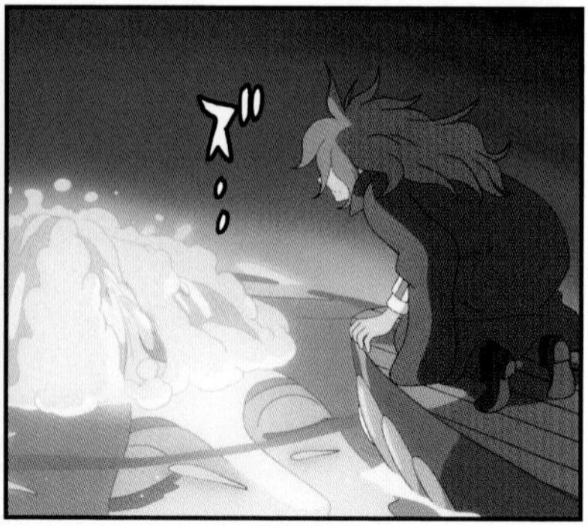
ズ…

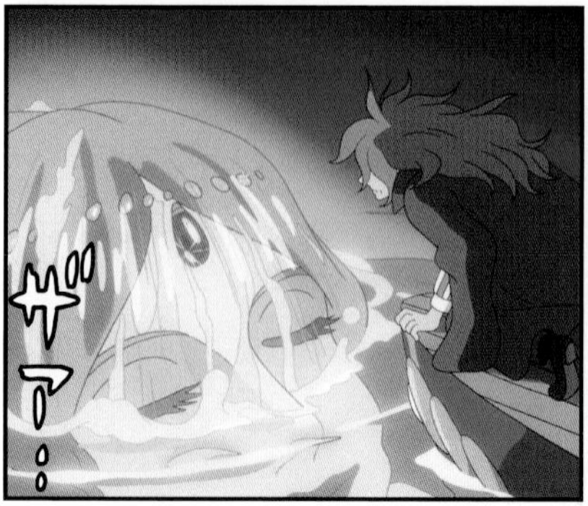
ザア…

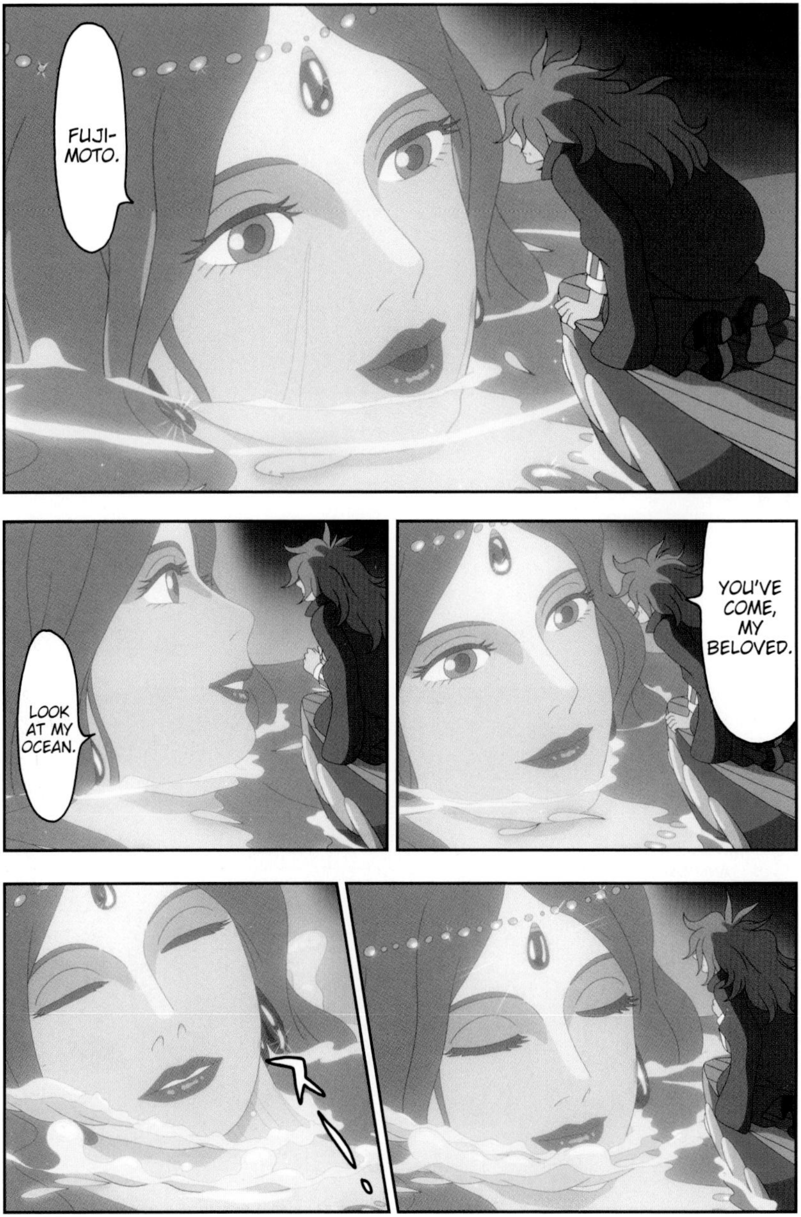
FUJI-MOTO.
YOU'VE COME, MY BELOVED.
LOOK AT MY OCEAN.

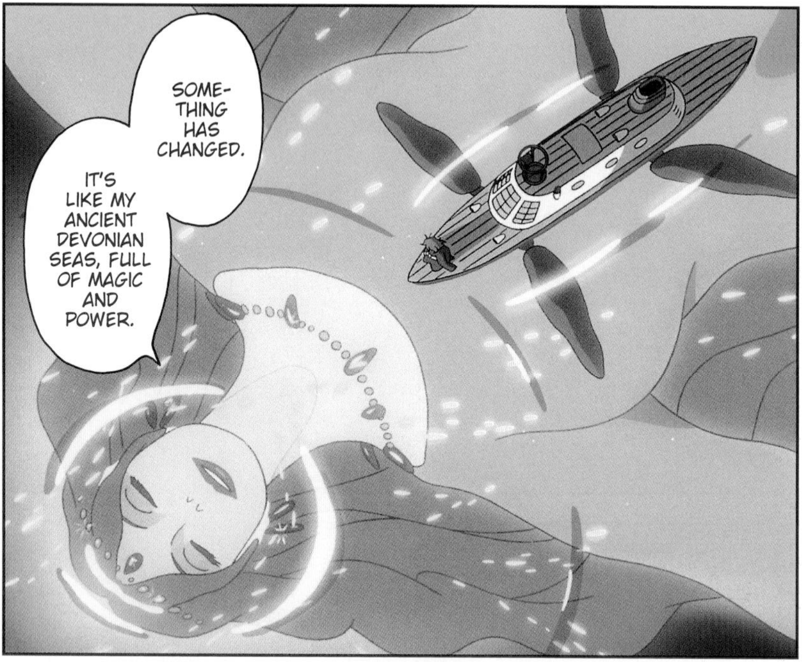
SOME-THING HAS CHANGED.
IT'S LIKE MY ANCIENT DEVONIAN SEAS, FULL OF MAGIC AND POWER.
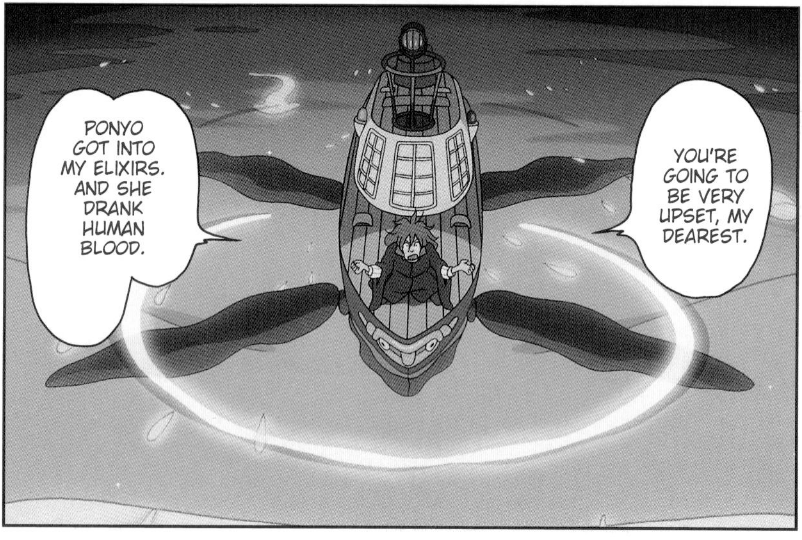
YOU'RE GOING TO BE VERY UPSET, MY DEAREST.
PONYO GOT INTO MY ELIXIRS. AND SHE DRANK HUMAN BLOOD.

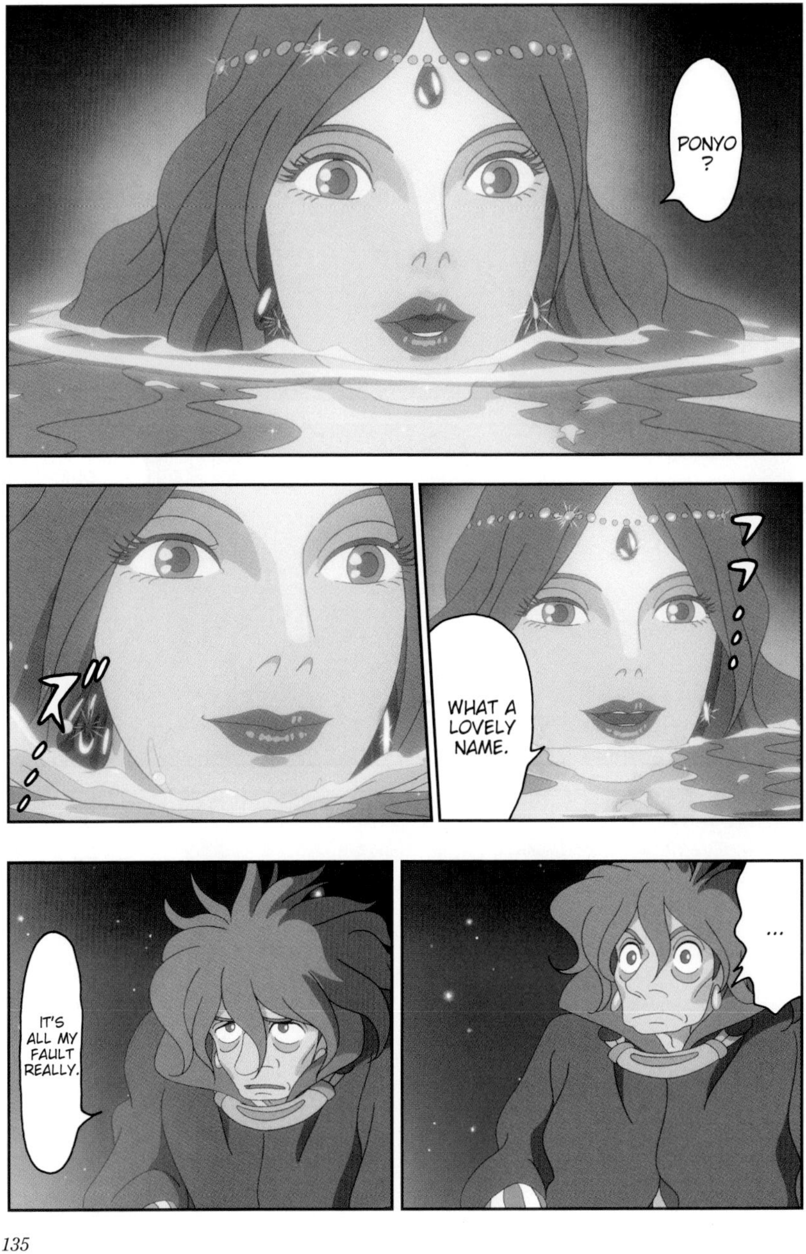
PONYO ?
WHAT A LOVELY NAME.
...
IT'S ALL MY FAULT REALLY.

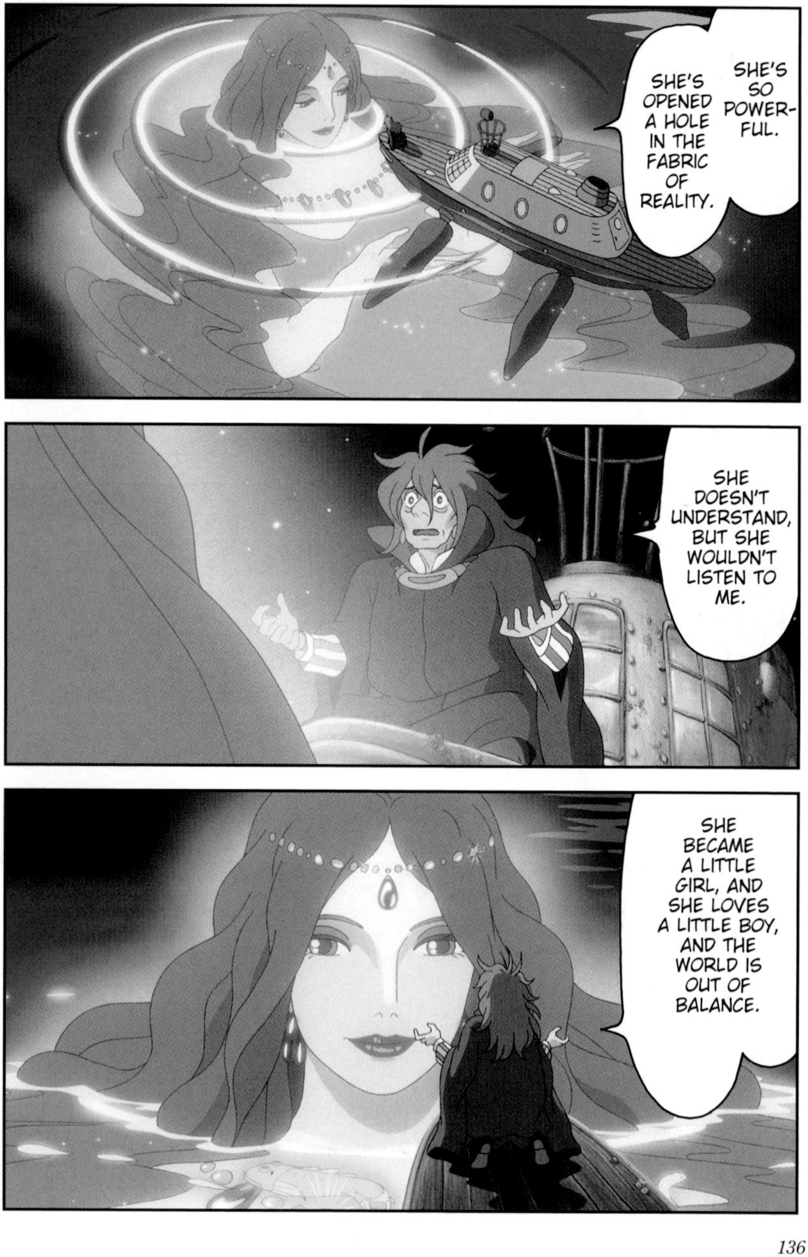
SHE'S SO POWER-FUL.
SHE'S OPENED A HOLE IN THE FABRIC OF REALITY.
SHE DOESN'T UNDERSTAND, BUT SHE WOULDN'T LISTEN TO ME.
SHE BECAME A LITTLE GIRL, AND SHE LOVES A LITTLE BOY, AND THE WORLD IS OUT OF BALANCE.

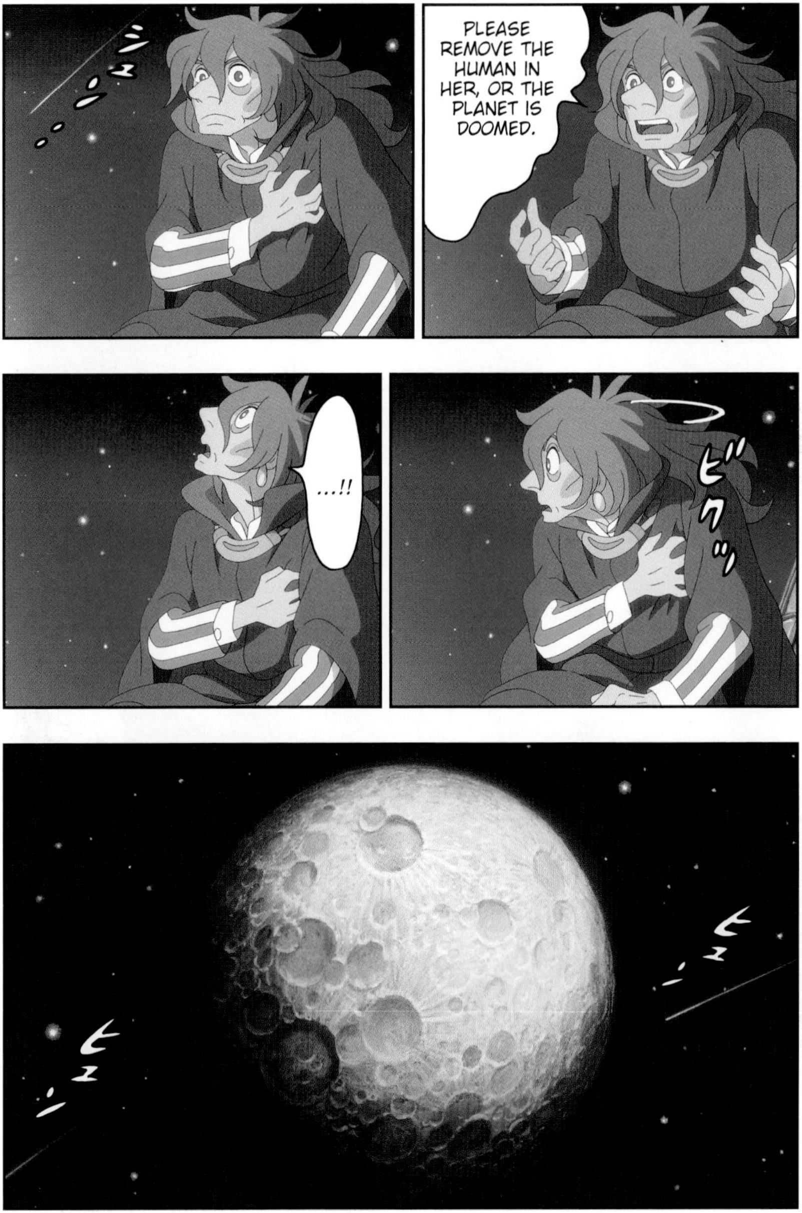
PLEASE REMOVE THE HUMAN IN HER, OR THE PLANET IS DOOMED.
ビクッ
...!!

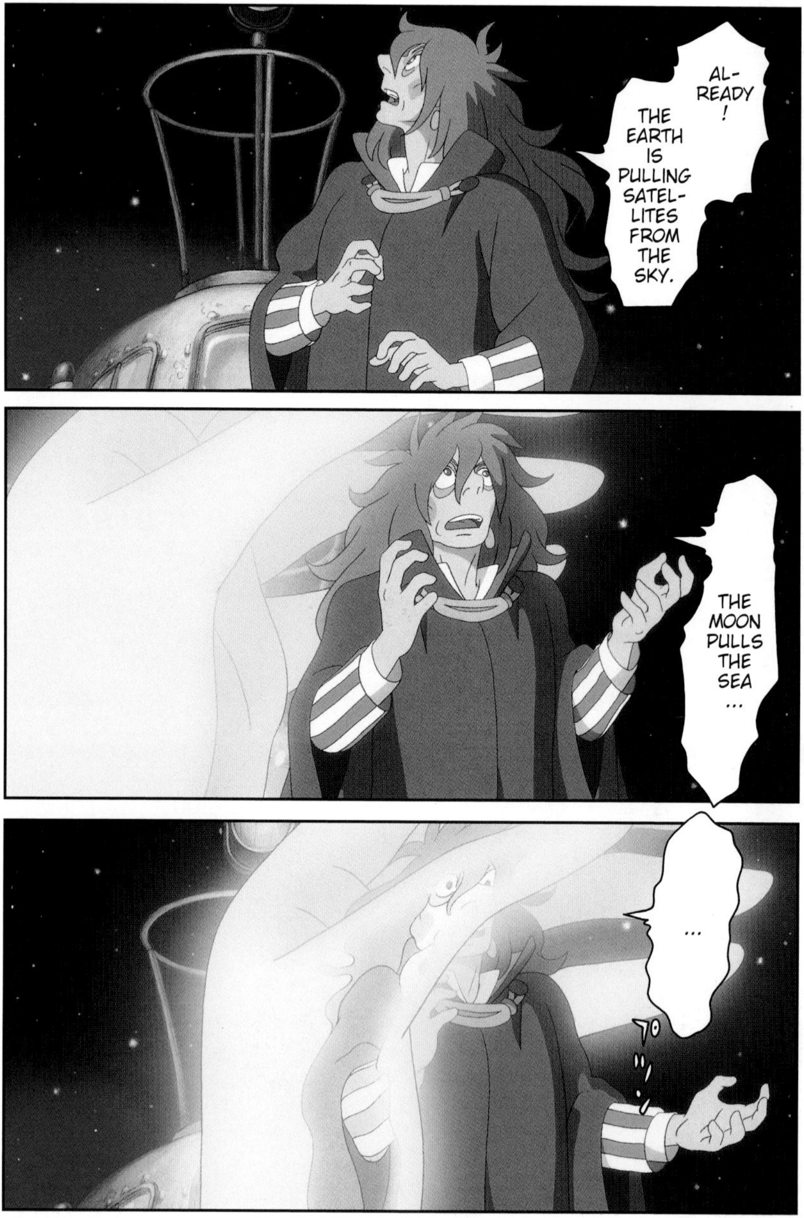
AL-READY!
THE EARTH IS PULLING SATEL-LITES FROM THE SKY.
THE MOON PULLS THE SEA ...
...

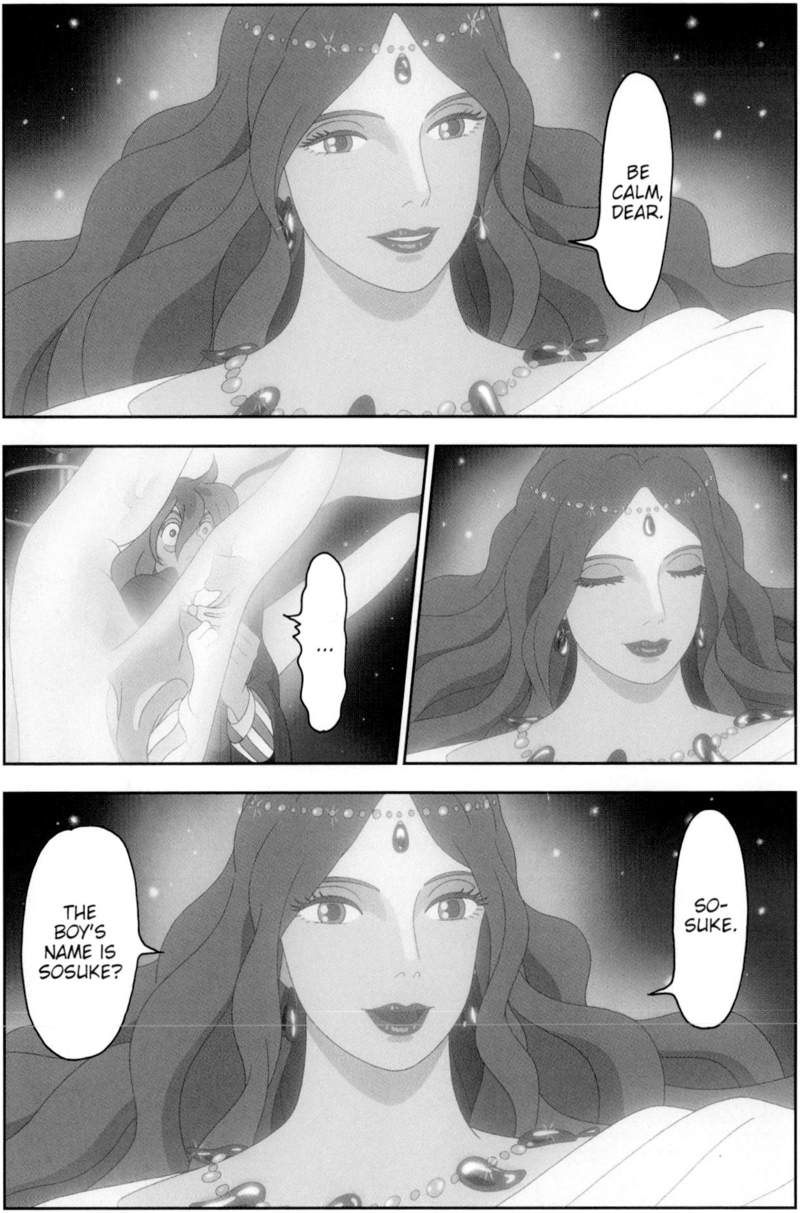
BE CALM, DEAR.
...
SO-SUKE.
THE BOY'S NAME IS SOSUKE?

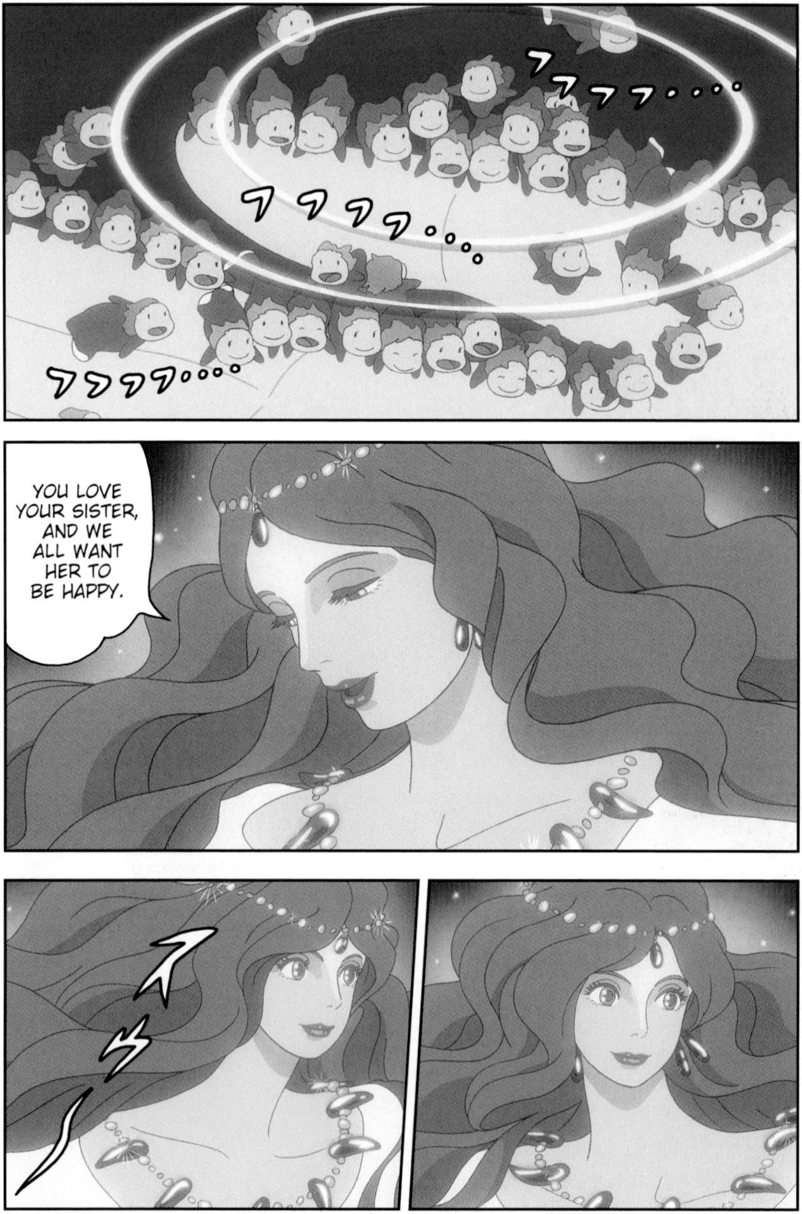
フフフフ・・・・
フフフフ・・・・
フフフフ・・・・
YOU LOVE YOUR SISTER, AND WE ALL WANT HER TO BE HAPPY.

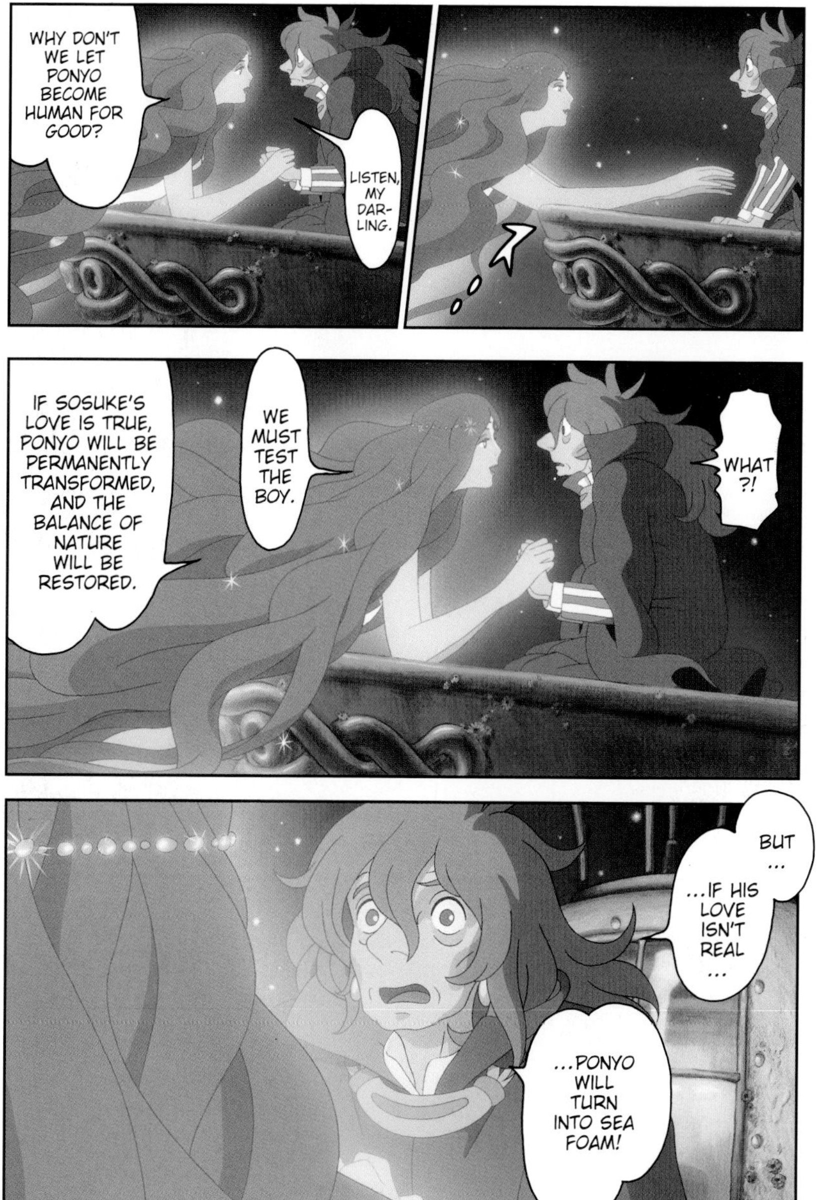
WHY DON'T WE LET PONYO BECOME HUMAN FOR GOOD?
LISTEN, MY DAR-LING.
IF SOSUKE'S LOVE IS TRUE, PONYO WILL BE PERMANENTLY TRANSFORMED, AND THE BALANCE OF NATURE WILL BE RESTORED.
WE MUST TEST THE BOY.
WHAT?!
BUT ...
...IF HIS LOVE ISN'T REAL ...
...PONYO WILL TURN INTO SEA FOAM!

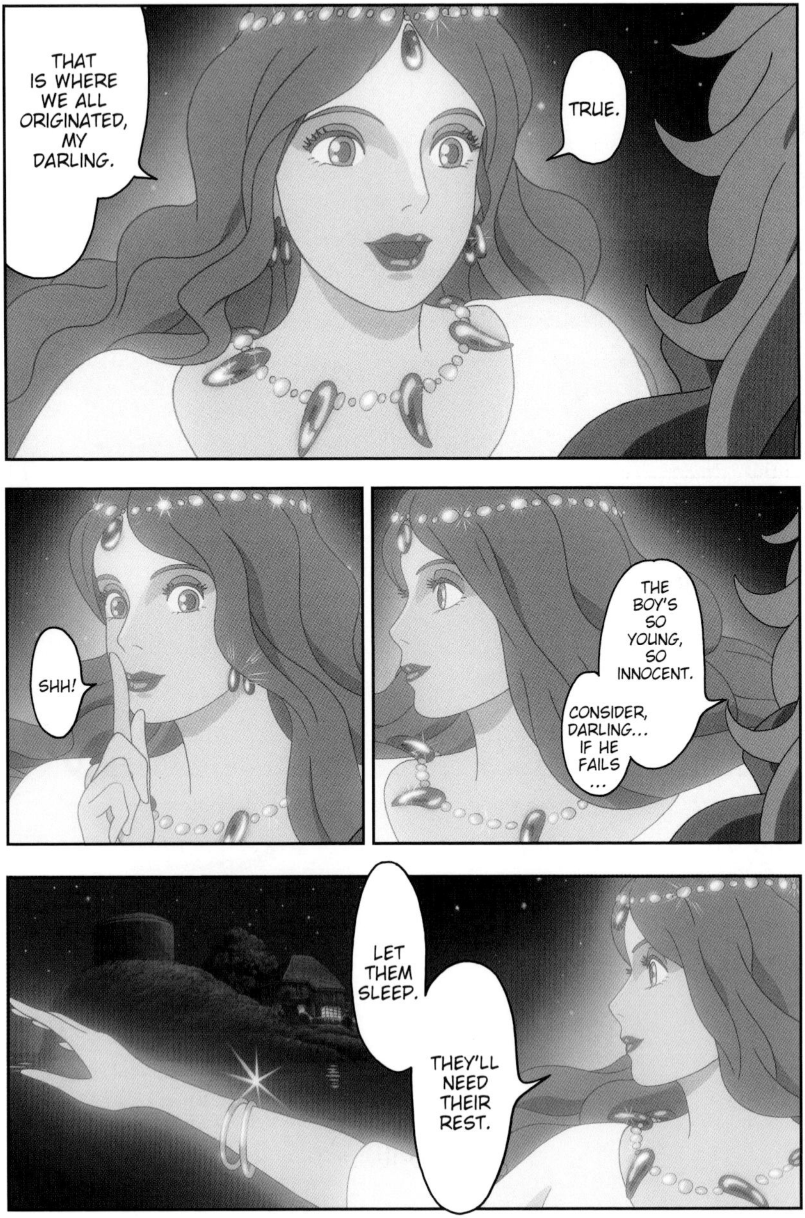
THAT IS WHERE WE ALL ORIGINATED, MY DARLING.
TRUE.
SHH!
THE BOY'S SO YOUNG, SO INNOCENT.
CONSIDER, DARLING... IF HE FAILS...
LET THEM SLEEP.
THEY'LL NEED THEIR REST.

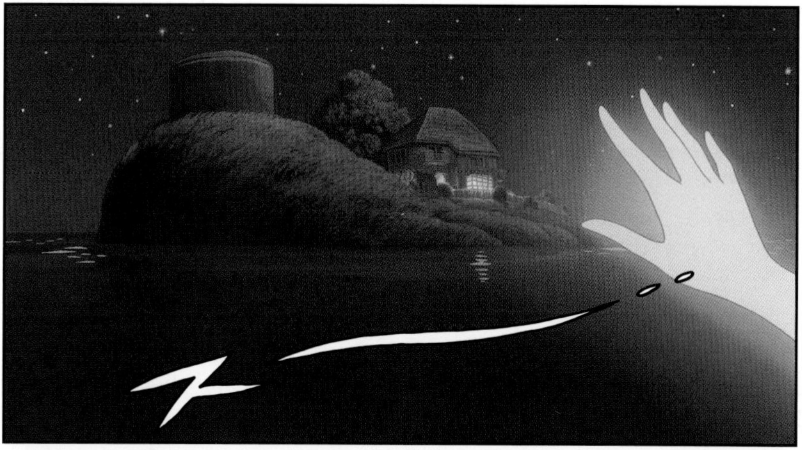
スー
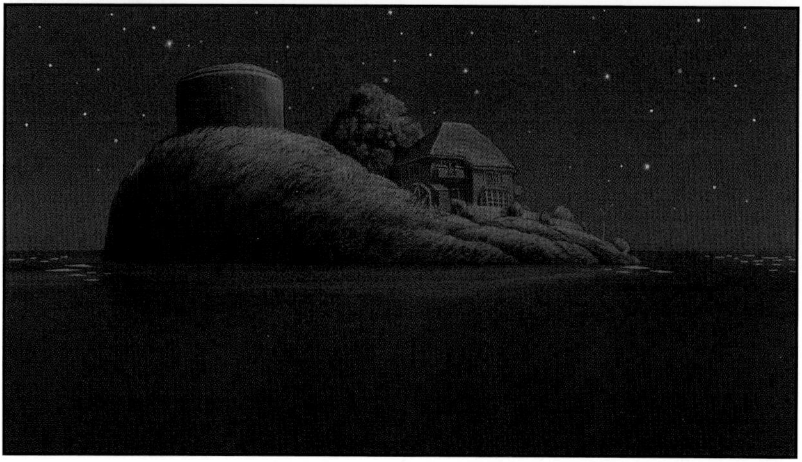

To be continued…

# Your Guide to *Ponyo* Sound Effects!

To increase your enjoyment of the distinctive Japanese visual style of *Ponyo*, we've included a listing of and guide to the sound effects used in this comic adaptation of the movie. In the comic, these sound effects are written in the Japanese phonetic characters called *katakana*.

In the sound effects glossary for *Ponyo* sound effects are listed by page and panel number. For example, 4.1 means page 4, panel 1. And if there is more than one sound effect in a panel, the sound effects are listed in order (so, 22.1.1 means page 22, panel 1, first sound effect). Remember that all numbers are given in the original Japanese reading order: right-to-left.

After the page and panel numbers, you'll see the literally translated sound spelled out by the katakana, followed by how this sound effect might have been spelled out, or what it stands for, in English—it is interesting to see the different ways Japanese people describe the sounds of things!

You'll sometimes see a long dash at the end of a sound effects listing. This is just a way of showing that the sound is the kind that lasts for a while; similarly, a hypen and number indicate the panels affected.

Now you are ready to use the *Ponyo* Sound Effects Guide!

| | |
|---|---|
| 4.1.1 | FX: DWODWOOO [woosh] |
| 4.1.2 | FX: GIGIII [errk] |
| 4.2 | FX: ZUBABABA [brwwww] |
| 5.1-3 | FX: BASHAAA [sphshh] |
| 6.1-3 | FX: KI KIIII [squeee] |
| 6.6 | FX: GWOO [woosh] |
| 6.7-8 | FX: DWOOO [bwooosh] |
| 7.1 | FX: SHAAAA [shpppp] |
| 7.2 | FX: GWOO [woosh] |
| 7.3 | FX: DWOOO [bwoosh] |
| 8.1-3 | FX: DO DO DWOOO [bwo bwo blwooo] |
| 8.4-5 | FX: SHAAA [shppp] |
| 8.5-6 | FX: DWOOO [bwoosh] |
| 11.1-2 | FX: KI KIII [squeee] |
| 11.4 | FX: KI KIII [squeee] |
| 12.1 | FX: KI KIII [squeee] |
| 12.4 | FX: BWOOO [vrrooom] |
| 13.1-2 | FX: BWOOO [vroom] |
| 13.2-3 | FX: ZABAAAN [crash] |
| 21.3-4 | FX: BWOOO [vroom] |
| 21.5.1 | FX: DODOUU [bwassh] |
| 21.5.2 | FX: ZABAAA [crash] |
| 22.6 | FX: GANN [wham] |
| 22.7 | FX: KIIII [squee] |
| 23.1-2 | FX: GWOOO [woosh] |
| 23.3 | FX: DO DWOO [bwo bwoooo] |
| 23.4 | FX: GWOOO [woooosh] |
| 24.6 | FX: GWOOO [woooosh] |
| 25.3 | FX: BYU BYU [whish whish] |
| 25.4 | FX: BUWA [flop] |
| 26.1 | FX: GGU [grab] |
| 26.5 | FX: DWOOO [bwooo] |
| 27.1 | FX: GWOOO [woosh] |
| 27.4.1 | FX: DO DWOO [bwo bwoo] |
| 27.4.2 | FX: BWOOOO [vroom] |
| 28.2 | FX: ZABBA [crash] |
| 28.3 | FX: BWOOO [vroom] |
| 28.4 | FX: DWO [bwo] |
| 28.5 | FX: ZZA [shpa] |
| 28.6 | FX: BAAAA [shpp shpp] |
| 29.1 | FX: BYOOO [shwooosh] |
| 29.2 | FX: GOOOOO [bwhoooo] |
| 29.3 | FX: KATA KATA [rattle rattle] |
| 29.4 | FX: DWOOO [gwooosh] |
| 30.2 | FX: KORO KORON [roll roll] |
| 30.3-5 | FX: DOWAAAA [bwooosh] |
| 31.1 | FX: BWOOOO [vroom] |
| 31.3 | FX: HA [hupp] |

| | | |
|---|---|---|
| 45.1 | FX: | GUI [pull] |
| 45.2.1 | FX: | CACHA [cltch] |
| 45.2.2 | FX: | PPA [fwa] |
| | | |
| 46.3 | FX: | SHA [shlpp] |
| 46.4 | FX: | SUTA SUTA [tmp tmp] |
| 46.5.1 | FX: | PPA [flip] |
| 46.5.2 | FX: | CACHI [cltch] |
| | | |
| 47.1 | FX: | CACHI [cltch] |
| 47.2 | FX: | SSU [slp] |
| 47.3 | FX: | TA TA [tp tp] |
| 47.4 | FX: | DA [tmp] |
| 47.5 | FX: | KURU [spin] |
| 47.6 | FX: | DA DA DA [tmp tmp tmp] |
| | | |
| 48.1 | FX: | TA TA [tp tp] |
| 48.2 | FX: | PYON [hop] |
| 48.3 | FX: | DAN [bmmp] |
| 48.4 | FX: | DA [tmp] |
| 48.5 | FX: | BAAN [smack] |
| 48.6 | FX: | KURA [flop] |
| | | |
| 49.2 | FX: | PYON [hop] |
| 49.3 | FX: | DOSU [fwmp] |
| 49.4 | FX: | DO TA TA TA TA [tmp tmp tmp tmp] |
| 49.5 | FX: | BOWA [fwpp] |
| | | |
| 50.1 | FX: | WASHI WASHI [rub rub] |
| | | |
| 51.2 | FX: | KOKURI [nod] |
| 51.4 | FX: | SUUUU [sniff] |
| | | |
| 52.3 | FX: | DA [tmp] |
| | | |
| 53.3 | FX: | KUI [turn] |
| 53.4 | FX: | ZAAAA [shpaaa] |
| | | |
| 54.2.1 | FX: | KACHI [flip] |
| 54.2.2 | FX: | BO [shpa] |
| | | |
| 55.1 | FX: | GOSO GOSO [fromp fromp] |
| 55.2 | FX: | PATAN [shut] |
| 55.3 | FX: | DOTA DOTA [bwomp bwomp] |
| 55.4 | FX: | DA DA [tmp tmp] |
| 55.5 | FX: | DA [tmp] |
| 55.6 | FX: | TON [jump] |
| 55.7 | FX: | PYON [hop] |
| | | |
| 56.2 | FX: | DOTAN [blpp] |
| 56.4 | FX: | IYA IYA [no, no] |
| | | |
| 57.1 | FX: | MUNI MUNI [wiggle wiggle] |
| 57.2 | FX: | MUNI [wiggle] |

| | | |
|---|---|---|
| 32.1.1 | FX: | KI KIIII [squee] |
| 32.1.2 | FX: | KARAN [roll] |
| 32.4-5 | FX: | DOBAAAA [splshh] |
| | | |
| 33.1-2 | FX: | ZAAAAA [shwaaaa] |
| | | |
| 34.6 | FX: | DA [tmp] |
| 34.7 | FX: | TA TA [tp tp] |
| | | |
| 35.3 | FX: | TA TA [tp tp] |
| 35.4 | FX: | TA TA TA [tp tp tp] |
| 35.5 | FX: | SHURU [slip] |
| | | |
| 36.1-3 | FX: | TA TA TA TA TA [tp tp tp tp tp] |
| 36.6-7 | FX: | TA TA TA TA [tp tp tp tp] |
| | | |
| 37.1 | FX: | TA TA [tp tp] |
| 37.2 | FX: | BA [bwpp] |
| 37.3 | FX: | GYUUU [squeeze] |
| 37.4 | FX: | HA [hpp] |
| | | |
| 38.1 | FX: | YORO [wobble] |
| 38.2.1 | FX: | UUUUNN [urrrr] |
| 38.2.2 | FX: | YORO [wobble] |
| 38.3 | FX: | ST [slp] |
| | | |
| 39.2 | FX: | KOKURI [nod] |
| 39.4 | FX: | PYON [hop] |
| 39.5 | FX: | PYON PYON [hop hop] |
| | | |
| 40.1.1 | FX: | KYA HA HA HA HA [ha ha ha ha] |
| 40.1.2 | FX: | PYON PYON [hop hop] |
| 40.2 | FX: | GABA [hug] |
| 40.4 | FX: | ZABA [crash] |
| 40.5 | FX: | DWOOO [bwooo] |
| | | |
| 41.1 | FX: | DWOOO [bwooosh] |
| 41.2.1 | FX: | ZAAA [shwaa] |
| 41.2.2 | FX: | KYA HA HA HA HA HA [ha ha ha ha ha ha] |
| | | |
| 42.1 | FX: | ZAAAA [plp plp] |
| 42.2 | FX: | DA [tmp] |
| 42.3 | FX: | GABA [grab] |
| 42.4 | FX: | SSA [shp] |
| | | |
| 43.1 | FX: | SUTA SUTA [tmp tmp] |
| 43.2 | FX: | GGU [urr] |
| 43.3 | FX: | CACHA [cltch] |
| 43.4 | FX: | KUI [clp] |
| 43.5 | FX: | BATAN [shut] |
| | | |
| 44.1 | FX: | SSU [slpp] |
| 44.4 | FX: | KOKURI [nod] |

| | | |
|---|---|---|
| 76.2.3 | FX: | ZAA ZAA [shaa shaa] |
| 76.2.4 | FX: | KIIII [quiii] |
| | | |
| 78.1 | FX: | ZA [shp] |
| 78.2 | FX: | GOTON [flpp] |
| 78.4.1 | FX: | GUSHA [grpp] |
| 78.4.2 | FX: | BAKI BAKI BAKI BAKI [brk brk brk brk] |
| | | |
| 79.1 | FX: | CHARA CHARA CHARA [fwp fwp fwp] |
| | | |
| 80.1 | FX: | JOBO JOBO [glpp glpp] |
| 80.3 | FX: | SSU [spo] |
| | | |
| 82.2 | FX: | SO [fwa] |
| 82.3 | FX: | PAKU [clop] |
| 82.4 | FX: | DOKI [babmp] |
| | | |
| 83.4 | FX: | GYU [squeeze] |
| | | |
| 84.3 | FX: | SSA [flip] |
| | | |
| 85.3 | FX: | HYOI [grab] |
| 85.4.1 | FX: | MM [hmp] |
| 85.4.2 | FX: | PAKU [swallow] |
| 85.5 | FX: | HAFU HAFU [huff huff] |
| | | |
| 86.1 | FX: | CHURU [sip] |
| 86.3 | FX: | TORONN [ahhh] |
| 86.4 | FX: | FUUU [whew] |
| | | |
| 87.1 | FX: | MMM [hmm] |
| 87.2 | FX: | TORONN [ahhh] |
| 87.3 | FX: | FUUU [whew] |
| | | |
| 88.1 | FX: | FUUU [whew] |
| 88.2 | FX: | ZURU ZURU [slurp slurp] |
| | | |
| 89.2 | FX: | SSU [fwop] |
| | | |
| 90.1 | FX: | SUUU [swuuu] |
| 90.2 | FX: | PICHA PICHA [plip plip] |
| | | |
| 91.3 | FX: | CHIKA CHIKA [blink blink] |
| | | |
| 92.1 | FX: | FU [fww] |
| | | |
| 94.4 | FX: | SSA [slp] |
| | | |
| 99.3 | FX: | GYU [hug] |
| | | |
| 100.1 | FX: | BURURURURU [vroom vroom] |
| 100.3 | FX: | BWOOOO [vroooom] |
| | | |
| 101.2.1 | FX: | BWOOO [vroom] |
| 101.2.2 | FX: | BASHA [splash] |

| | | |
|---|---|---|
| 57.4 | FX: | GUNI [grip] |
| 57.5 | FX: | KOTON [plopp] |
| | | |
| 58.2 | FX: | SSU [slp] |
| 58.4 | FX: | TORO [dropp] |
| 58.5 | FX: | TARA [dripp] |
| 58.6 | FX: | KASHA KASHA [stir stir] |
| | | |
| 59.1 | FX: | KOTO [plop] |
| 59.5 | FX: | KASHA KASHA [stir stir] |
| | | |
| 60.3 | FX: | NI [he he] |
| 60.5 | FX: | TON [thmp] |
| 60.6 | FX: | KASHA KASHA [stir stir] |
| | | |
| 61.4 | FX: | HOWAAN [frmmp] |
| | | |
| 62.5 | FX: | OKU OKU OKU [gulp gulp gulp] |
| | | |
| 63.1 | FX: | OKU OKU [gulp gulp] |
| | | |
| 68.4 | FX: | KACHI [flip] |
| 68.5 | FX: | KUI [cltch] |
| | | |
| 69.1 | FX: | GGU [grp] |
| 69.2.1 | FX: | SHU [slpp] |
| 69.2.2 | FX: | TARURU [grmm grmm] |
| 69.3.1 | FX: | GUI [yank] |
| 69.3.2 | FX: | TARURURU [grmm grmm] |
| 69.5.1 | FX: | GUI [yank] |
| 69.5.2 | FX: | TARURURU [grmm grmm] |
| 69.6.1 | FX: | GUI [yank] |
| 69.6.2 | FX: | TARURURU [grmm grmm] |
| 69.7 | FX: | HAA HAA [huff huff] |
| | | |
| 70.5 | FX: | KON KON [knock knock] |
| 70.6 | FX: | KUI KUI [cltch cltch] |
| | | |
| 71.2 | FX: | KUI [glpp] |
| | | |
| 72.1.1 | FX: | GUI [yank] |
| 72.1.2 | FX: | BURURURURUN [vrom vrom vrom] |
| 72.2 | FX: | PPA [shpa] |
| 72.5 | FX: | PYON PYON [hop hop] |
| | | |
| 73.3 | FX: | TA TA [tp tp] |
| | | |
| 74.3 | FX: | TA TA [tp tp] |
| | | |
| 76.1.1 | FX: | ZA ZA ZA ZA [zp zp zp zp] |
| 76.1.2 | FX: | JI JI [ggi ggi] |
| 76.1.3 | FX: | PIII [piiii] |
| 76.1.4 | FX: | ZAAA [shaaaa] |
| 76.2.1 | FX: | BARI BARI [blp blp] |
| 76.2.2 | FX: | JI JI [ggi ggi] |

| | | |
|---|---|---|
| 125.1 | FX: | GUNYA [twist] |
| 125.2 | FX: | GUNYA [twist] |
| 125.4 | FX: | GUYNA GUNYA [twist twist] |
| | | |
| 126.1.1 | FX: | GUNYA [twist] |
| 126.1.2 | FX: | KUCHA KUCHA KUCHA [nibble nibble nibble] |
| 126.3 | FX: | GURA [wobble] |
| 126.4 | FX: | VWOHO VWOHO VWOHO [glbb glbb glbb] |
| | | |
| 127.3 | FX: | DOBON [splash] |
| 127.4 | FX: | BUKU BUKU [bubble bubble] |
| 127.5 | FX: | ZABA [shpa] |
| | | |
| 128.4 | FX: | CHAPU [jump] |
| | | |
| 129.3 | FX: | SSA [flip] |
| 129.4 | FX: | ZABA [plopp] |
| | | |
| 132.3 | FX: | ZZU [blpp] |
| 132.4 | FX: | ZAAAA [shplaaa] |
| | | |
| 133.5 | FX: | SUUU [sssss] |
| | | |
| 135.2 | FX: | FU FU [he he] |
| 135.3 | FX: | ZU [zpp] |
| | | |
| 137.2 | FX: | SHUN [shoot] |
| 137.3 | FX: | BIKU [startle] |
| 137.5 | FX: | HYUN HYUN [shoot shoot] |
| | | |
| 138.3 | FX: | PUTSUN [ptsnn] |
| | | |
| 140.1.1 | FX: | FU FU FU FU [he he he he] |
| 140.1.2 | FX: | FU FU FU FU [he he he he] |
| 140.1.3 | FX: | FU FU FU FU [he he he he] |
| 140.4 | FX: | SUUU [slpp] |
| | | |
| 141.1 | FX: | SU [slp] |
| | | |
| 143.1 | FX: | SUUU [wave] |

| | | |
|---|---|---|
| 101.3 | FX: | BWOOO [vroom] |
| 101.4 | FX: | SAAAA [shaaaa] |
| | | |
| 102.1 | FX: | SAAA [shaaa] |
| 102.2 | FX: | FU [fwp] |
| 102.4 | FX: | GARA [grpp] |
| 102.5 | FX: | PISHAN [shut] |
| | | |
| 104.1 | FX: | GOON GOOON GOOON GOON [bwaum bwaum bwaum bwaum] |
| | | |
| 107.1 | FX: | DWOOOO [bwooosh] |
| | | |
| 108.2 | FX: | BUSUN [shwmp] |
| 108.3 | FX: | PITA [stop] |
| | | |
| 110.4 | FX: | ZUSAAAAAA [shpaaaa] |
| | | |
| 111.3-4 | FX: | ZAAAAA [shpaaaa] |
| | | |
| 112.1-3 | FX: | ZAAAAA [shpaaaa] |
| 112.4-5 | FX: | GWOOO [wooosh] |
| | | |
| 113.1-3 | FX: | GWOOO [wooosh] |
| | | |
| 115.1-2 | FX: | ZAAAAA [shpaaaa] |
| | | |
| 117.2 | FX: | GUNYA [smush] |
| 117.3-4 | FX: | GARA GARA GARA GARA [rumble rumble rumble] |
| 117.4 | FX: | BSHA [splsh] |
| | | |
| 118.1.1 | FX: | BWO [poof] |
| 118.1.2 | FX: | GUHYE GUHYE GUHYE GUHYE [grmm grmm grmm] |
| 118.2 | FX: | UYIII [spin] |
| | | |
| 119.1 | FX: | GWOOO [wooosh] |
| | | |
| 120.1 | FX: | PICHA [splish] |
| 120.2 | FX: | SUUU [sssss] |
| 120.4 | FX: | CHAPUN [plip] |
| | | |
| 121.1.1 | FX: | CHAPUN [plipp] |
| 121.1.2 | FX: | SUU [ssss] |
| 121.3 | FX: | FUNYORO FUNYORO [shwmp shwmp] |
| 121.5 | FX: | PITA [stpp] |
| | | |
| 122.1 | FX: | SOOO [careful] |
| 122.2 | FX: | PACHI PACHI [snap snap] |
| 122.3 | FX: | CHIPA CHIPA [flick flick] |
| | | |
| 123.1 | FX: | PIRI PIRI [pling pling] |
| 123.2 | FX: | MOZO [turn] |
| 123.3.1 | FX: | SUUU SUUU [zzz zzz] |
| 123.3.2 | FX: | KUUU [zzzz] |

This book should be read in its original Japanese right-to-left format.
Please turn it around to begin!

# PONYO

## Volume 3 of 4

### Original story and screenplay written and directed by
### Hayao Miyazaki

Translated from the original Japanese by Jim Hubbert
English-language screenplay by Melissa Mathison

Film Comic Adaptation/Mai Ihara
Lettering/Rina Mapa
Design/Carolina Ugalde
Editor/Megan Bates
Editorial Director/Masumi Washington

VP, Production/Alvin Lu
VP, Publishing Licensing/Rika Inouye
VP, Sales & Product Marketing/Gonzalo Ferreyra
VP, Creative/Linda Espinosa
Publisher/Hyoe Narita

Gake no Ue no Ponyo (Ponyo on the Cliff by the Sea)
© 2008 Nibariki - GNDHDDT
All rights reserved.
First published in Japan by Tokuma Shoten Co., Ltd.
PONYO title logo © 2009 Nibariki-GNDHDDT
The stories, characters and incidents mentioned in this publication are
entirely fictional.

Printed in Singapore

Published by
VIZ Media, LLC
295 Bay St.
San Francisco, CA 94133

First printing, September 2009

PARENTAL ADVISORY
PONYO is suitable for all ages.
ratings.viz.com

# A ROYAL
# MEOW!

## BARON
## The Cat Returns
### Story and Art by Aoi Hiiragi

When Haru rescues a cat, she gets drawn into a world of talking cats! Haru wants to go back home, but the feline royal family wants to make her the next Cat Princess. Can the dapper cat Baron help her before she becomes the cats' meow?

*The original graphic novel that inspired the film and picture book*

## The Cat Returns
### Picture Book

A hardcover children's book that recounts Haru's adventures using actual images from the original movie—perfect for storytime!

## Get the COMPLETE Studio Ghibli Library
## The Cat Returns collection today at store.viz.com

# THE ART OF HOWL'S MOVING CASTLE

A hardcover book generously packed with concept sketches, character and background drawings, paintings, and cell images!

**208 FULL COLOR & 48 B/W pages $34.99!**

A FILM BY HAYAO MIYAZAKI

# HOWL'S MOVING CASTLE
## Picture Book

An attractive hardcover for the whole family with scene-by-scene film footage and character dialog!

**$19.99**

## STUDIO GHIBLI LIBRARY

Breathtaking. Visual. Magical.

© 2004 Nibariki - GNDDDT
Howl's Moving Castle title logo © Buena Vista Pictures Distribution

**media**
www.viz.com